WINEM.
AND BREWING

Good wine and beer do not just happen, they have to be made. The amateur who uses his materials in a crafts-manlike way can produce at a low cost to himself wines at least as good as those found on supermarket shelves, and brew a variety of authentic beers.

Written from a wide knowledge of winemaking and brewing, this book tells the beginner all he needs to know to set about making a great variety of wines, from *vins ordinaires* to sparkling wines, aperitifs and liqueurs. Equipment, ingredients and methods are discussed in detail, and helpful advice given on bottling, storing and serving wine. The author has also included a selection of recipes for just some of the innumerable wines that can be made from the wide range of ingredients to be found in the shops, the countryside and the garden. The chapters on brewing give complete instructions on the different methods of making beer, and recipes are included for bitter, lager, stout and many other ales.

TEACH YOURSELF BOOKS

WINEMAKING AND BREWING

Duncan Gillespie

TEACH YOURSELF BOOKS

Hodder and Stoughton

First printed 1974
2nd edition 1980
3rd edition 1985

British Library Cataloguing in Publication Data
Gillespie, Duncan
Winemaking and brewing.—3rd ed.—(Teach
yourself books)
1. Wine and wine making—Amateurs' manuals
I. Title
641.8'72   TP548.2

ISBN 0 340 35655 3

Printed and bound in Great Britain for
Hodder and Stoughton Educational,
a division of Hodder and Stoughton Ltd,
Mill Road, Dunton Green, Sevenoaks, Kent,
by Richard Clay (The Chaucer Press) Ltd,
Bungay, Suffolk. Photoset by
Rowland Phototypesetting Ltd,
Bury St Edmunds, Suffolk

Contents

Abbreviations

cm = centimetre
cwt = hundredweight
ft = feet
g = gram
gal = gal
in = inch
kg = kilogram

lb = pound
m = metre
mill = million
ml = millilitre
pt = pint
tsp = teaspoon

Note: The imperial and metric measures in this book are independent and are not conversions.

1

Why Brew it Yourself?

Winemaking and home brewing are gaining converts fast. At the time of writing, six million people in Britain alone are said to be enjoying the craft. Ask them why they do it, and you will get a score of different reasons. Cost comes into it. You can easily make twenty bottles of red wine for the price of a comparable bottle from the wine shop, and beer costs less than a sixth of the pub pint.

There is an old Scots way of dismissing something cheap – 'If it's no' guid, it's no' dear'. This does not apply to well-made wines and beers. It is true that they are not dear – but they are good.

Many people find in the craft the chance to exercise their skill, for making your own wine and beer can be as simple or as complicated as you choose. In a world where food and drink are becoming more bland and uniform, the craftsman at home has a fine chance to preserve some of the old variety of styles and flavours, and to add individual zest to uniformity.

Pride is a factor. There is great satisfaction in watching the expression of pleased disbelief that grows on the face of a friend when he first tastes one of your wines, and that first very tentative sip proves to him that it is much better than he had anticipated.

Making your own wine and beer enables you to be lavish with your hospitality. As one writer put it: 'The owner of a fine wine cellar can be recognised merely by the way he smiles and puts out his hands to his friends.'

Convenience is one of the vital factors. The old methods, using baker's yeast, big bread-crocks for fermentation, and pieces of blanket for straining, would have been impractical in the small modern kitchen. Now, with plastic fermenting vessels, neat glass jars with clear fermentation locks, and (for those who prefer them) ready-made ingredients, the amount of inconvenience caused and space needed are much smaller.

Unlike the commercial winemaker and brewer, the home-brew enthusiast does not have to pay heavy duty, meet heavy overheads, and seek to make a profit. Nor does the do-it-yourself enthusiast have to turn out a consistent article for his 'customers' – he and his friends are delighted if a brew turns out good, even if it is a little different from previous attempts.

The sheer scope of the craft is another attraction. Someone once worked out that the permutations of a basic parsnip wine recipe totalled over three million. Some winemakers put on old clothes and go out to the hedges, the woodland corners, and the spoil-heaps of coalmines and other waste ground to look for ripe elderberries and blackberries. Others grow fruit and vegetables for the purpose – there can be few better ways of making a garden pay dividends. Those who live in the heart of a town or city can gather their winemaking ingredients off the shelves of specialist shops and supermarkets.

Even unwanted jam and jelly, transmuted by a little skill into something more stimulating, can find its way into the wine-bottle. That stimulus is found in all home-made wines and beers – all are alcoholic.

Most home-brewed beers are stronger than their pub equivalents, and it is possible to make brews so strong that a pint will send you weaving to bed. Making *good* beer is the real test of skill. Home-made wines also tend to be stronger than the average table-wine. So, if you have been drinking either in any quantity, beware of the breathalyser.

Because wine has been made for thousands of years, modern winemakers are standing on the shoulders of generations of their predecessors. Because of this accumulation of experience, the craft is far easier than ever before.

Plastic containers took the place of wooden casks, difficult to keep clean and tight, and crocks, which were heavy yet fragile. Cleanliness is easier, with Campden tablets and other sterilants taking the place of large quantities of boiling water and the fumes of burning sulphur.

Yeast nutrient now feeds the yeast and helps it to complete its task, and the proper wine yeasts can ferment the wine out to a strong, clear, enjoyable drink, instead of giving up half-way to leave it as a muddy cordial.

The biggest factor in changing the image of winemaking and brewing has been the development of kits.

Wine kits vary from fourteen-day and three-week kits, by way of straight grape concentrate, in a dozen wine types, to mixtures of grape and fruit juices. More and more people come into winemaking through buying such a kit and producing results good enough to encourage them to go forward and learn more.

They probably try the kit in the first place because of the cost of commercial wine. Good commercial wine can never be cheap – it is expensive in labour, and fewer and fewer pickers are available to toil in the sun for their plate of spaghetti, carafe of wine and meagre pay, yet mechanical pickers are still some way from perfection. Despite the existence of wine 'lakes', the price of the finest wines, the top growths, has risen astronomically, and the price of many other wines has risen in sympathy.

Once, either from sheer necessity or for the pleasure of getting something for almost nothing, winemakers took pride in producing wines which cost little more than a penny or two a bottle. Now, as is plain to see from some of the published recipes and from the cost of some of the best kits coming on the market, winemakers do not mind putting their hands much deeper into their pockets, provided that they can be sure that the result is comparable with commercial wine.

The difference between 'kit wine and beer' and 'real wine and beer' is often compared to the difference between instant coffee and 'real' coffee. The comparison is accurate, if one takes it far enough. Instant coffee is bought for convenience, varies from brand to brand, and is usually enjoyed even by those who also make the real thing. And instant coffee is often the first step to the enjoyment of 'real coffee', leading to the purchase of percolators, grinders, and then to experimentation with various sources of raw material.

There is, after all, no law that says you cannot make both kit wines and beers, and your own personal wines and beers. In our craft, as in Heaven, there are 'many mansions'.

Kits are not only for beginners. Those experienced in the craft continue to use them, for three main reasons:

1 Convenience – All the ingredients are in one tin or packet, and you do not need to search the shelves of the chemist or winemakers' supply shop.
2 Reassurance – Thousands of winemakers or home brewers have been this way before you, and found satisfaction, otherwise in a very competitive trade the suppliers would be out of business.
3 Simplicity – It is much easier and quicker to make wine from a kit

or a concentrate, or beer from a hopped-malt kit, than it is to make wine from fresh ingredients, or beer from malt grain which has to be cracked, mashed and sparged.

Those who use kits are generally advised to follow the instructions closely. This is certainly excellent advice until you get the measure of the kit and of the basic craft.

One maker, Tom Caxton, has encouraged beermakers to experiment by using extra ingredients – honey, for example, and barley syrup – and by varying the quantities. This is a recognition of the fact that kits often prove to be a springboard to more adventurous brewing and winemaking.

Just as some brewers make their 'weekday' beer from kits, and their 'Sunday' beers from purchased ingredients and a recipe, so winemakers can make wine for quick consumption from the proliferation of quick wines, usually summed up under the heading of 'three-week kits'.

To begin with those kits were despised by the 'real winemaker', and often despised without being tried. If they are accepted for what they are, they fill a valuable slot in the craft. Because they can be made and drunk so quickly, they are undemanding of storage space. They are drinkable as soon as they are clear, but improve with a month or two in store.

Over the years, too, interest has grown in the marriage of deep-freezing and winemaking. A deep-freeze was first advocated as a way of holding fruit until it was needed. For the first time, the fruits of early summer could be blended with those of late autumn.

Then it became clear that fruit which was 'badly' frozen – frozen slowly so that large ice crystals formed in the cells and burst them – yielded, when thawed, an abundance of juice of impressive clarity and flavour. In fact, the juice was so attractive that winemakers would set aside some to drink unfermented.

Sometimes the cross-fertilisation between the commercial wine trade and the suppliers of the home winemaker is slow to come about. Potassium sorbate (sorbic acid) was widely used to stabilise commercial wines before it became permissible to use it to stabilise home-made wines. It is interesting to note that a Campden tablet (the winemaker's friend) should be used in each gallon of wine stabilised in that way, otherwise a smell rather like the odour of crushed geranium leaves may develop.

The share of wine sold in boxes or dispensed by the glass from boxes has been growing steadily. Sir Guy Fison, chairman of the

Wine Development Board, commented when the boom began: 'The quality of the wines in the boxes is obviously acceptable to the public at large, otherwise the sales would not go on climbing in this remarkable way.'

The basis of those vessels is a strong multiple-layered collapsible container enclosed in a box, and they are available to the home winemaker in easily-filled forms.

This type of container should not be used for wine until it is fully stable otherwise a secondary fermentation may cause it to blow up and burst – the result, however, would not be as potentially severe as those caused by a bursting bottle.

For the same reason, anyone using them to hold sparkling wine or lively beer would need to be very skilful, very wary, and rather lucky.

Nevertheless, the commercial 'box' and the home winemakers' equivalent containers are surprisingly tough.

Economically-minded winemakers may scrounge empty wine-in-a-bag boxes from friendly licensed premises, but will find the taps very stubborn to remove and replace. There is something to be said for buying the easy filling and refilling Winemaid, Drafty or the like.

Professional winemakers in Europe and America have been developing the 'maceration carbonique' technique, in which whole grapes are enclosed in an atmosphere rich in carbon dioxide. When fermentation starts in the fruit, a very full and well-flavoured extraction of juice results. Winemakers in Britain have adapted the idea, using plastic sweet jars and other containers, and adding yeast before screwing down the lid. A technique, perhaps, for the well-experienced winemaker.

There are two points to be noticed about the proliferation of new ideas, techniques and equipment.

The first is that it is possible to be *too* elaborate for full enjoyment of our craft. The simpler you can keep your technique, the more likely you are to persist after the first flush of enthusiasm pales, and the more wine or beer you are likely to make for your enjoyment.

The second point is that over-elaboration conceals the fact that making alcoholic liquids is a natural and inevitable process, which was going on long before man arrived on the scene.

Fruit does not even have to fall into some hollow rock or log or other natural fermenting vessel to start to produce alcohol. Ripe fruit falling to the ground can ferment there and produce enough alcohol to intoxicate not only rats and other small ground animals but even elephants. They charge off, as one author described it, 'like runaway bulldozers, cutting great wavy paths through the bush'.

Throughout human history, such raw materials have been used to make wine to enable people 'to cope with their unique situation as men, animals with strange dreams, unfathomable sorrows, wild hopes' as J. B. Priestley put it.

Those raw materials can vary from the Zulu's marula berry (which makes a drink, smelling of turpentine, so potent that, having drunk it, a man is not allowed to bear arms in case he harms his neighbour) to the brewer's golden barley and the winemaker's grape concentrate or elderberries.

Not all the world's annual production of 23,000 million litres (5000 million gal) of commercial wine is good, though most is much better than the marula berry tipple. The best red wines in the world may be French, but some French red wine is so coarse that it has to be given to reluctant conscripts, distilled, or kept in wine 'lakes'. Italy is the world's largest producer. Most of her wines are good and sound, but there *was* that Tuscan wine described as tasting like raspberry wine in which an ancient tomcat had been steeped!

One great advantage of 'do-it-yourself' is that you can tailor your wines and beers to your own taste. As a general rule, young people and beginners in winemaking prefer sweet, even luscious, wines. As they grow older and more experienced in the craft, especially if they drink wine regularly, they tend to prefer drier wine.

But there is no virtue in drinking what you feel you *should* enjoy – nor, for that matter, in making the kinds of wines other people tell you that you should enjoy. These preferences are a more complicated matter than most people realise. There is, for instance, some evidence that the wine we most enjoy contains some element our body craves – that a woman with mild anaemia will find the iron-hard flavour of Australian Burgundy very attractive until her body chemistry comes back into balance.

It seems too good to be true that the winemaker who uses good materials in a craftsmanlike way can produce something at least as satisfactory as a branded wine on the supermarket shelf, and that we are free to make as much wine and beer as we wish, for our own consumption and that of our family and guests. Many have that feeling, even after years of experience . . .

A natural byproduct of the growth of interest in winemaking and brewing has been the great expansion in the number of Winemakers' Circles. Some are mainly social and 'self-lubricating', some treat the craft with an almost religious seriousness, while others blend instruction and social enjoyment very happily.

It is certainly worth while for the novice to join the nearest circle. If, after a fair trial, you do not feel that you fit in with its style, then try another, where you may feel more at home. You will find folk with similar interests to yourself and eager to pass on their greater experience. Owing to the greater availability of good books on the subject, and the expansion of trade facilities in almost every area, however, circle libraries and shops are less common than when they started.

Wine circles will add to your wine-tasting experience. Never (prudence permitting) turn down a chance to taste wines – home-made or commercial, good, bad, indifferent – in friends' homes, in restaurants, at commercial wine-tastings, on holiday, or going round shows at which samples of wines for sale by the case may be on offer.

But do not drink only mature wines. Taste your own wines at every stage of the process, for in this way you build up a mental library of tastes and smells which in the course of time will tell you many things about the progress of your winemaking that you cannot learn from the printed page.

2

Tools of the Trade

Containers

Goatskins, pigskins, huge clay jars, wooden barrels, bread crocks – all these have been used in the past, and still survive somewhere in the world. Happily, however, the modern winemaker and brewer has the great advantage of living in the 'Plastics Age'.

Plastic

When the craft began to expand, enthusiasts were quick to discover the virtues of plastic dustbins as 'primary fermentation vessels', for they could hold from 20 to 150 litres (4–30 gal) or more. They were used in every available colour – bright yellow ones with black lids seemed particularly favoured. Then came a scare that poisonous substances (cadmium and lead, in particular) could be leached out of the plastic by the alcohol and acid in the brew, and these dustbins began to fall out of favour. Subsequent experiments proved that one would need to drink an incredible amount of beer or wine fermented in such vessels to absorb a measurable amount of toxic substances. Nevertheless, the scare did bias some people against the containers they had been using for years as fermentation vessels, and they turned them to their original use, as dustbins, or lined them with a polythene bag for each new brew.

Now that the pure white food-grade containers are readily obtainable through the larger chemists and the trade suppliers there seems to be no reason why a winemaker or brewer, kitting out for the first time, should revert to the plastic dustbins that served his predecessors for twenty years or more.

The ideal size for these primary fermentation vessels is something that only you can decide. A 25 litre (5 gal) vessel may seem huge to the beginner – a smaller version of the Great Tun of Heidelberg, which held 17 000 litres (37 500 gal). But in time you may find that you wish to make much larger quantities. A container of that size does have some advantages: first, it is not too heavy to lift around (anything over the 25 litres (5 gal) mark can be a strain to move) and, second, if anything goes wrong with the batch you have lost only that limited amount.

On the other hand, if you have the kind of fermentation box or cupboard that will hold a 150 litre (30 gal) container there is no doubt that a batch that size is more economical in time, effort and probably cash than six batches of 25 litres (5 gal) each. If anything goes wrong, however, you are left with a large total loss, or, almost as bad, with 180 bottles of wine or beer not quite bad enough to pour away but not quite good enough to enjoy.

To begin with, then, you can reasonably restrict yourself to the 25 litre (5 gal), white, food standard buckets with tight-fitting press-on lids. These are for use in the pulp-fermentation stage of making wine, or for making a 25 litre (5 gal) brew of beer.

For the next stage, fermentation in bulk, there are many types of container to choose from. Jerricans, as bought by campers for use as water-carriers, are good for both brewing and winemaking, and (in

Assorted large containers for fermenting: fermenting bins, dustbins lined with polythene bags, plastic 'jerricans' and 'ex-wine fives'

many winemakers' experience) for storing wine in bulk. Being slab-sided, they can be stored side by side on suitable strong shelving with very little loss of space.

Not all these containers, however, can be trusted to resist boiling water, unlike most polythene vessels. There are few more dismal experiences for a home-brewer than to pour boiling wort (beer in the making) into a jerrican and watch it leak out through all four corners of the base and run steaming across the floor. Other plastic vessels, though not cracked or melted by boiling water, may soften and buckle alarmingly – another reason for buying strong-walled vessels rather than the cheapest you can find.

Excellent containers (discarded perhaps by breweries or food manufacturers) can sometimes be picked up very cheaply; but beware of any plastic container that has held insecticide, salad cream, rat poison, petrol, paraffin, vinegar, hair-oil or creosote – it is simply a matter of common sense.

Glass
Plastic containers have the great advantage of being light and easy to clean, but few winemakers would turn down the chance of a good glass carboy (though they are difficult to find nowadays, since they have been snapped up for use as miniature gardens). Carboys are excellent for making wine in bulk; but, being great glass bubbles, they are fragile and need to be kept in their well-packed iron or wicker cages.

Carboys, and glass jars, are preferred by some winemakers for maturing wine after the first fermentation; they find that plastic gives the wine an off-flavour. This is contrary to the experience of other winemakers, who have stored wine in, for example, plastic galloners from the local café selling fruit drinks and have had no trouble. They could both be right – different palates, different techniques, different storage conditions and, very probably, different plastics may make the difference.

If you do not wish to run the risk, then, when the time comes to move the wine from the 25 litre (5 gal) second-stage vessel, rack it into glass jars. Glass will certainly not taint wine. Used with care, glass jars should last indefinitely – and many winemakers use no other container for their wine, from the pulp-fermentation stage to the bottle. And for those who like their hobby to look craftsman-like, a shelf of glass gallon jars, each fitted with its fermentation lock, does look better than one covered with an assortment of plastic containers, large and small. In addition, glass containers are not as readily permeated by air and by strong smells as are some plastic containers.

Although glass vessels may not take kindly to being dropped or banged together, or being filled suddenly from a kettle of boiling water, they have the great advantage that you can see into them and follow what is happening – how well the wine is clearing, whether the sediment is thick enough to warrant racking, whether flowers of wine have begun to make their tissue-fine little islands on the surface of the liquid.

Some plastics stain very badly. Glass, for all practical purposes, is inert – although sometimes a strong elderberry wine seems to etch itself so thoroughly into the surface that it leaves a very stubborn coloured film.

Plastic is flexible. If, after the last racking, you fill a plastic galloner up to the neck and screw the cap on, the plastic will stretch a little if refermentation begins. A glass jar, on the other hand, will blow its bung or (as sometimes happens when a rubber bung is used and the rubber sticks to the glass) will burst messily when pressure builds up inside it.

On balance, plastic wins for the early stages of winemaking and brewing, and glass for long-term maturing.

Metal
Plastics and glass, then, have their advantages and their advocates, but metal containers have neither. Do not put any fermenting or fermented material in a metal container, otherwise you may spoil the brew or even poison yourself. Although stainless steel is often excepted from this ban on metal, it is noticeable that commercial wineries and breweries generally use stainless steel for piping, and for vessels with which the liquid will only be in contact for a short time, rather than for long-term storage vessels.

Wood
And what about the traditional oak cask for maturing wine in? There is no doubt that a year or so in an oak cask will often put extra quality and polish into a red wine in particular. A good oak cask, properly treated and kept in use so that it does not dry out and start at the seams, will last at least a lifetime, so that when you divide the initial cost of a cask into its years of life or the number of gallons it will hold it works out very cheaply.

A good cask is a pleasure to look at, and a testimonial to the skill of the craftsman who shaped, bent and hooped the staves so that the vessel is wine-tight. And anyone with a feeling for tradition will relish the fact that he is using a cask, for casks have been in use since Roman times.

But casks do have their disadvantages. They are very heavy when empty, and much heavier when full; the wood they are made of has thousands of crevices in which unwanted organisms can lurk; they are difficult to keep tight; and even when they are not leaking, or weeping a little, they are losing water and alcohol to the atmosphere through the pores of the wood.

You need a strong, well-shaped stillage on which to stand the barrel, and especially with a small cask you have the trouble of oxidation. Wine benefits from the limited amount of air that can permeate the wooden walls of a large cask; but the smaller bulk of wine in a small cask is likely to be affected by the excess of air reaching it. You can, of course, varnish the outside of the cask, but this defeats part of the purpose of using a cask at all – you might as well mature the wine in glass or plastic, except for any benefit of tannin the wine might draw from the wood.

Casks, new or second-hand, need to be carefully 'commissioned' by being thoroughly washed with successive amounts of boiling water and washing-soda, and then sterilised with sulphur dioxide solution. Even then, you will not be sure that you have bought yourself a sound cask until you use it, so the first brew to go into it should not be one you care greatly about. If you are buying a second-hand cask, reject at once and without any hesitation one that smells musty (like an old rain-barrel) or has a taint of vinegar.

Having pointed out the snags in using casks, it is only fair to repeat that the very best wines (commercial or otherwise) are matured in wood for a year, or sometimes for many years. If your aim is a large silver cup, then think in terms of using good casks, with all their attendant difficulties.

Fermentation boxes and cupboards

All the time that your wine or beer is fermenting it needs a cosy place. When you begin, a corner of a kitchen shelf may be adequate; but as the months go on, and the jars and containers multiply, you will need to find somewhere to keep your brews alone.

The first fermentation box you make will not be big enough; this is axiomatic. You may begin with something the size of an old-fashioned tea-chest, but a few brews later you will turn your eyes to the cupboard under the stairs. Either glass-fibre wool or polystyrene sheet should be used to insulate the walls and roof. It has been reckoned that a polystyrene sheet has the insulating value of 170 times its thickness in brick, so even an outhouse or a shed can be converted to suit our purpose.

As with so many aspects of winemaking and brewing, a little ingenuity goes a long way, and possibilities range from the dead-end of a corridor to a large wardrobe. The essentials are warmth, darkness (when a light is not in use) and reasonable convenience; a loft, for instance, unless it is reached by broad steps and not by a ladder, is seldom convenient.

The importance of convenience is rarely stressed enough. If your fermentation cupboard or room is convenient, then your brews will get the attention they deserve even after the first flush of enthusiasm has died away. If, however, you have to move furniture or put on your hat and coat before you can see how your brews are faring, you will naturally tend to neglect them. Make everything, from door catches to light switches, as convenient as possible and you will enjoy the craft much more.

Heaters and thermostats

Having found a place for fermenting your brews, how are you to heat it? The ideal form of heating is the tubular electric heater coupled to a thermostat used in greenhouses. If the thermostat is properly fitted, it does not matter (apart from the initial cost) how big the tubular heater is. A long tube will be just as economical to run as a short one and will be better able to cope with any sudden cold spells.

Ideally, the thermostat should be the kind that is immersed in liquid, not the kind that monitors the heat of the air; it is the heat of the liquid in the wine jars that we are interested in, and we wish the thermostat to switch on the power whenever the liquid begins to cool off, no matter how much the air temperature may vary.

Some people, home-brewers in particular, carry this a stage further and supply a source of heat in the liquid itself. A little tube heater of the kind sold for fish tanks can be submerged in a brew, linked to the type of thermostat that pet shops also sell for that purpose. Given care in handling, the heater and thermostat combination can last for years and never fail.

Some people have found that the heaters leak at the plastic cap if fully submerged, but that if hung with their caps above the liquid they do not work as efficiently as they should. Others worry that the plastic on a heater intended to be immersed in water may be affected by the complex mixture of acids, alcohols and other substances in which they now find themselves. Now that submersible heaters, intended for the purpose, are readily available from home-brew suppliers, there is much to be said for leaving the aquarium heaters to the tetras and guppies.

One point to note with all immersion heaters is that, if lowered right to the bottom of a plastic fermentation vessel, they can weld themselves to the bottom, creating a little hot spot which leaves a weakened thin crater on the bottom of the bin or, much worse, makes a hole when the heater is hauled up.

Winepresses and strainers

Many of the small items needed for winemaking and brewing are available at home: a coarse strainer, such as a large colander, and a fine strainer, such as a large nylon sieve; plastic funnels of all sizes, preferably ones that will neatly accept the strainer and sieve; and spoons, large and small. But not every home has a winepress, and not every winemaker needs one.

At one time, winepresses for the amateur were difficult to find. Now they are easy to find but difficult to pay for, and it is worth pointing out that you can make many gallons of wine without one.

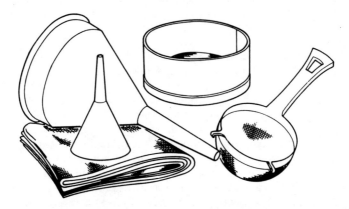

Funnels of all sizes are useful; so are fine nylon flour sieves and nylon netting for straining

The strainers mentioned above and a piece of strong terylene net – perhaps a metre square – will extract nearly all the juice from fruit pulp with a little strong-arm assistance. Terylene is recommended because of its strength and its ease in cleaning and sterilising. After pressing fruit, you will find that a brisk shake will remove most of the material from the netting, and a rinse under the tap will remove the remainder – a much easier task than cleaning the piece of blanket that is sometimes recommended for straining.

Some winemakers, when they finally decide that they are hooked on the hobby, will buy a small press; others will enjoy employing other skills to make themselves a press, perhaps using a car jack as the source of pressure. Such a press needs to be extremely strong, for the pressure when the pulp is dry can be measured in tons, not pounds.

If you devise your own press, make sure that metal cannot come in contact with the fruit juice. Iron is the commonest metal to use for bolts, the hoops of the press barrel, corner-pieces and other furniture. With luck, the action of the citric acid in the wine and the natural tendency for the iron to settle out in the course of fermentation will dispose of any contamination, but it is a risk not worth taking.

Copper bolts and other furnishings are more dangerous, since the acids in the fruit will react enthusiastically with copper and the resulting salts may still be present when you pour your wine into the glass. And zinc from galvanised metal is dangerous to both the wine and the winemaker, so do not use galvanised bolts or fixtures – these will be brighter anyway after the fruit has been pressed because the surface coat will have been removed by the acid.

Liberal use of polyurethane varnish on the wood and the metal of the press will help to prevent many troubles. Alternatively, you can seal the metal by heating it, rubbing on paraffin wax (from a white candle, for example) and polishing it up, but this is more laborious, and no more effective, than using polyurethane varnish.

Polyurethane is resistant to acids, boiling water, sulphite solution and weak alcoholic solutions, and it seals some of the crevices which might otherwise be colonised by bacteria and moulds. When you put the varnish on presses or other equipment, give it a week to dry before you use the apparatus.

If the spars of the press barrel are fairly close together it is not necessary to use a press-bag, but putting the fruit in a strong bag of this kind does help to strain the juice and to cut down the number of long-range jets of pulp that shoot out from between the spars!

If a bag is used, however strong, care must be taken in applying the pressure, for even the strongest material when crimped between the sharp edges of the spar will burst if too much force is applied.

If you do not use a press-bag, then strain the juice running from the press through a thickness of coarse net. This will catch the largest particles of pulp and prevent them from reaching the fermentation vessel.

Nylon bags of approximately the right size can be bought from winemakers' supply shops. The price will encourage you to be gentle with them!

Boilers

Both winemakers and brewers should equip themselves with a boiler of some kind – home brewing usually requires a larger boiler than winemaking.

Some people use heavy iron pots, close relatives of the kind in which Macbeth's witches did their home brewing. They certainly last well, and the contents do not burn as easily as in a thinner vessel, but their weight is a disadvantage if you have to lift them on and off a stove, particularly when they contain hot liquid.

Good boilers, suitable for use on a gas ring, can be bought through the trade. Not every ironmonger stocks similar boilers, but in the larger towns they can be found in shops supplying professional caterers.

In the same way that every vacuum cleaner is a 'Hoover', every electric boiler in the home-brewing world is a 'Burco'. A Burco boiler, of the kind once commonly used for boiling up 'whites', is very useful. In theory, it should be one lined with pure tin, since a wash-boiler is not intended for food production; but in practice, as long as you keep any acid out of the boiler, no harm should result.

Thermometers

Both winemakers and brewers should invest in a good brewing thermometer – you do not really need one that reads below freezing-point or much above boiling-point. The thermometer will be used, as a matter of course, to make sure that the basic liquid – the wine must or the beer wort – has cooled to below 26°C (80°F) before the yeast is added. You can guess instead, and if you are within 10° either way no harm will be done. But it is easy to make a bigger mistake than that, and scalded yeast dies, while cold yeast will not multiply.

In brewing, if you are using more advanced methods and mashing the ingredients, you will also need your thermometer to check the mashing temperature.

Spoons

Both the winemaker and the brewer will require a really long spoon – the kind traditionally needed to 'sup with the Devil or a native of Fife'. It can be made of wood or plastic (polypropylene), but, whichever it is, err on the side of length and avoid the irritation of ingredients sticking to the bottom of the boiler and the pain of scalded fingertips.

Hydrometers

Another very simple device, the hydrometer, scares some people away from the craft because its name sounds technical and scientific. It is, in fact, easier to use than a clinical thermometer, yet people who can confidently interpret a slide rule fight shy of it. The hydrometer simply measures the specific gravity of the liquid in which it is placed. Its use is desirable in winemaking and essential in home brewing.

Fermentation locks

Although fermentation locks are associated mainly with winemaking, they also have their use in home brewing. Their purpose is to allow the carbon dioxide created by fermentation to escape without permitting air (and airborne infection) or insects to find their way into the wine.

The same purpose can be achieved in other ways: a piece of polythene held in place over the mouth of the vessel with a rubber band, a firm wad of cotton wool in the neck of the vessel or a layer of paper tissues tied over the mouth. But none of these devices has the craftsmanlike appearance of fermentation locks, and none gives the same indication of how fermentation is proceeding.

First in the field was the traditional glass 'bubbler', which looks very smart and gulps away in a fascinating manner when the gas pushes through the liquid in the trap but which is very easily broken.

A makeshift fermentation lock with polythene, cotton wool and a
rubber band

Then came a variety of plastic traps, some being a close copy of the
glass original and others being drum-shaped. The principle behind
them all is the same – they retain a little sulphur dioxide solution in
such a way that all gases passing in or out have to bubble through
the liquid.

At one time, winemakers showed great ingenuity in converting
pill bottles and test-tubes into fermentation locks. Now, with such a
variety of locks in glass and plastic on the market at reasonable
prices, the time spent on this mini-plumbing seems wasted.

When using the conventional 'bubbler' with its two globes, it is
tempting to be liberal with the sulphite solution and almost fill both
glass balls. All that is required is sufficient solution to fill the U-tube
below the globes, which are in effect expansion chambers. Similarly, with the drum-shaped plastic lock, all that is needed is a little
more solution than will fill the cup up to the skirts of the cap. If an
airlock is overfilled, there is a danger that the sulphite solution may
be drawn back into the wine if the lock 'goes into reverse'. This is a
phenomenon that can be puzzling until you know the reason for it.
A fermentation lock bubbles 'backwards' when the pressure inside
the jar falls below the atmospheric pressure outside. This can
happen in cold weather when the wine will shrink fractionally in the
jar, or when a rising barometer shows that the pressure of the

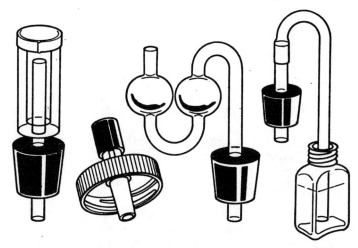

Various fermentation locks, the right-hand one being home-made using
an aspirin bottle containing a little water or sulphite solution

atmosphere outside the lock is greater than that on the surface of the
wine.

If you have difficulty in fitting the stem of a fermentation lock into
a rubber bung, wet the stem and the bung thoroughly. If this fails, a
drop of glycerine will provide lubrication.

Locks can be fitted to containers with plastic screwtops by very
carefully reaming out a hole in the plastic. Bore a hole that is too
small and then enlarge it very carefully with a sharp-pointed knife
until the stem of the lock is a tight, drive-home fit.

Siphons

To move wine from one container to another, or finally to bottle
your wine or beer, you will need a siphon. There are several patent
siphons on the market, each with its own advantage – a pump to
prime it or a device to stop the flow when the lower container is full.
To start with you will be well served by a simple length of rubber
tubing sold for the purpose – 1·2 m (4 ft) may be ample if you are
using only gallon jars, but a little extra length causes no problems
and can be very useful. Try to buy tubing that needs a good hard
pinch to close the flow – anything with lighter walls is liable to kink if
it is bent.

Filters

If you wish to enter your wine in shows, or if you wish to drink it early, you will probably join the increasing number of people who fine and filter their wine.

The Harris filter, designed to cope with about a gallon at a time, came on the market in 1971 and proved so popular that within two years the firm produced the Major model to cope with larger quantities.

Another filter, the Vinbrite, is marketed by the grape concentrate specialists Southern Vinyards. It, too, is simple to assemble and clean, and puts a good polish on a wine, particularly if it has been fined previously so that there are no big particles left to clog the filter.

Another firm, who made their name with their selection of wine yeasts, market a very simple type of filter in which the filtration is carried out by a porous tube (a tube of the correct fineness can be selected).

Corkers

When one considers that corkers can be bought for less than the price of one heavy round of drinks in a pub, it seems a poor economy to struggle away with a flogger and a length of plastic-covered wire. How much should be put on the debit side for every split bottle or bashed fingertip? Better by far to buy a proper corker, as soon as you know that you will have plenty of wine worth bottling. Better still, drop hints as your birthday draws near or Christmas approaches.

Labels

A well-corked bottle of good wine deserves a good label, and there are attractive labels on the market. Ready-gummed labels have the shortcoming that if they become even slightly damp they set into one big, thick, unusable label. If you buy ungummed labels, you will find that a packet of Polycell wallpaper paste will last for years – make up half an egg-cupful at a time and use it to stick on the labels. Polycell has the additional advantage that labels applied with it can be soaked off empty bottles in hot water in a minute or two – scraping reluctant labels off bottles is even more wearisome than washing dirty bottles.

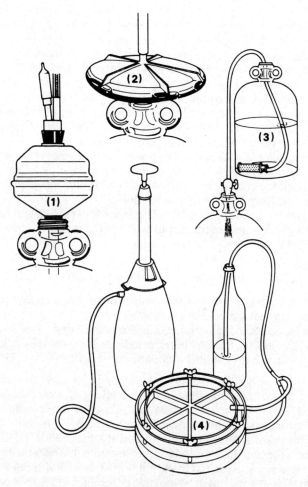

Popular proprietary wine filters available to the amateur and now widely used: (1) the Harris, which gives extremely fine filtration and polish; (2) the Vinbrite, easy and quick to use; (3) the tube filter, obtainable in various grades; and (4) the Vinamat pressure filter

Capsules

To give even more class to a gift bottle of wine a coloured aluminium-foil capsule can be very simply applied to the neck of the bottle. The capsule is bought as a little aluminium cup, which is popped over the neck of the bottle and crimped in place with a strong rubber ring. If the neck of the bottle is first moistened, the foil will stick all the closer to the glass.

Another type of capsule, the 'Viscap', sticks even more closely. Viscaps are sold submerged in a preservative liquid, and are fished out as necessary and slipped over the neck of the bottle. They do not have to be pulled or crimped in place but shrink tightly as they dry. Such capsules are used by some winemakers whenever they lay down an especially good wine for long maturing – the Viscap helps to prevent the cork from creeping out, from being attacked by cork moths and from drying out or perishing.

Another type of capsule, 'Visplas', is made of plastic, and is put in place by being dampened and pushed over the cork onto the neck of the bottle.

Some useful items you can make yourself

One ingredient in winemaking costs nothing but pays ample dividends, and that ingredient is *ingenuity*.

We all can find ways of making the work easier. For instance, W. H. T. Tayleur, founder of the firm Brew It Yourself Ltd, devised for his own use the simple bathboard. He describes it like this:

'It is simply a board or boards just long enough to go across the bath and strong enough to support a full 5-gallon carboy. Mine is made from three oak boards each 26 by 6 by ½ inches. The battens are positioned to lie just inside the sides of the bath so that if the sides are accidentally pushed it cannot slide far enough across the bath for one end to slip down into it. The 6-inch boards are spaced ¼ inch apart to permit drainage, so that spilth will run into the bath and not down outside it; the gaps should not be wide enough to allow small glass items such as U-tubes to slip through.

'The bathboard provides a working surface that is ideal for racking, bottling, compounding worts and musts, and every other brewing and winemaking job. There is plenty of hot and cold water to hand, the drop from the board to the bottom of the bath is just right for siphoning, and the inevitable spilth trickles down the plughole. Most important of all, this very simple gadget

The Tayleur bathboard and Gillespie swiller in use

liberates the only alternative site, the very much less convenient kitchen sink and draining board. A bathside chair or low stool is helpful especially for the tall.'

Another simple gadget, also making use of the bath, is the 'swiller'. A piece of hose, long enough to reach from the washbasin tap to any part of the bath, is fitted at one end with a hose-tap connection, preferably the kind that is locked in place by tightening a butterfly nut. At the other end the hosepipe is fitted with a piece of copper or plastic tubing small enough to go easily through the neck of a bottle.

Beer bottles to be washed can be ranged along the bottom of the bath, the swiller can be connected up and the tube placed in the first bottle. The force of the water is sufficient to break up any yeast deposit in the bottle and swill it out, making it easy to rinse out the bottles.

Without the fine tube, the swiller can be used to wash out containers that have been treated with bleach and need many changes of water to dispel the last of the chlorine smell.

3

Scope for Experiment

'The discovery of a wine is of greater moment than the discovery of a constellation – the universe is too full of stars.' Brillat-Savarin, whose name is associated with gastronomy rather than astronomy, used to quote that approvingly.

Home winemakers have ample scope to discover new wines, though the number of existing recipes must already run into thousands. Not so many years ago someone discovered the possibilities of bananas for winemaking, and there must be other sources of good wine as yet untapped. For instance, if you tie the flowers of a palm tree so that they cannot open and then bruise the tip of the bundle, it drips a gallon a day of sweet sap, cloudy, brown and capable of fermenting to a toddy of 8% alcohol. The sunbirds love it – and pass out on the grass below the tree.

Beware of being *too* adventurous. Among the plants that are likely to send you on a 'trip' – possibly a one-way trip – are poppies, thornapple (which occurs as a sinister-looking weed in the south of England), hemlock (the foliage of which is sometimes mistaken for herbs like parsley and the seeds picked in mistake for anise), and the attractive berries of privet, deadly nightshade, woody nightshade and ivy, the peas in laburnum pods, the glossy horse chestnut, yew berries (the sweet pulp is harmless though insipid, but the seeds are deadly), foxgloves, all parts of the rhododendron and azalea, lily of the valley, the berries of the shrub daphne or spurge laurel, all parts of the tomato other than its fruit and all parts of the potato other than its ungreened tubers, the flowers of lilac, and the flowers and seeds of sweet peas, honeysuckle, buttercups, bluebells and delphiniums.

And one cannot assume that, because one member of a plant

family is harmless, its relatives will also be harmless. Elderberry wine may be the classic country wine – and the white elderberry gives an equally pleasant wine, though quite different in character – but the red fruits of the related *Sambucus racemosa* have harmful seeds, and all parts of the dwarf elder or danewort are very unwholesome.

The very wary have warned winemakers not to allow the kernels of fruits like apricots, peaches, plums or almonds into their wine. It is true that the almond flavour of those kernels is linked with a trace of hydrogen cyanide, but the wine would have to contain a great many kernels and you would need to drink a great deal of it before you came to serious harm. It is worth remembering, however, not to include more crushed fruit stones in your wine than you can avoid.

If you wish to make winemaking your hobby, there is everything to be said for making many different wines, from single-gallon sample batches upwards. If, however, you want a regular supply of good, wholesome wine, there is an equally strong case for experimenting for a season or two, until you know the capabilities of the basic materials and your own preferences, and then making two or three big batches every year. For example, you might make 150 litres (30 gal) of mixed fruit wines, adding your raspberry, blackcurrant, elderberry and blackberry wines one after the other so that, by autumn, you had a blended bulk brew of red wine; then make another similar quantity of apple wine.

The ideal solution, as so often in life, is probably a compromise: two or three substantial batches of reliable bread-and-butter wines and as many experimental batches as you can find time for.

You will never make exactly the same wine twice, whether from bought ingredients or from hedgerow fruits. The reasons for the variations are as infinite as the permutations of the recipes. Winegrowers will tell you that their wines vary on each side of the line to which autumn mists rise from the valley floor, and no doubt elderberries (for instance) also vary from place to place and from bush to bush.

Recipes give you the chance to come close to the target – though you can always follow the example of the expert but slightly crack-brained revolver-shot who found that the way never to miss was to shoot first and then draw a target round the hole. In a similar way, you can do what some of the great Australian vineyards do – wait until a wine is mature and then decide whether it is a 'burgundy' or a 'claret'.

A wine that is intended for quick drinking should be low in acidity, low in tannin and low in fruit content. One that is intended for maturing, possibly for three or four years, should be very much higher in acidity, tannin and body, for wines that taste impossibly harsh at six months can, if shut away in a cool, dark place for years, make the quick wines taste juvenile and uninteresting. There is a place in your winemaking and your cellar for both.

If you do experiment with something improbable – turnip-tops or the like – do not be too surprised if it has a disconcerting resemblance in bouquet to a well-made compost-heap. In a way this is only natural, for yeasts are among the organisms we find in a compost-heap or in any decaying vegetable matter. Their place in the order of things is to break complicated dead matter down into less complicated substances which can be used by growing plants and by soil organisms and so give the wheel of life another spin. When we make wine or beer, we check that process (temporarily) at the point we choose.

One of the reasons that winemaking can be almost infinitely variable is that there are no firm rules that fresh fruit may only be used with other fresh fruit or dried with dried – fresh elderberries and dried figs marry very happily.

Do not be in too great a hurry to condemn one ingredient on the strength of the fact that you dislike one sample of one wine made from it. There is an old cliché that there are no good wines, only good bottles (which does not mean, as one person ironically put it, that a good bottle of wine is one with a good label but that a wine can only be judged by the sample from that one bottle in your glass). Next time you drink, say, fig wine you may be very impressed, and may resolve to make some yourself.

Remember, too, that you can adjust the finished wine until it comes nearer to your wishes, either by blending it with other complementary wines or by adding other substances such as glycerine. Analyse the average commercial wine and you will find that (after alcohol and water) the most common constituent is glycerine, which softens and rounds out the wine – hence it can be used, with discretion, to soften and round out a home-made wine, especially a strong wine that drinks like the proverbial whiplash.

In devising recipes and methods, do not follow the advice of the 'experts' too slavishly. One man, who knows more about our craft than most, has said that you cannot make good wine out of ripe gooseberries, whereas, in fact, you can make a wine that, if not

Château d'Yquem, will compare more than favourably with Spanish Sauternes.

The following three chapters are no more than a look at some of the items on a very varied menu.

4

Wild Harvest

No matter how easy it is nowadays to buy the raw materials for good wines straight off the shelves of the specialist shops or the supermarket, there is a special satisfaction to be gained from gathering the ingredients from the countryside. Part of that satisfaction stems, perhaps, from the fact that man was a hunter and food-gatherer for many thousands of years before he turned to agriculture and commerce – part, too, from the pleasure most of us feel in getting 'something for nothing'.

It is not only people who live in the country who take advantage of the wild harvest – for them, it is easier to pick some elderberries than it is to make their way to the nearest shop selling canned elderberry juice or dried berries – but town and city people, too, make a holiday of their 'vintage'.

Cars from the towns discharge family parties dressed in their oldest clothes, with bicycle clips or pieces or string round their trouser cuffs to ward off the exploring stems of nettles, wearing their strongest shoes or wellington boots, and hampered by polythene pails and picnic-baskets. Country folk, by and large, do not grudge them their pickings, though they may be amused by their enthusiasm and by their lack of local knowledge. What farmers and gamekeepers do object to are gates left open, polythene bags abandoned where cows can eat them and choke, branches of cherry trees wantonly broken in order to reach a handful of fruit, laybys used as toilets, lanes fouled with litter and standing corn trodden down. A farm is not simply space out of doors: it is the farmer's factory, hobby, home – and obsession.

So, if you are venturing onto enclosed ground, remember the old nursery motto 'It's manners to ask'. Generally you will be greeted with civility, and often your own good manners will pay dividends, for you will be directed to richer picking-grounds than you would ever have found for yourself. You may even find yourself returning season after season to the same farm, with your 'thank-you' bottle of wine, for your own harvest of winemaking materials, and will come to realise that the 'Farmer Giles' image is a caricature of the real countryman and that wit and wisdom are not monopolies of one side or the other of the speed limit signs.

It is highly unlikely that, however much the winemaking boom continues, winemakers will ever overpick elderberries to the point of extinction (if they do become extinct it will be by chemical spray or bulldozer), but even some of the commonest wild flowers are at risk of being overharvested, as will be made clear several times in the tally of plants available from this wild harvest.

Is there any danger to winemakers? Fortunately, very few British plants are deadly, though some are unwholesome, and most of the deadly plants are fungi, with which not even the most adventurous winemaker is likely to experiment. But the prudent attitude is 'If you don't know what it is, don't make wine with it!' One foraging party that ignored this warning was stopped just in time from going off with baskets full of 'elderflower heads' for wine, happily ignorant of the fact that the flower heads were those of the deadly hemlock plant. A little knowledge would have saved them from that risk, since elders are large bushes and hemlocks stemmy plants.

At one time, the crop of wild flowers, fruit and vegetation close to a busy road was the only one that had to be avoided since it might be contaminated by petrol and diesel fumes, and by dust or tarry and oily deposits. Now, even far from the main roads, there is some risk of contamination from weedkilling and pesticidal sprays. The risk is slight, and most of these sprays would be unlikely to cause even an opalescent haze in the finished wine. However, when you realise that some sprays are applied by specialists wearing gas masks who are warned to wash thoroughly if they feel the smallest splash of liquid on their bare skin, it is surely prudent to avoid plants that show signs of distortion or are close to the margin of fields containing crops. Farming is a business, so it is unlikely that money will have been wasted on spraying wild vegetation more than a few yards from the edge of the crop itself.

Hedgerow fruits obviously have their bad seasons and their vintage years, just as grapes do. Obviously, too, the soil, the subsoil, the rainfall, the drainage and the sunny aspect or shade all have their effects. Despite the many interested winemakers who are now paying heed to these matters, the answer to most questions about the ideal conditions for winemaking fruits is 'We just don't know'. Perhaps a detailed analysis of the possibilities of even the familiar elderberry must wait until elderberries are grown commercially in Britain (as they now are in the Maritime Provinces of Canada), but when that day comes, the amateur winemaker with his old clothes and his basket will not be welcome in the elderberry groves!

Sometimes, however, it is possible to gather soft fruit, or top fruits like apples and plums, on the fruit farm. Such an opportunity is given by the farmer when pickers are hard to get, and he is glad to clear his crop with the minimum of trouble.

'Pick-it-yourself' prices vary widely and sometimes the cost per pound works out at not much below the farm-gate price, or even the price you might pay in your local shop.

It is an open secret that fresh fruit on sale at the farm gate is sometimes bought in for resale, and that some of it was picked a couple of days before elsewhere in the Common Market. If the price is right, this fact need not deter the winemaking buyer.

Looking through the possibilities of the wild harvest, one finds that some are obvious and lavish sources of wine (the elderberry being the outstanding example) but that others repay time and effort very poorly. They are listed here in alphabetical order, not in order of preference.

Apples

The wild apples of hedges and woods are sometimes garden escapees or have grown from seeds dropped by birds, and can be quite sweet and palatable. They blend well with the native crab apple, which by definition is a shrub apple (for the crab has nothing to do with the sea) but which can be found as a woody shrub, as a large, handsome tree or as trees of intermediate shapes and sizes. Although harsh, high in tannin and acid, the crab apple, discreetly used, is a good source of wine.

Barberries

The spiny bushes of the barberry, with long, bright coral berries, are familiar in British hedges, yet the name is exotic, meaning the plant of the Berbers. The Berbers are armed with sharp daggers, and strong gloves are needed if you wish to reach into the heart of the bushes. Because the berries are small and painful to pick, they are best used to make up quantities in a mixed-fruit autumn wine.

Beech leaves

The bright young leaves of the beech are used to produce a liqueur called beech-leaf noyau. It is likely that they would make at least as good a wine as other herbage, but if they have been used for that purpose the fact does not seem to have been publicised. An opportunity for the adventurous experimenter?

Bilberries

Bilberry means 'the dark berry', and after you have been picking them for a while the staining on your fingers indicates the sound reason for their name. They grow in heathy places and, because they mix with the heather, can be hard to find. You may have to comb a wide moorland to obtain the berries for half a dozen bottles of wine – that fruity social wine may mean an August day of searching and gathering. Perhaps a day on the moors should be regarded as its own reward, with the bilberry wine as a happy memento and bonus?

Birch

The birch is famous as the source of one of the more unusual country wines, for the basic material is the clear and slightly sweet sap of the tree. Old methods involved cutting grooves in the trunk and fitting little tin spouts, or boring holes and inserting pipes made of elder branches with the pith removed. Nowadays, a hole can be bored in the trunk, just through the outer bark, and a piece of plastic tube inserted. This tube runs to a plastic galloner, or even to a polythene bag. A large and healthy tree, tapped like this in the month of March as the leaves begin to swell in the buds, will yield pints of sap in a few days, to be treated as the recipe given later indicates. An even simpler method, which was once employed with glass bottles but is much easier with plastic bags, is to cut off the end of a pencil-thick branch and firmly tie the neck of a bag round the cut end. Once again, an impressive amount of sap will gather in a day or two.

The birch leaves, picked very young and tender, can also be used to make wine after the style of a tea wine. The young leaves, picked on a fine spring day, can be dried on white paper or on fine cloth in a light, airy place, being shaken up daily so that they do not dry unevenly. They are ready to store if they rustle when stirred – and, being brittle to the touch, they should be handled carefully when put in dry, clean tins or polythene bags for storage. Amount per litre/gallon? Try a practice brew with 100 gm per 5 litres (4 oz per gal) and adjust the amount in future, upwards or downwards, to suit your taste.

Other leaves (raspberry, for example) have been similarly treated. Birch-leaf tea and wine is supposed to help rheumatism sufferers, but raspberry-leaf tea and wine aids in the troubles of childbirth, which means that at least half the winemakers will drink it purely for enjoyment. Although it might be amusing to make holly-leaf wine (especially a semi-sparkling wine which could be truthfully said to have a prickle), it has been found that the leaves, like the bright berries, have proved unwholesome to some experimenters in the past.

Blackberries

The bramble or blackberry is one of the best wild 'feedstocks' for wine and is readily available within a short distance almost everywhere in Britain, though it is sometimes difficult to arrive first on the scene. Traditional brambling-grounds are well known and visited every season by folk who may prefer picking brambles to spending an extra hour or two in front of the television set. The berries vary very much in their size and juiciness from area to area and from bush to bush, but this matters more to the jellymaker, who depends on a free run of juice, than to the winemaker, whose methods leach the flavour and colour from even hard, ripe fruit. Indeed, the flavour the winemaker seeks is probably to be found more, weight for weight, in the hard, seedy berries than in the plump, juicy ones.

It is said to be unlucky to pick blackberries after the middle of October – some say firmly 11 October, because when the Devil was thrown out of Heaven he spat on the berries and comes back to do so again on his unhappy anniversary. The effect of the Devil's spit on fermentation is unknown, but since berries ripening after that date are likely to be the homes of wild yeasts and bacteria it would be prudent to give the pulp a whiff of the Devil's own sulphur at a rate of at least one Campden tablet to the gallon.

Since the bramble season and the elderberry season overlap, it is a happy fact that the two berries (one easy, one difficult) can be picked on the same autumn expedition and blended together in any proportion to make a fine red wine. The higher the proportion of brambles, the shorter the pulp-fermentation period should be, for brambles yield a high amount of tannin – even more than the elderberries themselves.

Bramble shoots are used by those winemakers who enjoy wines made from vegetation. Their herbal use is to cure diarrhoea.

Broom

Although the flowers of the broom bush have been used to make wine for many years, it has to be put on record that there is some doubt about their wholesomeness. A pity, because, unlike gorse, which it resembles, the broom flower has no prickles to guard it and, unlike cowslips and primroses, it will not be wiped out by overpicking. The plant does contain traces of an alkaloid poison. How big is the risk? You will search the world in vain for a tombstone with the inscription 'Here lies a winemaker killed by his broom wine!' Whether you feel that the labour of gathering the flowers (approximately one measure of flowers is needed to make an equal measure of wine) is worth while is another matter.

Cherries

The cherry orchards that foam into blossom in England in April and May provide the sweet cherries of the fruitshops. The equally lovely trees that bloom in the hedges and around the edges of woods at about the same time of year yield (if you can get to them before the plundering beaks of birds) smaller and more astringent cherries, which can be used in winemaking but are more economically used in another way. Half fill a preserving-jar with the ripest sound cherries, well washed, and cover them with your strongest wine, either white or red. Screw the top on tightly and leave the jar where you can give it a shake from time to time, for as long as your patience lasts. The bitter-sweet fruit and vinous juice make an ideal accompaniment to ice-cream or otherwise uninteresting milkpuddings. (If there is some doubt about the soundness of the cherries, it may be prudent to add half a Campden tablet along with the wine in order to prevent unwanted refermentation or bacterial action.)

Clover

Clover blooms can be used as the base for a surprisingly successful, though seldom seen, country wine. The sweetest smelling species is the low-growing, wild white clover, the perfume of which competes with exhaust fumes along the embankments of miles of motorway, where unfortunately the law discourages winemakers from parking and scrambling up the banks after the blooms. Nor, of course, is it fair to trample into fields of clover to pick the big red mop-heads. But here and there, sometimes right on the edge of the biggest towns and cities, one can find patches of clover in bloom and can set to on the back-breaking task of picking enough of the flowers for a bottle or two of wine.

Coltsfoot

Coltsfoot is a familiar weed, the bright yellow flowers, like minia-ture dandelions, appearing before the leaves in spring. It grows best on bare land like neglected garden ground, for it is choked out by close-growing vegetation such as grass. Its Latin name *Tussilago* comes from *tussis*, a cough, and the flower has been traditionally used as the base for a cough-cure. If you need an excuse for sampling your coltsfoot wine, just say 'I'll take a drop or two for my cough'.

The traditional gallon of flowers needed to make a gallon of wine takes a surprising amount of finding, even in the most neglected garden, and this can be a cold task in early spring.

Cowslips

The dainty cowslip takes her name from the observation that the flower grows best where cow-dung has fallen. This fact need not discourage winemakers, for these humble origins will long since have been transmuted by the processes of growth and fermentation! What is more serious is the fact that the flowers, which look like bunches of little primroses on slender stems, are being picked to death in some parts of Britain, and to gather a gallon of them strips a large area of grassland of its dancing flowers. It is a matter for the winemaker's own conscience.

Cowslip wine is regarded as a cure for sleeplessness, and for some of the infirmities that far too much wine might cause (such as headaches, decay of memory or madness). In tribute to this, the plant was called 'St Peter's Keys of Heaven' – and it would be pleasant to say 'Have a drop of St Peters Keys'. But if we cull the cowslips now, there will be few or none for the future.

Currants – black, red and white

Currant bushes are often to be found growing in untended parts of Britain, perhaps as relics of a gamekeeper's garden deep in a wood, or by a lock-keeper's ruined cottage. The commonest is the black currant – the bushes are often full of aged black wood and the berries are borne, sometimes high above the ground, on short stubs of newer growth.

Since the berries are small, they take much longer to pick than the lush strigs of garden berries, but they can yield worthwhile baskets-ful to the winemaker who is willing to plunge into the undergrowth and take his chance with the thistles and nettles.

These currant bushes (black, white or red), whether garden escapees or survivors, or sown by birds, are an ideal source of fruit for wine, for, as with most fruit grown hard and wild, the flavour tends to be stronger than in fruit from well-tended gardens.

Dandelions

The undisciplined dandelion still blazes by the golden thousand on roadsides and waste ground, and yields for the patient gatherer the makings of a mild-flavoured wine. If only the yellow parts of the flower are used, the wine lacks the bite one might expect from a flower whose name means 'lion's teeth' – though the properties that give the flower its popular name of 'pee-the-bed' are still detectable! The whole plant, dug up and washed, is used in dandelion beer as the principal flavouring agent, and could perhaps be used to make a bitter, coffee-like wine.

Dandelions are not only prolific and the source of one of the classic country wines, they are also, to the unprejudiced eye, strikingly beautiful.

Elderberries – red and white

Outstanding among the classic sources of country wines is the elderberry, which is often misused by winemakers. It is said, with gallant exaggeration, that so transparent was the skin of the lovely Mary Queen of Scots that, when she drank red wine, the wine could be seen through her slender alabaster throat. Some wines, made from too high a weight of elderberries, might well be visible on their way down the throat of a Ghanaian stoker!

Most winemakers, on a fruit-gathering expedition, tend to take the elderberries as they come, but research in the last few years has shown that there is a wide variation between bush and bush. Some have a catty taste, some woody, some weedy, some fruity. It may be that selected bushes give the best wine, or it may be that the usual random blend, arrived at by the members of a happy family shouting 'Oooh! here's a good bush', is just as satisfactory.

White elderberries, which when fully ripe look like tiny green grapes, make a wine of distinctive flavour which repays long maturing. The wine is almost as colourless as gin, instead of an attractive ruby-red, and its flavour is tantalisingly different from that of the red elderberry.

Do not be tempted to experiment with berries from other species of elder, for the danewort and the red-berried *Sambucus racemosa* (which grows luxuriantly in quarries and similar places mainly on high ground and in the north of England and in Scotland) are very unwholesome.

The familiar elder is a blessed bush for winemakers, for its flowers and fruit rarely fail altogether, even in the worst years, and provide abundant materials for wines, which can vary from light and brisk to big, deep red and full bodied. Perhaps we should spill a libation of elderberry wine each season to Hulda, mother of the good fairies, who lives under the roots!

If frosty weather overtakes you before you can pick your harvest of elderberries, remember that berries which have been frozen on the bushes give a rich but rather harsh juice if picked before they thaw and spoil. Some winemakers reproduce this condition deliberately by deep-freezing ripe berries, then proceeding with a pulp fermentation. Because of the harshness of flavour and the high tannin of wine made from frozen berries, it is advisable to reduce the period of fermentation on the pulp to two or three days, to cut back drastically the weight of fruit to the litre/gallon or be prepared to wait some years for the wine to mature into something really big, worthwhile and mouthfilling.

The flowers, when used with discretion, also have their place in winemaking, for their flavour has been summed up in the aphorism 'Right amount, muscat; too much, tomcat'. A couple of heads of fresh flowers, or a teaspoonful of dried flowers, can greatly improve the nose of other wines.

And elderflowers are the basis of the traditional 'elderflower champagne', which was intended to be drunk within a week or two of bottling. Since the recipes involved large quantities of sugar, no yeast, almost immediate bottling and sometimes the addition of vinegar, over the years the proportion of burst bottles and spoilt brews must have been disappointingly high. Yet, for all that, through the years the light, refreshing, sparkling wine, fragrant of the creamy froth of the blossoms, has been relished in many a summer garden. As can be seen from the recipe section, more controlled methods can now be used.

Gooseberries

A clump of wild gooseberries can give that enjoyable something-for-nothing feeling. They are found here and there all over Britain, and although the wild bush is, if anything, better armed than the garden varieties the best of the berries are small, soft, sweet and highly flavoured, ideal as the basis of a social wine. The small, hard berries can also be used for dry wines of a very different character. Gooseberries, wild or cultivated, are among the most versatile of feedstocks.

Gorse

The prickly bushes of gorse – whin to the North-countryman and the Scot – usually have a scattering of yellow flowers, but it is in late spring that the bushes come into full bloom, when the fragrance on a sunny day can be almost choking in its intensity. It is then that the hardy winemaker, at the cost of a multitude of jags and scratches, laboriously gathers the flowers. A wine made at such a cost deserves to be superlative – it is, in fact, pleasant, but no pleasanter than many a wine made without the shedding of a drop of blood.

Hawthorn

Hawthorn is one of the most familiar British trees, but it is generally kept cropped back as a hedge plant (its name means the hedge thorn). In these conditions it does not flower and fruit as freely as when it is allowed to grow into a tree, but the red haw berries (so like little apples when looked at closely) are more freely accessible. The flowers and the fruit are both traditional materials for country wines, although the *Amateur Winemaker* puts the hawthorn in the doubtful class, saying that its berries contain a toxic substance. However, a species of hawthorn, the azarole, is grown for food in southern Europe.

For those willing to brave the iron-hard thorns, the haws yield a very acceptable fruit wine and can be used with others to make a mixed-fruit autumn wine. The experimental winemaker may care to try to make a foliage wine with the first green leaves, which country children munch as 'bread-and-cheese' – though perhaps the laxative effect of the green leaves may be more concentrated in the wine!

Heather

Heather stains the hillsides with wine, and legend says that 'from the bonnie bells of heather they brewed an ale long syne' and that the last two men who knew the secret were slain rather than divulge it. Perhaps that legend is true, for any recipes for heather ale have a contrived air about them.

Hops

Hops, though principally associated with brewing, have been used in country wines for centuries. The hop scrambles wild through the hedges in many areas of England, and the use of two or three heads of green hops to 5 litres (1 gal) gives zest to some of the old recipes for vegetable, herb or grain wines.

Meadowsweet

Meadowsweet, or queen of the meadow, is one of the commonest flowers in Britain's marshy places and riversides, the heavy perfume of its frothy flowers hanging in the summer air. Its dried leaves have been traditionally used to give a bouquet to drinks of all kinds, and both the leaves and the flowers can be used (discreetly) in wine.

Nettles

The young tops of nettles were a welcome supplement to the diet of country folk in the days before the can-opener and the deep-freeze.

Whether they have any place on the modern menu, or in the modern wine cellar, is a matter of personal taste, but many people find that the traditional brews, with their accompaniments of goose-grass and dandelions, taste disconcertingly like a thin soup. But they are well spoken of as health drinks.

Oak

The oak tree, the emblem of old England, provided not only timber for the 'hearts of oak' men-o'-war but also leaves for oak wine. Some of the old recipes recommended such quantities that the resulting wine must have contained more tannin than the writing-fluid in Victorian school inkwells. A discreet use of six fresh new leaves per 5 litres (1 gal) of wine lacking in tannin can add necessary zest and flavour. And if you do make pure oak-leaf wine, following one of the foliage recipes, and it turns out to have a mouth-puckering amount of tannin in it, do not throw it away. Keep it for blending, for sooner or later you will make a bland and flabby wine with which the tannin of the oak leaf will marry happily.

Oregon grape

The name of the Oregon grape is puzzling when you see it in flower, for the bush looks like a relative of the barberry (which it is) and its yellow flowers give no hint of the grape-like miniature clusters to come later in the year. These berries even have a bloom on them, similar to the bloom on black grapes. Winemakers are not likely to be popular if they pick the Oregon grapes in the public park, where the bushes are often found in shrubberies, but one may encounter them in the grounds of country estates which have reverted to wilderness. The fruit can be used to augment a mixed-fruit wine.

Primroses

Primrose wine is one of the classic country wines, but it is difficult to recommend the flower as a basic ingredient, not because of its flavour, or lack of flavour, but because, over large areas of Britain, the wild primrose is literally being picked to death. Winemakers are not generally to blame, but thoughtless people swoop on a mossy bank covered with the pale yellow flowers, rape it to make posies and then, as often as not, drop the wilting bunches before they leave

the woodland. If you know a place where primroses grow un-
molested and you feel you want to take some for wine, at least ration
yourself on the 'pick one, leave one' basis so that the colony can
survive for the future.

Raspberries

The wild raspberry is usually smaller and more seedy than its garden
kin, and does not grow in convenient weedless rows. Instead, the
canes shoot up in semi-shaded places at the edge of woods, often in
the company of nettles and thistles. An expedition to gather wild
rasps is an occasion for old clothes that cover the flesh, not for
Bermuda shorts and brief skirts.

These small wild raspberries seem to give a wine more flavour and
bouquet, but perhaps this is partly due to the solid satisfaction of
obtaining the basic material at the cost of nothing but time, effort,
stings and scratches.

Those who prefer their wines not to taste distinctively of their
origins should note that wine made from these full-flavoured berries
is strongly raspberry in character – they may prefer to use the fruit in
a batch of mixed ingredients.

Roses

There are many wild rose species, the fruits of which are all
wholesome. The commonest British wild rose is the dog rose, *Rosa
canina*. This is the rose that provides the rootstock for our cultivated
roses, and which we curse when it sends up strong spiny suckers.
You may also find other wild species, such as sweetbriar (*R.
rubiginosa*) and Scotch rose (*R. spinosissima*). All have hips which
can be used for winemaking. Leave them to ripen fully, until the first
hard nip of frost has softened them, because they are then better
flavoured and easier to work with.

Picking rose-hips on a dry sunny day with just a hint of frost in the
air is a pleasant autumn pastime, with the promise of good wine to
come; but it is only fair to say that the wine can have a characteristic
tang which not everyone likes. Try a sample of rose-hip wine made
by someone else before you invest too much time, material and
effort in a big batch of your own.

Rowan

The flowers of the rowan or mountain ash look temptingly like elderflower heads, but the smell is pungent and discouraging, and it is obviously worth while leaving the flowers to develop into the bright clusters of red berries. The magical fruits (a guard against evil spells, snake bites and witchcraft) make a fine wine, refreshingly astringent, and they can also be used to give character to mixed-fruit wines. Because of the astringent flavour, as little as 500 gm (1 lb) to 5 litres (1 gal) can be used – and it is easy, on an expedition to the hillsides or sandy heaths where the neat trees grow, to pick a big weight of berries in a sunny autumn afternoon. The rowan is one of the neglected crops in the wild harvest as far as winemaking is concerned, but you may find competition from the birds, who do not need convincing of the berries' attractiveness.

Sloes

The sloe, the little black plum which is an ancestor of the garden plums, is covered in white flowers before the leaves appear. Unfortunately, the bloom does not always set, so the bushes are not always covered with the round grape-like berries after the flowers have gone. Sloes are so tart and acid that they are inedible raw, but they can be mellowed by long steeping in a sweet, strong wine to make a less-potent cousin of the well-known sloe gin. They can also be used, alone or in a blend of other autumn fruits, to make excellent wine. The dark berries, however, do not give the richness of colour that you would expect.

Strawberries

Wild strawberries make a beautiful wine. The plants are certainly common, on heaths, railway embankments and commons, and in the fringes of woodland. In most years there is a good crop of fruit. But the berries are so small and light, and take so much back-breaking gathering, that they are better kept to savour one at a time, perhaps with a glass of sweet white wine.

5

Gardening for Wine

Not every winemaker has a garden, but even those who have only a small plot have the opportunity to grow the feedstocks for a great deal of wine.

The most prolific garden crops can yield the makings of many bottles of wine to the square yard of ground – examples, each making very different types of wine, are black currants, rhubarb and parsnips.

Just as there is some controversy in winemaking between those who favour the old traditions and those who believe in scientific methods, so in gardening there are those who prefer to use compost and manure (sometimes summed up scornfully as 'muck and mystery') and those who favour artificial fertilisers. No impartial investigation has ever been made into which school produces the best raw materials for winemaking, but the advocates of artificials tend to boast of yields and the compost fans of flavour.

Nearly every garden fruit and vegetable, and many flowers, can be used to make wine. Not all are equally satisfactory, yet it is true to say that sometimes astonishingly good wines are made from such unlikely bases as peapods and turnips. Once again, it is a matter for the individual to decide whether the skill and enthusiasm deployed on using such materials would not be better expended on making wine from more tractable foodstocks.

Apples

The first fruit to be listed is one of the most satisfactory – and most flexible in the styles of wine that can be made from it – the apple.

Crab apples, which are mainly self-fertile, lovely in flower, hardy, compact, less tempting to boy raiders and yield a fruit that gives an extra tang and character to more insipid varieties, are worth growing. However, a big tree laden with fruit can yield a surprisingly small weight of apples.

A mature tree of a vigorous variety like the cooker 'Bramley Seedling' can yield, on the other hand, hundredweights of fruit – and since around 10 kg (20 lb) of apples will give 5 litres (1 gal) of juice for cider and about 3·5 kg (7 lb) will form the base for 5 litres (1 gal) of apple wine, one or two cooking-apple trees can supply a household with a year's drinking.

Neither crabs, nor cooking apples, nor dessert apples are ideal by themselves – a blend of all three, it is generally agreed, makes for a balanced wine.

Beetroot

Beetroot wines are among the country classics, and yet most winemakers would admit to misgivings about them. Although they may be pleasant and acceptable, they are rarely comparable in quality to the best of fruit wines. Beetroots are easy to grow on reasonably fertile soils which do not dry out, and a small bed will provide roots for gallons of wine. Traditionally, the old and wrinkled beets are used in the spring, but by making the wine from young, sweet roots one can extract the colour and flavour by osmotic pressure, and make a wine that matures more quickly.

The sliced raw beets are covered with hot sugar syrup, and the combination of heat and the 'pull' of the strong sugary liquid burst the cell walls, liberating the contents. The method is described in more detail in the recipe section. The reason why the juice is boiled after extraction is to remove any persisting soil organisms, which, it has been suggested, may be responsible for the earthy taste of root wines – for there are more organisms in a half-teaspoonful of healthy soil than there are people in the world. Nobody would deliberately allow soil to contaminate their wine at any stage, but the risk of this is obviously greater when you are handling beetroot, parsnips and the like. Usually, the thorough boiling required to extract the juice will effectively deal with soil-borne bugs on the chunks of vegetable.

Incidentally, even the more disappointing country wine made from beetroots by granny's methods is not the most devastating drink made from the roots – in Persia they are a source of vodka.

Blackberries

Brambles or blackberries do well in gardens and form almost impenetrable frontier fences – just as effective as barbed wire where such a screen is needed, and much more fruitful than barbed wire! 'Himalayan Giant' is one of the best varieties for this purpose, being very vigorous and thorny. Those who prefer to gather the berries with less risk will plant 'Merton Thornless', or another of the thornless varieties. Brambles, though native to Britain, are choosy about situation and soil, preferring a rich but well-drained soil in a position where they will not be battered by strong winds or burned by salt spray or frost.

The cultivated bramble is no better flavoured than its wild relative, and winemakers who have ample access to wild berries should consider growing other cane fruit (say, raspberries) in their gardens.

Enthusiasts for herbal wines may be interested to note that wine can be made from bramble tips, at the rate of a measure of tips (lightly pressed down) for every measure of wine. Here again, it is probably better to harvest from wild bushes rather than domestic ones.

Blueberries

Blueberries, associated in the British mind with American pies, are likely to become more and more popular in gardens in this country, especially where the soil is moist and acid – the kind of land one does not associate with good fruit crops. Blueberries, planted out at a spacing of about 2 m × 2 m (6 ft × 6 ft) produce upwards of 2·5 kg (5 lb) per bush of juicy, easily picked fruit, which with their dark blue colour and bright bloom look (as, indeed, they are) very suitable for winemaking. They are even more attractive to birds than to winemakers, so you will have to net your bushes.

Broad beans

Broad beans, which are among the easiest of garden crops to grow in most parts of the country, are used by some winemakers as a basic material. They boil up the hard, dried beans for an hour, then strain the boilings and make wine from the liquid. More a way of using up a stock of surplus broad beans than of making a superb wine!

Carrots

Carrots make, if not a superb wine, a very presentable one, though many a glassful offered as 'carrot whisky' has no obvious resemblance to Glenlivet or Cameron Bridge. Carrots grow easily to a great size in some gardens, in others, carrot-fly destroys the plants before the roots begin to form. If you are lucky enough to have good carrot soil, you can certainly produce the makings of many gallons of wine from a small bed.

There seems to be little to choose between the many varieties on offer in the catalogues – though 'Red Elephant Wine' has a certain ring to it, and the carrot of that name grows to a great size yet stays succulent. Such juicy roots not only carry flavour but also contain sugar.

Catnip

Catnip is worth a mention as a curiosity. The Chinese used to add it to their rice wine to increase the euphoria it created, but since the plant's attraction to cats is due to a drug, Metatibilacetone, which has been used to tranquillize the big cats in zoos, it is safer left out of our wines.

Currants – black, red and white

Currants – black, red and white – are an excellent source of wine, used by themselves or in blends of other fruits. Black currants, well grown, must be top of the league for productivity, for in theory a small garden planted exclusively with black currant bushes could produce 5000 litres (1000 gal) of light wine a year – somewhat more than the average family consumes. Black currants can be used to make heavy, fruity wines, with as much as 2·5 kg (5 lb) of dead-ripe berries to 5 litres (1 gal), or light, fresh wines, with 500 gm (1 lb) of fruit or even less to 5 litres (1 gal).

The new varieties, 'Ben Lomond' and 'Ben More', are to be commended. They fruit abundantly and are less subject to frost damage. 'Laxton's Giant' has fruit as big as cherries. The 'Hilltop' strain of 'Baldwin' holds its berries till the last one is ripe, enabling the winemaker to clear his plot in one vintage pick. 'Wellington XXX' makes a big sprawling bush, which fruits early and heavily on most soils. If you like the flavour of black-currant wine (and not everyone does), this is a fruit to consider planting deliberately for wine. Big bud and its accompanying virus disease, reversion, are the only two severe troubles that afflict the bushes, although sometimes disappointingly the fruit will run off and leave bare strigs.

Red currants and white currants, which belong to races related to the black currant, yield berries that can be transformed into wines capable of deceiving the knowledgeable – unlike black currants, they do not betray their origin. Red and white currants fruit on the old wood and can readily be trained into cordons or a formal fence. They are practically everlasting, outliving the gardener who plants them, and they are almost disease-free. So what is the snag about them? They are tedious to pick, and even the most enthusiastic berry-picker might weary of the job before he has gathered enough for his 30 bottles or so of fine wine.

Dahlias

Grown in their native South America for food, dahlias can be used to make wine. The tubers are washed, cut up and boiled like beetroot or parsnips, and the resulting juice (balanced with acid and tannin, sugar, yeast nutrient and Benerva tablets) is fermented out. It is more a novelty for dahlia-show dinners than a serious wine.

Figs

Home-grown figs make a superb wine, but even the most enthusiastic winemaker is likely to find that his family appreciates their honey sweetness too much as dessert fruit to enable him to make wine from them. But, of course, dried figs are always available.

Goldenrod

A weed in America, and in Britain one of the easiest of perennials to grow, goldenrod is used to colour and flavour wine, at a rate of a couple of handfuls of petals to 5 litres (1 gal).

Gooseberries

Gooseberries are nicknamed the hairy grape, and not for nothing. They can be used when hard and green to make wines comparable to at least some of the blended Rhine wines, and at every stage of ripeness in some way, until at last, when so ripe that they can scarcely be picked without bursting, they can make big, fruity wines of the Sauternes and Tokay type. Gooseberry wine, made from such ripe berries, may need a year or two to mature and to lose a certain oily unctuousness.

The bushes lend themselves to training, and a gardener whose space is limited can grow them as cordons up a wall facing in any direction.

There are many hundreds of varieties, not all of which are now available commercially. The commonest varieties are fruitful, hardy, long-lived and disease-free. 'Careless', a 'white' variety, which can be used green or as golden balls of sweet juice, deserves mention; so do 'Keepsake', one of the earliest varieties, 'Leveller', *the* dessert variety, and 'Whinham's Industry', a red berry that tolerates heavy soils and produces dark red, hairy, sweet fruits which hang well.

In searching through the list of garden plants and fruits for future winemaking, do not overlook the obvious – and gooseberries are obvious because (prickles apart) they are so suitable for our purpose.

Houseleeks

These succulent plants, which grow on walls and even roofs, are not used in winemaking but must surely be the badge of the less discreet members of our craft, for the popular old name is 'Welcome home husband however drunk you be'!

Huckleberries

The garden huckleberry is grown from seed. It is listed in some catalogues as Wonderberry, which would look well on a label. The compact bushes, which result from early sowing under glass, bear up to 3 kg (6 lb) of fruit in a good season. The fruit, low in acidity and tannin (and also in pectin), can be blended with other autumn fruits, particularly apples.

Lettuces

Lettuces have been used to make foliage wines, but do not be tempted to use a row of shot lettuces to make a big batch. The bolted plants are rich in narcotic juice, and the resulting wine may be more of a knock-out than you had anticipated. Lettuce wine, to sum up, is one that is worth trying by the experimental winemaker – trying once.

Loganberries

The loganberry, cousin of the blackberry, is a fruit that it *is* worth growing for wine. It was discovered in the garden of Judge Logan in California, hence the name. The best thorny strain of loganberry is the virus-free LY59, but it is difficult to find – the thornless strain has obvious advantages. The canes need a substantial fence or trellis to grow on. In July and August they yield their tapering, dull-red, juicy berries, which are more acid than blackberries.

The Tayberry, a prolific new cane fruit with very large purple juicy berries, seems made for the winemaker's purpose. Culture is similar to the loganberry.

Marigolds

The marigold is one of the few flowers worth growing for winemaking, other than the rose. The flowers to use are those of the common marigold, the calendula, and since the petals are required to contribute colour as well as a little flavour the best varieties are the deep orange ones like 'Orange King'.

Marigolds could scarcely be easier to grow. Sown in the spring as soon as the soil is workable, they will establish themselves quickly and, if left to their own devices, will seed themselves all around.

Medlar fruits

The medlar, a handsome tree when in bloom, gives strange-looking fruits, rather like the prototype for a cross between a rose-hip, an apple and an outsize hawthorn haw. In this country the fruits are picked late and left to soften until they are on the verge of going rotten, a process known as 'bletting'. Only then can they be eaten, or successfully used for winemaking. Not a tree to plant deliberately with a view to future vintages, but a fruit to be used for wine when available.

Mint

Mint, the familiar flavour in drinks like Crème de Menthe, thrives in good soil in an open position and may even move out to invade adjacent garden ground. Almost the only ailment that affects it is rust, which can be treated by pushing dry straw or grass between the stems and setting it on fire.

There are several varieties and many unintentional hybrids, and flavours vary from *eau-de-cologne* to toothpaste and from chewing-gum to Chartreuse. Try a small batch with the mint you are going to use before you commit yourself to making a big batch whose flavour you may not like.

Mulberries

Mulberry trees may have been grown in Britain since the time of the Romans. The long-lived trees are seen at their best on old lawns, though their yield is better where the feeding is richer. Mulberries from a tree on a lawn are harvested very easily – you simply wait until the luscious fruits fall to the grass, then pick them up. The fruits are purple-black and the juice stains fabric permanently, so be careful of good clothes when winemaking. Most British mulberries go to waste – if you find someone with a fruitful tree, you may well get the mulberries for the taking. But carry them home in a polythene container, not in a basket, or the juice will certainly run away.

Parsley

Parsley wine is the one that converts those who are bigoted enough to say that vegetables never make worthwhile wine. Given a deep rich soil which holds the moisture well, parsley will produce lavish quantities of foliage for wine. 30 gm (1 oz) of seed sows 24 m (80 ft) of drill, and for winemaking purposes the best method is to sow in the spring, as soon as the soil is workable, and to harvest the entire row in September, digging the remains in. Parsley seed is slow to germinate – pour a kettleful of boiling water up the drill and sow the seed onto the steaming ground, and you may speed up the process a little. Ten days or so after sowing the seed, water the ground with paraquat weedkiller (Weedol) and this will ensure that the slow-sprouting seedlings will show through in weed-free surroundings.

Most herbs have their medical uses, and parsley is no exception –

it is a specific against rheumatism, but no excuse is needed for enjoying this herbal wine. Incidentally, parsley was reputed to have the curious property of weakening glass. The experimental wine-maker might care to note whether the proportion of burst bottles is higher with it than with other wines.

Parsnips

Well-made parsnip wine needs no apology, being probably the best of the root wines. Parsnips can produce a huge gallonage from a restricted area – 1 kg (2 lb) of roots to 300 cm (1 ft) of row is by no means a record. There is no need to go all out for size and produce parsnips like those on the show-bench. Roots of a ½ kg (1 lb) weight each are adequate.

The seed, which looks like flakes of breakfast food, should be sown thinly as early in the spring as possible. 30 gm (1 oz) sows 45 m (150 ft) of row, which could yield the basis for more than 150 litres (30 gal) of good wine. In most parts of Britain the roots can be left in the ground until they are sweetened by the first severe frosts. A little canker on the shoulders is almost the only trouble they are likely to suffer from, and the cankered marks are easily sliced away when you are preparing the roots for the pot. This is one wine where a discreet use of spice – root ginger, perhaps – enhances the character and flavour.

Peaches

Peaches, beautiful in bloom, crop heavily in the more favoured parts of the British Isles, and the resulting fruit makes fine wine. Since those who make wine from their home-grown peaches think in terms of one fruit to a litre or six to the gallon, a bush of 'Peregrine' producing over 100 marketable peaches would provide something like 1000 litres or over 160 gal!

Peach trees are pruned more like black-currant bushes than like other top fruit, old wood being cut out in May to stimulate new growth. Also like black currants, they are greedy plants and love plenty of nitrogen. It is unlikely that even the keenest winemaker will be allowed to make wine from every peach he grows, but when you have a bush or two in full fruit you may, generously, allow some to be eaten raw or even cooked.

Nectarines, which are fuzzless peaches, also make good wine. They do not tolerate dry conditions as well as peaches do and in a dry summer may need thorough watering.

Peas

Peapod wine, when it is good, is a sterling example of the triumph of skill over basically unsuitable material. But since peapods go on the compost-heap anyway, there is little harm in trying an experimental gallon as a bonus to the pleasure of eating small, sweet green peas from your own garden.

Plums

Plums in their various kinds need no such reservations – they are a source of good wine, and have been for centuries. 'Victoria', which can be enjoyed raw or cooked, is the best-known variety. It tends to crop irregularly, but when it does bear fruit it produces enough to make wine for the sparser years to come. Plum trees need plenty of room and should not be planted closer together than 4 m (18 ft).

The related damson is even more suitable for winemaking than the plum itself, though it has been described as 'much stone and little flesh'. Some have names that would look well on a label – for example, what could be more cheering than 'Merryweather Wine'? The hardy, dense bushes, by the way, make ideal windbreaks on the verge of a garden.

The bullace, a slightly more civilised version of the wild sloe, bears astringent fruit which can be left on the tree until the leaves have fallen and frost has mellowed the tartness.

Potatoes

Potato wine has a place in winemakers' mythology, being notorious for the hangovers it leaves one with. If you feel you wish to make potato wine, then include plenty of raisins, fresh orange juice and perhaps some cereal – and then leave out the potatoes! (The experimental winemaker may care to use the starchy liquid in which potatoes have been boiled as a basis, with diastatic malt extract, for a half-strength schnapps.)

Pumpkins

Pumpkins share with vegetable marrows the disability of not really being a good winestock, but they have the additional shortcoming of being much more difficult to grow, except in the more favoured corners of Britain.

Quinces

Quince bushes grow, unrecognised by that name, in many a suburban garden, for the flowering quinces are still thought of by most
gardeners as japonicas. The shrub is mainly grown for its flowers,
but its tart fruits are a welcome bonus and can be used along with
apples in an autumn wine, when their aroma and piquancy will add a
little subtlety to the result. Fruiting quinces provide their fruits as a
crop and their blossom as a bonus.

Raspberries

The idea that the raspberry is one of the most useful plants in the
winemaker's garden is not shared by everyone – some winemakers
think that its flavour is too dominant. Those who favour raspberries
can argue that the flavour, though distinct even in low-fruit wines, is
pleasant and vinous, and that the berries are easy to grow, straightforward to pick and simple to use in wine.

Mechanical picking, though well past the experimental stage in
the commercial raspberry fields, is unlikely to reach the winemakers' gardens in the foreseeable future – the winemaker will still have
to depend on the skill of his own fingertips and those of his
pressganged family, relatives and acquaintances.

Since from well-grown, healthy raspberries you can harvest 1·5 kg
of fruit for every metre of row (1 lb to the foot) and since 1 kg to
5 litres (2 lb to the gallon) makes quite a fruity wine, it can be seen
that even a small patch of raspberries will fill many wine bottles. The
plants thrive in a wide variety of soils and climates but appreciate
shelter from the wind, for the leaves are bruised and the canes
broken by rough weather.

The canes should be picked over regularly, but there is no need to
start a gallon of wine every time you gather a basket of berries. They
keep very well if covered with a strong solution of sulphur dioxide –
say, four Campden tablets dissolved in a litre (quart) of water and
stirred into the berries in a plastic bucket.

By preserving the berries – which is what the professionals do,
and for much longer than a day or two, since raspberries used in jam
may not even have been picked the year they were boiled – you are
able to make your raspberry wine in one big batch, instead of in
awkward small amounts.

A raspberry bed can be made to look quite ornamental if the

canes are neatly tied to supporting wires and the alleys in between the rows are grassed down and kept close cut.

To sum up, raspberries are definitely a worthwhile addition to any garden. But if you are establishing your own raspberry vineyard, do not scrounge young plants, however healthy-looking, from a neighbour. Buy strong, certified young plants from a nurseryman.

Rhubarb

There are few plants that, generously treated, can give such a gallonage of wine from a limited area as rhubarb. The wine you make from it is unlikely to be superb, but there is no reason why it should not be very drinkable as well as plentiful. To make the best of your rhubarb, do not wait until September when the patch is a jungle of huge stems as thick as your wrist. Instead, start your vintage when the stems are still young, tender and less acid.

Rhubarb contains oxalic acid, and oxalic acid is poisonous, but the danger can be grossly exaggerated. Folk who cheerfully sit down to large wedges of rhubarb tart without any fear of ill-effects, except to their waistlines, will sheer away from rhubarb as a winestock because of its 'poisonous' acidity.

There are ways of reducing that acidity. Calcium carbonate – powdered chalk – can be stirred into the juice, until fizzing ceases and the juice is bland and neutral. Others prefer to use potassium carbonate, finding that this neither throws a sediment nor impairs the flavour. But the simplest way is to pick the rhubarb early and use one of the cold methods which do not dissolve the nodules of oxalic acid, and forget all about such treatments.

If you have space, it is best to earmark one or two plants for supplies for tarts and jam and to reserve the remainder for one big, early pulling for wine, leaving the bed to recover for the rest of the year, perhaps with a top dressing of compost to help next year's vintage. To avoid damaging the crowns when picking, slide your hand down the stalk, with your thumb in the hollow side, and then twist gently.

Cut off all the leaves – do not be tempted to make rhubarb-leaf wine, for the oxalic acid *is* concentrated dangerously in the green leaves.

More than one recipe, and method of preparation, has been given in the recipe section because, although rhubarb wine may never hit the heights, it is so cheap and easy to make that it deserves detailed mention. And it lends itself to blending – for example, rhubarb and black bananas are in season at different times of the year, and there may be a gap of more than six months between the day when you pull your first lavish gathering of rhubarb and the day when your friendly greengrocer tips you the wink that he has a box of very overripe bananas. The two very inexpensive wines complement each other nicely and can be blended at any stage – the rhubarb wine, which is likely to be thin and acid, matches the banana wine, which is full-bodied and smooth, and can be made with only a little added acid.

Even the smallest suburban garden, though shaded and sooty, can produce a worthwhile bulk of wine from a well-tended rhubarb patch.

Roses

The rose, the queen of the garden to her lovers, is so familiar throughout Britain, yet it is not appreciated as a source of wine. Deep-red roses give their colour and fragrance to wines made from them, but there is no reason why a white wine could not be made from the lighter blooms (white, yellow, gold and flame). The petals must be picked as freshly as possible, before the heat of the sun draws the scent from them.

Ideally, a bed of selected roses – 'Fragrant Cloud', 'Wendy Cussons', 'Josephine Bruce' and 'Papa Meilland', for example – should be planted especially for wine, so that the winemaker can gather the petals just as the blooms begin to open without being loudly accused of spoiling the display.

Remember that rose-petal wine, which by itself may seem too intensely scented and lacking in body, can be used with great success to blend with other wines that lack a good 'nose'. Rose petals can also be incorporated into almost every wine recipe to give the other ingredients the aroma they may lack. In fact, although rose-petal wine may be enjoyed as a 'single' wine, it is in mixed wines that rose petals play their most useful part.

Roses can also be grown for their fruit. It is not a good idea to let hybrid tea and floribunda roses set and ripen seed, but some of the shrub roses can be grown as informal hedges and will yield a good harvest of rose-hips. *Rosa rugosa*, in its various varieties, is the obvious choice, for the prickly bushes bear large tomato-red fruit which can be gathered when soft and ripe, perhaps after the first nip of frost.

The country hedgerows are well stocked with rose-hips, so shrub roses grown specifically for their fruit are essentially for the wine-maker with a large garden. But there is scarcely a garden, however small, that cannot offer a handful of fragrant petals to enhance a wine.

Sugar beet

Sugar beet, which is, in fact, a sugary white beetroot, can be grown from seed – a few seedsmen offer it. The method of growing is no more complicated than for its red kinsman, but when you come to make your wine some allowance should be made (preferably by taking a hydrometer reading) for the sugar liberated by boiling. Like most roots, sugar beet has a persistent 'rooty' flavour which can take up to three or four years to mellow.

Swedes

Swedes certainly have this quality, for the wine can have that unpleasant flavour detectable in milk from turnip-fed cows. Their place in the winemaker's menu is not in his decanter but on his plate.

Tomatoes

If you have a surplus of tomatoes you can try converting them into wine. Home-grown tomatoes tend to be more intense in flavour and therefore less likely to make a watery, insipid wine, but even with high-flavoured varieties such as 'Gardener's Delight' the result is apt to be bland.

Turnips

What has just been said about swedes applies particularly to turnips, although some enthusiasts for strange feedstocks have contrived to make a turnip cider from the expressed juice of the roots.

Vegetable marrows

This vegetable has its place in the mythology of the craft. Everyone knows that if you take a huge marrow, hollow it out, stuff it with Demerara sugar and sling it in a net with a woollen wick stuck into it, it will drip the best of West Indies' rum all winter. What a pity it isn't as easy as that! You *can* make vegetable-marrow wine by cutting the marrow into even-sized chunks, boiling them like beetroot or turnips and then straining off the juice. The result is certainly better than with turnips. But probably most marrow wine is made because the gardener, having grown a huge example of 'Long Green Trailer', does not know what to do with the monster after he has shown it to all his admiring friends.

Vines

A place might have been found at the end of this by no means exhaustive list of garden sources of wine for the *Worcesterberry*, a very thorny bush similar to a gooseberry but with berries like black currants, but it seemed only fitting to end the list with the vine, with which, as far as we are aware, winemaking began.

Vines, though found in less hospitable parts of North America, are not native to Britain, but there seems no doubt that grapes have been grown here since the time of the Romans. In recent years, interest has greatly revived and the first commercial vineyards have been established. (One could not realistically call the Castell Coch vineyard, north of Cardiff, a commercial vineyard. It was the toy of the rich Marquess of Bute from 1871 to 1914, and the money he made from coal subsidised his red and white wines.)

The development of more precocious varieties has extended the vine's range northwards, and there are those who foresee the eventual establishment of vineyards on the more hospitable slopes of Scotland.

It was Virgil who said that 'Vines love an open hill', and this is true even at the northernmost extent of their range. Most winemakers, however, have to accept the garden they have and, inside it, give the grapes the best position they can.

The growing of grapes in Britain has been dealt with in detail and with some authority in recent books, though it is a subject that needs to be constantly brought up to date.

Winemakers, even in those parts of Britain unable to ripen the earliest grapes, may still make large quantities of wine from the foliage, young shoots and tendrils of a few vines. Although this is sometimes called 'folly wine', there is nothing foolish about the end result, for, skilfully made, it can be a light table wine capable of deceiving the knowledgeable.

Therefore, winemakers north of the line below which grapes may reasonably be expected to ripen – and this line is creeping north year by year – may take the lavish harvest of prunings as the basis for their principal wine and accept the occasional harvest of fully ripe grapes as a bonus.

Although a voluminous literature exists on the qualities of different varieties of grapes, nothing seems to have been published on the best varieties for 'folly wine'. A task here for an experimentally minded winemaker? If so, let us hope that he is not tempted to smuggle any vines in from abroad, in case he infects Britain's infant vineyards with the dreaded phylloxera, which devastated the European vines in the last century.

6

Straight from the Shelf

Not every winemaker has a garden, nor the time and inclination to harvest the wild vintage, but every winemaker can stock up quickly, easily and sometimes quite cheaply at specialist shops, grocers and supermarkets.

It is probably here too, rather than in the chapter on the Wild Harvest, that the 'pick-it-yourself' system belongs. The system started because farmers, faced with a glut of produce, sold it cheaply to those willing to gather it for themselves, or because an unexpected shortage of pickers occurred.

The method is much better organised now – and the produce is correspondingly dearer. So much so, that if you were to cost your own time and your travelling at realistic rates, you would not have gained financially.

The bonus comes in other ways.

You go home with the 'do-it-yourself' glow, as well as with baskets of the finest of fruit – and if it is not the finest of fruit you have only yourself to blame, having picked it yourself. You have had a day out in the country, which to those who live penned in by walls is a real bonus.

On the best 'pick-your-own' farms, the facilities – car parks, toilets, picnic sites – would do credit to many holiday and caravan camps. Some even run buses from the nearest big town. Many have their own shop. If the recipe for strawberry wine says 'Take the juice of two lemons', the lemons may be on sale just there.

Only some of the subjects suitable for conversion into wine are listed in this chapter – others appear, as single wines or as blends, in the recipe section.

Bananas

First in our list, and a surprising one to those outside the craft, is the ordinary banana. To most of us one banana seems very much like another, but as with potatoes, which we also take for granted, there are many varieties, ranging from small, sweet, dessert ones to large, starchy fruits, which in their native lands are used as vegetables.

Ideally, a wine banana should be dead ripe, black all over and going juicy at one end. Bananas that were unripe when a touch of frost hit them are also black all over and can give trouble because of their starchiness, which causes a persistent haze. But dead-ripe bananas (perhaps verging on the overripe) do not cause hazes – in fact, they help other wines to clear quickly when included in the basic ingredients.

Where a dominating banana flavour is not objectionable, the fruit can be crushed or chopped up, skins and all, and boiled. Where a more delicate flavour is desired, then the bananas may be peeled and only the flesh used. Another factor to take into consideration when deciding whether or not to use the skins is the amount of fruit you have and the amount of wine you wish to make. If you have a surplus of bananas, you may feel free to throw away the skins. If bananas and other ingredients are short, you may prefer to use the fruit entire and to take the chance that the banana flavour may mask some of the other tastes.

Often, when shopkeepers learn that you welcome overripe bananas, you will find that you can afford to be lavish, for you may be presented with as much as 25 kg (½ cwt) for carrying away. In that case, you *can* afford to peel the fruit and boil up the flesh for twenty minutes, straining off the juice and leaving it overnight to settle. The sludge will settle to the bottom, and the comparatively clear liquid on top can be poured off and used to replace an equivalent amount of water in wine recipes. This gives the wine a fullness and body that is difficult to achieve at home, unless you use hefty quantities of dried fruit or grape concentrate.

Bananas, then, do well in many wines ('dressed' in strong-flavoured wines like elderberry, or 'nude' in herbal wines or apple wine), but they also make a surprisingly good wine by themselves.

It is not to be wondered at that banana wine is a comparatively recent discovery – it took a flash of imagination on the part of some experimenter to say 'I wonder how overripe bananas would do, at 4 lb to the gallon?'

Crystal malt

Brewers are well aware of the body, colour and flavour given to beer by crystal malt. These qualities make it useful in a limited number of wines of the Brown Sherry, Marsala and Madeira type. All share the caramelised 'brown' flavour conferred by crystal malt. There is, of course, no regulation to prevent the experimentally minded using it in any other wine they choose, but it is advisable to make a trial jar first.

Dried fruits

By using dried fruits such as figs, dates, sultanas, currants, raisins, peaches, apricots and prunes, the winemaker could devise an almost endless range of wine styles – these fruits all have a sugar content of approximately 50%. He could extend his range still further by using bilberries, elderberries and sloes, which have a negligible sugar content. All these fruits are dealt with individually in the recipe section.

Fruit juices

Fruit juices are almost as good as dried fruits, and even easier to use. Generally, unsweetened juices are the best bargain because you can buy sugar more cheaply dry in a neat bag than in solution in a can.

When making wine with any juices or fruits (generally in bottles or jars) that contain preservatives like sulphur dioxide, it is wiser to bring the juices to boiling-point and to hold them at that temperature for a few minutes in order to drive off the surplus sulphur. Having done this, you will find that the fermentation establishes itself much more quickly than if the yeast had been left to multiply in the rather unfriendly atmosphere of a sulphured liquid.

A litre (2 pt), or even a little less, of juice (orange being the best example) and between 1 kg and 1·5 kg (2 lb–3 lb) of sugar will together produce 5 litres (1 gal) of a pleasant wine. And going on from there you can build up more complicated recipes – a pinch of grape tannin to give the wine a little extra zest, grape concentrate to give it a vinous roundness, barley syrup or bananas to add to the body.

Grain

Grain figures prominently in the older recipes, with names like 'wheat whisky'. It is wasteful to use such starchy materials as wheat and barley grains without first converting them (as is done in malting) into sweet, sugary substances that the yeast can make use of, since all you are using is some of the flavour, mainly from the husk, and some gummy materials which help to give the wine body, though they may also sometimes throw persistent hazes. However, some quite pleasant wines – and a few which deserve more complimentary terms than that – have been made from the old recipes.

One quite important point – if you buy your whole grain from a shop that specialises in supplying winemakers, it *should* be fit to use as it is. If you purchase it from a local corn merchant or from the pet shop, put it in a sieve and give it a thorough wash under the tap. This is not only to remove dust, and perhaps the traces of rats and mice, but also to wash off any seed dressings the farmer might have applied – and even the spores of the ergot fungus, which, though rare, can be distressing and dangerous if absorbed.

Grapes and grape concentrate

What about bought grapes? Unless you can contrive to get regular, cheap, bulk supplies, wine made from bought grapes is likely to be one of the more expensive and less satisfactory of your vintages. For a pure grape wine, something like 7 kg (14 lb) of fruit to 5 litres (1 gal) is needed. If you use less than that and stretch the juice with water, you will need to adjust the acid, tannin and sugar content, as with other wines. Where grapes (bought, perhaps, at the fruit market at the end of a day when there has been a glut of them) really come into their own is as a part of a mixed-fruit wine, for they give roundness and vinosity to what otherwise might be a thin country wine.

Grape concentrate is one of the most convenient base materials for wine, though at the time of writing the cost is high and likely to rise further as some of the cheaper sources begin to be phased out. The cost of the resulting wine may seem scandalous to the older school of winemakers, yet it has to be borne in mind that the cost of six bottles made from grape concentrate is not likely to be much more than that of a comparable bottle of wine enjoyed in a restaurant. (The comparative values, as against the comparative costs, are a matter for the individual winemaker to weigh up.)

Grape-concentrate wine is unlikely to be comparable to, for example, the great vintage wines of France. This stands to reason, for who, having a vineyard capable of producing one of the acknowledged 'great growths', would sell his grapes to make concentrate?

By and large, the grape concentrate that goes into the cans is a good commercial product, capable of producing a good, sound, commercial-style 'plonk'. But many winemakers have found that you can improve your country wines by adding a little grape concentrate to the brew.

Where currants, raisins and sultanas were once commonly used to give body and vinosity to a wine, it is now easier and not much dearer to substitute a cupful of grape concentrate for each 250 gm (½ lb) of dried fruit. The taste will not be identical – it may well be better. Those dried fruits each had their own distinctive flavour and could not be regarded as sterile, since their crevices could harbour a whole menagerie of organisms, which meant that the fruit had to be sulphited or covered with water and brought through the boil.

Concentrates can also vary in flavour, some having a distinct caramel tang as though they had been overheated. They are usually taken to be sterile, but the occasional briskly fermenting can or plastic container of concentrate shows that this happy assumption can be wrong. And it may be that, if the concentrate contains 'livestock', the yeasts are sound and desirable wine yeasts which have survived the process of concentration. While the concentrate remains concentrated, any organisms are normally held dormant by the very high percentage of sugar, but once it is diluted the organisms find ideal breeding conditions.

If you are prudent, then, you may wish to treat 5 litres (1 gal) of diluted concentrate with one Campden tablet just in case, or you may well go ahead, quite happy to take a calculated risk on the concentrate's sterility, on the assumption that a robust yeast culture will, in any case, crowd out any unwanted visitors before they can establish themselves.

Grape concentrates and juices vary widely, and if you find one that suits your purpose and your palate it is best to persevere with it. There are vintage years in sardines, when ideal conditions for the little fish are matched by ideal conditions for the olive harvest, so it seems certain that there are vintage years for grape concentrates and other years when the standard falls below the average. For all practical purposes, we can forget that possibility, unless, coming across a brand that impresses you favourably, you care to stockpile the cans or cartons for the future.

Because of the wide variation in quality and treatment, it is still worthwhile, when making grape concentrate into wine, to add yeast nutrient as usual and, if it is your custom, a Benerva tablet, and extra acid if the taste indicates the need for it.

Jam

One fruit concentrate that is rather despised by some winemakers as being a frivolous base for a wine is jam. Obviously, it would be a pointless enterprise to make a batch of jam and, immediately afterwards, convert it into wine, but many households at some time or another find themselves with a surplus. Then the jam makes a very acceptable wine. Or perhaps the local supermarket runs an offer of jam at loss-leader prices. It defeats their purpose if you go in and scoop a trolley-load of jam without buying some of the goods with a high profit mark-up, but that is their worry!

About 500 gm (1 lb) to 5 litres (1 gal) of wine is a good rule of thumb (a minimum figure rather than a maximum).

If you are using up surplus jam that has been lying in the cupboard for a couple of seasons and has some mould on the surface, scrape the mould off and bring the jam through the boil in a litre or so (2–3 pts) of water, stirring thoroughly. This should prevent any infection. Jam that is completely above suspicion can simply be dissolved in hot water.

The jammy must has to be treated with pectin degrading enzyme when it has cooled down – you are now undoing what you did when you made the jam, for you are 'unsetting' instead of setting it.

Jam wines are usually better to be sweet than dry, and acid and tannin will almost always be needed.

Malt extract

Malt extract tends to be neglected in winemaking, though (for example) 500 gm (1 lb) of malt extract and 1 kg (2 lb) of sugar make a basis for 5 litres (1 gal) of strong dry wine, ideal for blending and as a foundation for other wines using spices, fruit juices, herbs and so forth. Malt wine can be made sweeter by stepping up either the malt or the sugar content and can be varied by the choice of yeast. Tokay yeast, and a high fermentation temperature, can chase the gravity down surprisingly quickly to produce a fiery drink on the threshhold between wine and spirit in flavour and effect.

Oranges and orangettes

Oranges and orangettes have very different parts to play in wine-making. Oranges make a good basis for white wine, although, in view of the difference in cost and convenience, it is often worth considering buying orange juice instead.

Oranges, however, can sometimes be bought quite cheaply – for instance, when some in a case have begun to develop the familiar blue-mould patches. The mould is sometimes not much more than skin deep and has no adverse effect on the wine.

Many of the older recipes for orange wine advised peeling the fruit, then baking the peel in a slow oven until crisp and dry – this process dispels some of the oils in the skin, which can slow down fermentation. There is some argument as to whether fermentation slows down because the fine layer of oil seals the surface or because the oil is toxic to the yeast, but the end result is the same. Although wines made from fresh oranges and from whole-fruit pulp do give trouble in this way, a thorough rousing seems to get the fermentation moving again in almost every case.

Over the years, winemakers have reported that the white pith that lies between the skin and the fruity pulp causes bitterness in the wine. It is probably worth going to a little extra trouble to exclude the pith, though it is fair to add that other winemakers have consistently used the whole fruit, including the pith, and had no trouble at all.

Orangettes are small, dry, immature oranges, as hard as wood – they can scarcely be cracked with nutcrackers. They are ideal for adding zest and flavour to an otherwise dull wine. Drop them for a few minutes into a strong sulphite solution, or scald them, to deal with any lurking infections on the rind and then add them whole to a wine that has completed its fermentation. Used at a rate of one to a litre or six to a gallon jar, and left in the wine while it matures, the orangettes give a refreshing bitterness and a fine aroma of orange.

Because they provide so much flavour from so small a bulk, orangettes are a good basis for experimenting – from including one or two in a pulp fermentation to trying them, raw or cooked, as part of a liqueur formulation.

Peaches

Peaches have already been discussed, but they deserve to be mentioned again because many winemakers have been delighted by the wine they have made from peaches bought in bulk from a shop or a fruit market. Used to make a low-fruit white wine, they need not be expensive.

Rhubarb

This has also been mentioned before, but here again shops are a possible source, for tinned rhubarb makes good wine at any season of the year (not only in May and June) and is not at all wasteful. The amount of fibre left in the strainer is negligible – almost everything in the tin, including the added sugar, goes to good use. It isn't as cheap as rhubarb from the garden, but, as with other tinned or packaged foods, you are paying for the ready availability and the convenience.

Rice

When used in wine, rice should be the unpolished kind, to be found mainly in health-food stores. The reason for preferring this is not because you will get the vitamins that prevent beriberi but because rice, like other grains, is mainly used in wine to give flavour – and unpolished rice has much more flavour. It is on record that Marco Polo found fifty-four different varieties of rice wine in China when he went there – each, presumably, with its own reputation for leaving a hangover and a headache. In home-brewed beer and in wine, rice has a notorious name for causing drastic effects far beyond the alcohol content of the brew, and so it should be approached with caution at the recipe stage as well as in the glass.

Syrups

Now quite common in brewing, syrups can also be used in winemaking. The ordinary tinned golden syrup was used in the war years, and just afterwards during the winemaking revival, but it has little to commend it nowadays. Wheat syrup, barley syrup, maize syrup and the dextrinous products that give roundness to home-brewed beer can do the same for wines, particularly those made from vegetables.

Although the recipe flies in the face of the advice never to mix grain and grape, successful wines can be made by blending wheat syrup and grape concentrate. The experimentally minded winemaker might care to try a sparkling wine based on 500 gm (1 lb) of wheat syrup and 250 g (½ lb) of white grape concentrate to 5 litres (1 gal).

Tea

Tea wines were originally made as an economy measure – to screw the last of the taste and flavour from tea leaves which would otherwise have been thrown out on the rose-bed or washed down the sink – and made on this basis they are likely to be as unpleasant as they sound, unless bolstered up liberally with plenty of dried fruit and orange juice. They had to be made oversweet to mask the rank taste of tannin. One writer summed it up when he said that no doubt prisoners of war would be glad of tea wine.

But it is only fair to add that some winemakers, by buying high-quality tea for the purpose, and using grape concentrate and perhaps very discreet amounts of spice, produce tea wines of delicacy with a character of their own. It is a matter of personal choice whether you feel that the cash, the skill and the effort could not be better spent on some other wine.

Vegetables

Most vegetables bought from the greengrocer's are similar to those grown in gardens – beetroot and parsnip are obvious examples – but early experiments show that freeze-dried vegetables, particularly carrots, are worth considering. Once again, they are not cheap but they are convenient – a sentence that sums up most of this chapter.

7

Water and Sugar

Water

By far the bulkiest ingredient in wine and beer is water. Some home-brewers adjust the water they use with chemicals, but most winemakers take it as it comes, straight from the tap. This is almost always satisfactory, for few municipal supplies are infected with sufficient micro-organisms to spoil a wine, but although tap water is adequately sterile for winemaking, that used for making up a yeast starter should be boiled. The reason for this is that any organisms in the water, few though they may be, are likely to multiply in the starter liquid, just as the yeast cells do.

It is still possible to find recipes (even in newly published books) claiming that rain water is cleaner than tap water. For this to be true you would need to live in an area with very unsatisfactory tap water and very, very clean air. To carry the argument to absurdity, if you climbed Ben Nevis and melted down the snow from the summit, you would find that it contained particles from the smoke of Fort William, suburban smog from New York and volcanic fall-out from Hekla in Iceland.

So forget about rain water and use tap water. If you have reason to suspect its purity, boil it before using it.

Water, as it gushes from the tap, contains large amounts of air – so much that in some areas it looks milky in the glass until the air bubbles dispel. Some of this air is needed by the yeast while multiplying. Now, if water is boiled, either to sterilise it or to dispel excess chlorine, the air it contains is boiled out, and this can cause a fermentation to be slow to get under way. If you have boiled all the water for a wine, give it a good rousing, and this should get enough oxygen to get the yeast to work.

Water seems such a simple liquid to the layman, but because of the different rocks through which it passes every water is a mineral water, with its own blend of ingredients. Perhaps some day laboratory experiments will prove that water of one kind is ideal for fig Tokay and water of another kind makes the best basis for apple Sauternes. In the meantime, there is little data on the subject, although some winemakers are so convinced of the virtues of one particular source of supply that they will, for example, bring back a season's Highland water when returning from a caravan holiday.

The subject is less in doubt in brewing. The rule of thumb that hard water makes good pale ale and bitter, and soft water good stout and brown ale is all that most home-brewers need to know. Although you can easily add hardening salts to soft water when you make bitter or, conversely, soften hard water when you wish to make stout, it is well worth while, before you start experimenting in this way, to make several brews from untreated water straight from the tap. It is almost certain that you will enjoy the beer you brew, even though the purists may consider it contains 35 parts per million too much calcium sulphate.

Having established that the beer you make from untreated water is not only drinkable but also enjoyable, you can go on to experiment with proprietary products for hardening or softening the water as necessary – your local water board will tell you whether the water they supply is hard or soft. (Remember that hard water furs the inside of kettles, while soft water lathers beautifully with the minimum of soap.)

Fluoride added to public water supplies is highly unlikely to spoil beer or wine, as it has to be present in quantities of over 200 parts per million to check fermentation.

Sugar

The next ingredient is also common to both winemaking and brewing – sugar. This white sugar is remarkable in being the only pure chemical substance used as a foodstuff – a fact that explains the violence of the attacks of the whole-food enthusiasts.

Adding extra sugar – called chaptalisation or amelioration – is necessary in poor years in winemaking countries when the amount of natural sugar in the grapes has fallen short of what is required. It is necessary *every* year in home winemaking, except for those fortunate enough to have vineyards of luscious sweet grapes on a south-facing slope in the warmer parts of Britain. The other ingredients in home-made wines, in the quantities we use, do not contain sufficient sugar to make a balanced wine.

For winemaking and brewing, ordinary granulated sugar of the kind you buy from the grocer or supermarket is ideal. Cost is one factor – sugar still costs less than the alternatives because it is used as a loss-leader in many shops, the shopkeeper making little or no profit except on the goods people buy along with the sugar.

Invert sugar has its advocates in winemaking and brewing – they claim that with it fermentation is quicker and more complete, because the yeast does not have to invert the sugar for itself. Weight for weight, invert sugar is markedly more expensive than ordinary grocery sugar, and, since it contains more water than grocery sugar, 1¼ parts of invert have to be used to replace 1 part of grocery sugar.

The fact that commercial brewers use massive quantities of invert sugar has made many home-brewers wonder whether they are missing something by not following their example. Time means money to commercial brewers, and it may be that the extra through-put that they achieve by shortening each fermentation period more than pays for the higher cost of invert sugar. There would seem to be no convincing evidence that a home brew is improved by using invert sugar.

This is a matter that can be put to the proof by any experimentally minded winemaker or brewer. You can invert your own sugar quite easily by boiling 5 kg of granulated sugar with 1 litre of water and 3 gm of citric acid – stirring regularly – and holding it at the boil for half an hour. If, when cool, the syrup is made up to 5 litres, by adding water, each litre will contain 1 kg of sugar, inverted. The Imperial equivalent is 8 lb of sugar, boiled in 2 pt of water with ½ tsp citric acid and made up to 1 gal – each pint of syrup then contains 1 lb of invert sugar.

Invert sugar can also be bought in packs – more convenient but more expensive.

You may also wish to experiment with glucose chips, which have their enthusiastic advocates. Once again weight for weight and in relation to the relative sweetness, glucose chips are much more expensive than household white sugar.

Because of the difficulty of dissolving dry sugar in a wine or beer, the general practice is to make the sugar into a syrup of known gravity. For example, 1 kg of sugar boiled up with 365 ml of water produces a litre of syrup. The non-metric system is initially even simpler – 2 lb of sugar boiled up with 1 pt of water produces 2 pt of syrup, each pint equivalent to 1 lb of sugar.

But the simplicity of the metric system comes with its use – that litre of syrup can be divided into tiny portions, each equivalent of a weight of dry sugar. A litre of syrup = 1 kilo of sugar, therefore 1 ml of syrup = 1 gm of sugar.

Although in theory this syrup is of such a high gravity that no organisms can survive in it, experience shows that some unwanted organisms, moulds in particular, can multiply if it is stored for more than two or three weeks. It is therefore prudent to make up the syrup a batch at a time, as you need it, for if you do this you know that you are not 'seeding' your wine with some unsuspected infection.

8

Helpful Extras

In specialist shops winemakers are faced with shelf upon shelf of ingredients, some with long chemical names. Are they all necessary? Not strictly, though many help us to make better and clearer wine.

Yeast nutrient

One ingredient that has found a place in every winemaker's store-cupboard is yeast nutrient. Sometimes this takes the form of proprietary crystals or tablets, sometimes the winemaker simply buys the principal chemical loose. In almost every instance, the main ingredient is diammonium phosphate, in which both the nitrogen and the phosphorus aid the fermentation. Sometimes the nutrient is ammonium phosphate and sometimes ammonium sulphate. Diammonium sulphate may be best, but any of them is better than none and helps the yeast to achieve its maximum alcohol-producing potential.

So, always use yeast nutrient in wines. Use double quantities in mead, and it does no harm to use at least a little in the stronger home-brewed beers.

Acid

Acid needs to be added in many recipes, particularly those in which the main ingredients are flowers or vegetables.

Citric acid was the first to be used, and is still by far the most popular acid with the majority of winemakers. Used in excess, it can give wine a distinct hint of lemonade – which is natural, since citric acid is, as its name indicates, the principal acid of lemons and other citrus fruits. Nowadays, however, it is obtained from molasses rather than direct from lemons.

As the craft developed, other acids came to the fore, and you can now buy pre-packed mixtures, such as 3 parts of tartaric acid to 2 parts of malic acid and 1 part of citric acid.

Malic acid (once again, the name indicates the original source, for this is the acid of apples) needs time to do its work of improving the flavour and bouquet of the finished wine – two years is a reasonable minimum. Used in excess, it gives a distinct 'cider' taste to wine.

Succinic acid is another which has a disproportionate effect on the quality of a wine that has been given plenty of time in the cellar to mature but which is wasted in a wine made for quick consumption.

Lactic acid has its enthusiasts too. They argue that this is the natural acid in grape wine in which the tartaric acid has precipitated as tartar during maturation and the malic acid has been converted into lactic acid by a malo-lactic fermentation. The use of lactic acid will produce esters in the bouquet which will have the natural vinous character, whereas the use of 'foreign' acids like citric acid produce an alien bouquet. Lactic acid can be added at any stage of a fermentation, being biologically stable, and stable to sulphur dioxide, and throwing no deposit. This acid is sold as a liquid, and around 30 ml (1 fl oz) is needed in 35 litres (7 gal) of wine.

Once again, lactic acid comes into its own in wines that are going to be laid down for some years, and 5 ml (1 tsp) of the liquid can replace 3 gm (½ tsp) of citric acid in the ingredients of 5 litres (1 gal) of wine that you intend to allow to mature.

Tartaric acid seems to have no great advantages in winemaking. It is precipitated as tartrate crystals (argol), and these can often be seen in wines made from grapes or grape concentrate. They look like powdered glass and are sometimes mistaken for this, but they are, in fact, completely harmless, being simple cream of tartar, familiar in home baking.

Measuring acidity
The desirable level of acidity is very much a matter of taste, and as winemakers grow older they tend to enjoy higher acidity than they would have relished in their youth, 30 gm per 5 litres (1 oz per gallon) of citric acid is regarded as a reasonable amount for a sound wine by some winemakers, while others say that half that quantity is more than ample even in wines made from flowers and vegetables

which contain very little acid of their own. While gathering experience, it is as well to err on the low side, for acid can be added later. 15 gm in 5 litres (½ oz in 1 gal) is enough to sustain a healthy fermentation, and may be enough for a wine that will be drunk quickly. A wine that is intended to be enjoyed while young and fresh does not need as much acidity as one that will be left to mature for years.

Unfortunately, there is no simple answer to the question 'How much acid is already in my wine?', for it poses another question 'Do you wish to measure the amount of acid in the wine or the acid activity in the wine?'

The amount of acid is arrived at by titration, a process requiring some simple laboratory equipment, the use of a chemical called phenolphthalein and a certain exactness of mind. The chemical is added to a measured sample of the wine, then caustic soda solution (which is strongly alkaline) is dropped in. When the chemical balance of the wine moves from acid to alkaline, a colour change takes place and the amount of alkali added to produce this change gives a close indication (in careful hands) of the amount of acidity originally in the sample.

Measuring the acid activity of the wine depends on the pH of the liquid, and this is arrived at by using narrow-range indicator papers, which change colour at different pH values.

Although many a learned treatise has been written on the theory of the measurement of a wine's acidity by determination of the pH factor, there is, fortunately, no reason why the winemaker should know very much about the theory. The pH figure indicates the concentration of hydrogen ions in the liquid, but for all practical purposes, this is also an indication of how alkaline or acid the must or wort, or wine or beer, actually is.

What is difficult to understand, but important to remember, is that the scale reads downwards. Anything over pH 7 is alkaline, so the nearer to pH 7 the reading lies, the nearer to alkalinity and the weaker the acidity. Thus pH 6·9 is barely acid at all, but pH 3 is strongly acid.

Unhappily, a change of one unit up or down the scale does not mean anything as simple as a change of 1% or 10%. The pH scale is logarithmic, and those who (like the author) happily abandoned log tables some years ago will have to take it on trust that a change of one unit up or down the scale alters the alkalinity or acidity by ten times.

You do not need laboratory equipment to check the pH. You dip a slip of paper in the liquid and compare the resulting colour with the colours on a comparison chart supplied with the papers. The method is a more exact form of the old familiar test used in school laboratories, when litmus paper turned blue when placed in an acid solution and red in an alkaline solution.

Of the range of pH readings, winemakers are most likely to be interested in those between 3·4 and 3·2, which indicate an ideal level of acidity for wine-yeast activity, while home-brewers are dealing with a much less acid liquid (and therefore, remember, one with a *higher* pH reading) and their beer wort may be about pH 5.

Titration, narrow-range comparison papers or the acid-testing kits sold by suppliers to the craft will all tell you something about the chemistry of your wine. What they will not tell you is whether you will like the wine when it is mature.

The human palate, given a chance to learn, is a far more subtle method of measurement of the factors that interest us than even the most advanced gas chromatographic equipment. If you taste your wine at all stages, from the uncrushed fruit to the finished product, by way of the juice that runs from the press, the must as it ferments and the wine at each racking, you will learn how much acid is needed to make a wine that pleases *you*. As a rule, only wines that before fermentation are markedly acid, even acid enough to be sour and unpleasant, have sufficient acid for good balance when they are mature.

What if the wine is too acid? If you increase the amount of fruit in a wine, you do not only increase the fruitiness but the acidity as well. Excess acid *can* be disposed of in the way usually recommended for treating rhubarb (though not in this book) by discreet additions of precipitated chalk, ground cuttlefish bone or other alkalis. If you feel you must use this process, do be discreet, for 5 gm (1 tsp) of chalk can knock so much acid out of 5 litres (1 gal) of overacid wine as to render it unpalatably bland. And add the alkali little by little – this will reduce the amount of foaming caused by the liberation of gas, and will also allow you to check whether the acidity of the wine has fallen as far as you wish.

Tannin

With added nutrient and added acid, you can make a good wine without the help of any other 'chemical', for you can adjust the amount of tannin in the recipe with natural ingredients, such as oak leaves or fresh tea. Tannin occurs naturally in many places, from grape-pips to tan-bark and from oak-apple galls to elderberries. Added tannin is chiefly necessary in root wines, flower wines and other non-fruit wines. 150 ml (½ cup) of strong, freshly made tea or 1·7 gm (a scant quarter-teaspoonful) of grape tannin is sufficient in these cases. Tannin BP, which can be bought from the chemist, can also be used.

Each form has its advocates. Strong fresh tea has the advantage that if you use too much it does not seem to have the same mouth-drawing effect that excess grape tannin has.

Now for a look at the additives which, though not strictly necessary, have their roles to play.

Pectin degrading enzyme

The most important goes under the general name of 'pectin degrading enzyme', and under a variety of trade names such as Pectinol and Pectolase. Many of the fruits from which we make wine can also be used to make jam and jelly. The jam and jelly set satisfactorily because of the presence of a complex substance called pectin. This same substance, if permitted to do so, can cause a very persistent haze in wines. At worst, pectin can make a wine set like jelly, but more usually an opalescent sheen clouds the clarity of the wine. The taste is not affected, but the eye's pleasure in a star-bright wine and the craftsman's pride in a well-made product are both diminished.

It is unlikely that you will have any trouble if you add pectin degrading enzyme to the raw materials or the must at the same time as you add the yeast. Before the yeast has made any considerable amount of alcohol to check the work of the enzyme, the enzyme will have done its work and reduced the pectin chains to a manageable size.

Thiamine (vitamin B_1)

Wine had been made for many thousands of years before it was found that the vitamin B_1 group of vitamins was essential to fermentation, although only fantastically small concentrations of some of these vitamins were required to have an effect. Just as pectin degrading enzyme should be added as a matter of course to the early stages of a wine, so one should add enough thiamine (vitamin B_1) to ensure a healthy fermentation.

For wines, made from fruit for example, that have plenty of

natural nutrient in them, one 3 mg Benerva tablet to 5 litres (1 gal) is enough – add two tablets to grain and vegetable wines, and three to flower wines and mead. The tablets, which cost little, will have a good effect on the fermentation, but it is highly unlikely that they will have any effect on the baldness of the senior winemakers – there is some evidence that the vitamin helps to prevent premature baldness and greyness in rats!

Rohament P

Rohament P is one of the additives with a strange-sounding name (the name becomes more understandable when one realises that the originators were Rohm and Haas of Darmstadt). The 'P' stands for pectinglycosidase – a merciful abbreviation – and it is a natural organic compound, not a chemical. The enzyme it contains breaks down the connective tissue in fruit and frees the individual cells, quickly or slowly depending on the quantity used and the temperature of the ingredients. It is active at the usual acidity of fruits.

If you wish to extract the maximum amount of colour from the fruits, the suppliers recommend that the ingredients should be held at 104°F for one to two hours after Rohament P is added, with frequent stirring, but the enzyme will work at room temperature, when it will require a day to do its work – once again, with frequent stirring.

Some people heat the treated pulp to 60–70°C (150–160°F) to deactivate the enzymes, but experience has shown that this is not necessary.

Rohament P, then, does give substantially more juice per pound of fruit because of the way it breaks down the cellular structure of the fruit. However, you have the trouble of maintaining the right temperatures and heating the pulp to inactivate the enzyme. In addition, you may find that, on pressing the fruit, you have trouble from the fine sludge caused by the enzyme's success in breaking down the structure of the fruit. It is, on balance, easier to obtain more juice and more flavour by using more fruit rather than by using Rohament P.

Stabilisers

It is easy to make a strong sweet wine, a strong dry wine or a weak dry wine. It is much more difficult to make a weak sweet wine because there is always the danger of renewed fermentation, with its sequel of cloudiness and, possibly, of burst bottles.

Stabilisers are obtainable that will inhibit any further fermentation. Potassium sorbate, at a concentration of 1 g to 5 litres (1 gal), will hold further fermentation in check. It is available to winemakers through trade suppliers, and its advocates say that this amount is far below the level of any possible health hazard. It is up to each winemaker to decide whether to stabilise his wines in this way. Another stabiliser is benzoic acid, which is also a permitted preservative and can, in very small quantities, stop a fermentation in its tracks.

Most winemakers using stabilisers will prefer to buy the commercial brands and use them according to instructions.

Glycerine

Some substances have an effect on the texture of wine, rather than on its taste or its fermentation, and glycerine is one of them. It is an alcohol, although not usually thought of as such, and is produced as a by-product of fermentation. Used in small quantities, it can give a good wine extra roundness and mask the harshness of a bad wine. As much as 60 ml to the litre (1 fl oz/pt) is sometimes recommended, but some palates can detect a sticky oiliness before even half that concentration is reached. 5 ml (1 tsp) to the bottle is a good level at which to start.

Glucose polymer

Another body-builder which can be used is glucose polymer, at about 500 g (8 oz) to 5 litres (1 gal) of wine – it gives body without much additional sweetness. It is best added early in the fermentation so that it becomes integrated with the wine, but it can be added towards the end of the process, when it is unlikely that the small amount of fermentable sugars in the glucose polymer will cause a renewal of fermentation.

Fungal amylase

Small quantities of starch sometimes cause very persistent hazes in wines, particularly those made from roots, cereals, and under-ripe apples and bananas. Another enzyme product, fungal amylase, is available to deal with this.

If starch is suspected when you begin to make the wine, test for it with iodine solution – one drop in several drops of the liquid will cause a characteristic change of colour to a harsh blue. Fungal amylase can be added at that point, or at any time onwards – it can even be used in a finished wine that proves to have been marred by a starch haze. The enzyme is active at room temperature and at the usual level of acidity in wines and fruit juices. The instructions accompanying the product give an indication of the quantities needed, but as little as 2·5 g will treat 20 lb of fruit or 5 gal of juice or wine.

9

Hygiene

Beginners to home brewing and winemaking, when told of the importance of hygiene, are apt to bridle and say indignantly, 'Of course, I keep everything clean – I wash all the equipment as carefully as I wash the crockery and cutlery!' The more experienced (perhaps having bought that experience at the cost of a batch of spoiled wine) know that even this standard of cleanliness is not enough.

Fermenting vessels and other equipment have to be sterilised to reduce the chance of infection by unwanted organisms. This is very important in winemaking, although the alcoholic content of the wine has a discouraging effect on these organisms. It is even more important in brewing, when not even the preservative effect of the hop makes up entirely for the low alcohol content.

Some winemakers go to such extremes as using, for example, a pressure cooker as an autoclave to sterilise the smaller items of equipment.

Sulphur, in various forms, is the winemaker's friend, as it has been for many centuries. The Romans used to burn sulphur in their cellars as a purification rite, and this can still be done if no one in the neighbourhood is going to be affected by the choking fumes. Light a small heap of flowers of sulphur on a tin lid – low blue flames will appear, and a chest-catching smoke. Equipment that has been washed and exposed thoroughly to the sulphur fumes while still wet will be effectively sterilised. Sulphur sticks, candles, strips and tapes can be bought for smoking the interior of casks too.

Campden tablets supply the active chemical, sulphur dioxide, in a less haphazard way. Each tablet represents, when dissolved in 5 litres of liquid, 46 parts per million of sulphur dioxide (or 50 ppm in 1 gal). At this concentration the tablets have other purposes in winemaking, which will be dealt with later.

If you are sterilising equipment that you know to be already reasonably germ-free, then two Campden tablets and a pinch of citric acid dissolved in ½ litre (1 pt) of warm water will be strong enough for rinsing the equipment (bottles, jars, siphons and the like). When you are dealing with something more suspect – bottles just collected from a heap at the back of a hotel, for example – then a solution twice as strong can be used.

Campden tablets (like winemakers and home-brewers) suffer in the course of time from old age – they age more quickly when they are not stored in a dark place and in an airtight container. Although they cost less when bought in bulk, it is safer to buy small amounts and use them while they are still fresh.

Fresh or old, some Campden tablets are so soft that they fall to powder in the jar and some so hard that they might have been chipped from the proverbial nether millstone. The hard ones can be ground down between two *old* teaspoons, or folded in paper and gently but firmly crushed with pliers, and even the most obdurate will dissolve in time if left to steep in a little warm water.

Household bleach, which is not expensive when bought by the bottleful and is cheap when bought in bigger bulk, has its place in dealing with really suspect containers. Glass jars, for instance, left to steep overnight in a 9:1 solution of water and bleach will really sparkle when they are rinsed out. They will be sterile too – it would be a hardy bug that could withstand that solution. However, the jars will then need very thorough rinsing to get rid of the 'swimming-pool' smell.

Various detergent substances (Silana p.f. is one of the most familiar) also have some sterilising effect and give equipment a sparkle. But be wary of using household detergent lavishly, for some are very persistent and may taint successive batches of wine with a sweet and sickly scent. They may also knock the head off every brew of beer made in that vessel.

Campden tablets are ideal when you begin practising the craft, and they should certainly be kept to hand at all times, but once it becomes plain that you will be winemaking or brewing regularly, and therefore constantly having to wash up equipment, you should make up a stock solution of 'sulphite'. Buy 60 gm (2 oz) of sodium metabisulphite or potassium metabisulphite from your winemakers' supply shop or chemist and dissolve it in ½ litre (1 pt) of water. Keep this stock solution in a tightly stoppered bottle and use it for rinsing all equipment. Better still, buy ½ kg (1 lb) and make 5 litres (1 gal) of this useful solution.

Be careful when you use the solution, for it has a most unpleasant effect when one breathes the fumes. Choking and weeping, but unharmed, you will resolve to be more careful in future. Winemakers and home-brewers who suffer from chest and heart conditions, however, might be justified in fighting shy of using this powerful liquid and restrict themselves to Campden tablet solution.

There is one difference in the uses of the two – the sulphite solution can be used again and again for months, but the Campden tablet solution should be flung away after it has been used once on, for instance, a batch of a couple of dozen bottles.

Sulphite solution has another use – after you have steeped or rinsed equipment with bleach, and rinsed it again under the cold tap to get rid of the bleach, as an added precaution give it a final swill with sulphite solution to neutralise any bleach that may be left.

Be liberal with your use of hot water and sulphite solution and you will not be much troubled with infections from your winemaking and brewing equipment.

One piece of gear that is sometimes forgotten by winemakers, yet is in contact with every drop of many wines, is the straining net or cloth. Make sure that it is sterile before use by boiling it in a pan of water for ten minutes or more, or by soaking it thoroughly in sterilising solution.

10

Keeping the Yeast Happy

The greater part of success in making good wine or beer lies in 'keeping the yeast happy'. Louis Pasteur, in 1862, summed it up accurately when he said: 'When the sweet juice of a plant or fruit is abandoned to itself, air brings to it yeast which transforms the sugar into alcohol and carbon dioxide; then other microbial agents intervene which oxidise the alcohol to acetic acid, and still others which complete the process of oxidation to carbon dioxide, thereby turning practically all the carbon originally present in the sugar back to the atmosphere where it becomes once more available for the growth of plants. It is by interrupting the oxidation of sugar either at the alcohol or acetic acid stage that man has established empirically the industries which give him wine, beer or vinegar.'

Yeasts are very simple single-celled plants, containing ferments (enzymes) which break down sugar into almost equal weights of carbon dioxide and alcohol. By and large, they prefer temperatures around 21°C (70°F), growing sluggish if the temperature falls much below 10°C (50°F), and dying if it is held much above 38°C (100°F).

There are very many different species and subspecies of yeasts, from the kind that turn oil into protein for a protein-hungry world to those that cause dandruff and athlete's foot. Yeasts occur on men, on shrimps, on soil and as the bloom on grapes.

A survey of the bloom on the grapes of fifty-eight vineyards in the Gironde isolated over two thousand strains of fermenting yeasts, belonging to twenty-eight different species. One of those species, *Kloeckera apiculata*, although regarded as an enemy by home winemakers and able to ferment to around only 4% alcohol, is believed by some winemakers to contribute valuable fruity esters to the wine. As the percentage of alcohol increases, our friend the wine yeast, *Saccharomyces ellipsoideus*, takes over and can produce a very much higher level of alcohol than any of the other species.

The primary part of the fermentation, as far as we are concerned, is the sugar-to-alcohol role of the yeast, but running parallel to this process are others which produce substances like methyl alcohol (from the breaking down of pectin) and fusel oil (from the breaking down of amino acids). Both are unpleasant or even harmful in quantity, but in small amounts have their part to play in the balance and the maturing of our wines.

It is now customary in winemaking and home brewing to use specialised types of yeast – not the putty-like substance from the baker or the dry bread yeasts from the chemist.

Just as in poultry farming, where named breeds of hens like Rhode Island Reds and Leghorns have been replaced by hybrids known by letters and numbers, so the now familiar wine yeasts, bearing the name of their original source (Burgundy from France, Port from Portugal, Tokay from Hungary), are being supplemented by yeasts with trade names.

An early arrival on the scene, and a good one, was the CWE67 yeast, which made a name for itself by the speed with which it got to work. Vinkwik is another notable arrival equally dedicated to the philosophy that the quicker a fermentation gets off its mark and completes its course, the better. With some proprietary yeast mixtures this speed is amazing. You put a teaspoonful of the yeast-and-nutrients mixture in a bottle of water that has been boiled and allowed to cool, and it 'comes to life' so quickly that it can be added as a starter inside five hours. The Unican Superyeasts are a good example.

Yeasts now come in a variety of forms – as powders or granules, as tablets, as liquid cultures in little bottles or in plastic sachets, or as grey squiggles on the surface of a wedge of agar jelly in a test-tube. 'Now that we are offered two dozen pure yeasts bearing memorable names, it is worth seeing that these thoroughbreds get the pasture they want', one writer commented. In other words, the yeast must be kept happy.

Except for the experimentally minded, there is a great deal to be said in favour of finding a wine yeast that suits you, and which produces good wine, and using it for the rest of your winemaking career.

Yeasts multiply by dividing, but not into two equal parts like some organisms. Yeast cells develop little buds on the surface, and sometimes this 'daughter' bud remains loosely attached to its 'mother' while it produces little buds of its own. Usually the buds break away, leaving a scar on the surface of the 'mother' cell, and some yeast cells may have two dozen scars or more.

Since each cell has such fantastic powers of reproduction, it is as well that they are kept in check. (If a yeast cell budded and kept on budding every two hours, and each bud did the same, and each of those new buds . . . within about a fortnight the world would be up over the head in yeast.) No matter how good a yeast you use, and how well balanced a wort you make up, the yeast is unlikely to go on the rampage like that. What can happen is that the yeast may multiply more quickly than you expected, and your wine or beer may froth over onto the fitted carpet. Some people stand the vessel in a tray to catch any fall-out, but a thick layer of newspaper will mop up a surprising amount of overspill.

And what if your yeast does not seem as happy as it might be? Sometimes, if you have added the yeast direct, without making up a starter bottle, the organism you think is fermenting your wine may not even come to active life – the brew may have been invaded by an unwanted visitor which has hitched a lift with the yeast, or dropped out of thin air, or emerged from a snug cranny somewhere in the fermentation vessel. It may be *Kloeckera apiculata*, which will produce its 4% of alcohol and then die out. Perhaps by the time that stage is reached your wine yeast may have woken up and you will never know the difference, but if the wine yeast is not ready to take over, you will be left with a weakly and oversweet cordial containing 4% alcohol, instead of a sound robust wine containing perhaps 12%.

Sometimes a slow or stuck fermentation is due to a weakly yeast – perhaps it has been lying on a shelf in the shop or in a cupboard in your home for far too long. Faced with a fermentation that does not start, or with one that is obviously unsatisfactorily slow, make a vigorous starter with a new yeast and add it – the improvement is often dramatic – or simply scatter an energetic yeast like CWE67 on top of the must. There is no need to worry about using two different strains of yeast. You might be criticised for producing an insipid half-wine containing one strain of yeast but not for producing a good wine containing yeast of mixed 'racial purity'.

It is easy to worry too much about an apparently stuck fermentation. If the wine has started fermenting briskly, so that it is over the 4% alcohol point, has sugar to work on and is safely protected by a fermentation lock, a couple of weeks can pass without activity, and no harm done. A little of the yeast will break down and supply the trace elements to promote new yeast growth and enzyme action, and away the fermentation will go again. That kind of 'stop-go' fermentation, at its most extreme, is to be seen in the big, heavy, sweet wines like Tokay, which can tick over literally for years. For a fast-driving fermentation is not all clear gain – the resulting wine is certain to be strong, and very likely to be sound and healthy, but some of the imponderables that add up to a subtle and delicate wine will have been driven off in the brisk 'boil'.

If stuck fermentations are to be avoided, the temperature should not be allowed to creep above 26°C (80°F), since it is at this point that the yeasts cease to produce the enzymes necessary for fermentation, although the yeasts themselves do not normally perish until the temperature rises to about 38°C (100°F).

It is the temperature of the liquid that matters, not the air temperature. Making wine in bulk has the advantage of evening out swings in temperature, and when the room temperature is a little low one has the advantage of a lift of 5°C or so in the warmth of the wine because of the heat generated by the process of fermentation (even inside a jar, the difference in temperature between the outside of the jar and the heart of the liquid may be as much as 3°C (or 5°F)). If, however, the temperature of the fermenting room is already around 26°C (80°F), the warmth of fermentation can push the temperature of the wine above danger level.

Cold is a far commoner cause of a stuck fermentation, and here again it is the liquid temperature that matters. On a frosty night the air temperature in a room may fall low enough to chill the wine, and when the warmth of the day takes the chill off the air the wine may still be far too cold for the comfort of the yeast.

Another cause of stuck fermentation, showing that the yeast is unhappy, should rarely occur when well-balanced recipes are used: 'starvation' or 'malnutrition' due to lack of acid, yeast nutrient and, sometimes, vitamins. Mead, because honey lacks some of these, is the most likely type of wine to stick like this, and for that reason (as well as for reasons of flavour) there are sound grounds for including a quantity of grape concentrate, though this technically turns the mead into a melomel.

Remember the experiments in the school laboratory which showed that liquid will pass through a semi-permeable membrane from a weak solution into a strong solution in order to equalise the balance? If yeast is put into a strong sugar solution, some of the liquid in the yeast cells will be pulled by osmosis through the semi-permeable cell walls. The cells will crumple and will cease to carry on with their work until the balance is redressed by diluting the solution outside the walls. If, then, as in some of the old recipes, something like 2 kg (4 lb) of sugar is shot into each 5 litres (1 gal), the yeast cells will shrivel because of the difference in pressure. Even if the concentration is not as high as this, the fermentation will be slow to start and may limp on for months.

An occasional cause of a slow start to a fermentation is oxygen starvation. Suppose a winemaker has boiled the ingredients (beetroot, for example) in order to extract the colour and flavour, and boiled the rest of the water because it is strongly chlorinated and he wishes to drive off the chlorine. The yeast, when added to this, finds itself unable to multiply, since yeast, like most organisms, needs oxygen if it is to multiply. A good rousing, so that the liquid is well aerated, will prompt the yeast colony into life, and after a few days the gas will once again be cheerily bubbling through the airlock.

By far the commonest cause of a fermentation ceasing is that the process is complete. In the case of a dry wine, all the available sugar has been converted, and in the case of a sweet wine, the alcohol content has reached the upper limit that the yeast can tolerate and it ceases to work.

One way of ensuring that a fermentation gets off to a good start is to use a starter-culture.

Grandmother's method of spreading baker's yeast thickly on a piece of dry toast and floating the toast, yeast downwards, on the surface of the liquid was, in effect, adding a primitive starter. The toast fell apart, the yeast was dispersed in the must and fermentation started quickly. Some winemakers used to cream the baker's yeast (as is done when making bread), and in this case fermentation started even more quickly and vehemently – a great advantage if, as sometimes happened, the old methods were rather less than sterile. The millions of active yeast cells invaded the must, and other organisms were shouldered aside and starved out.

More and more, professional winemakers resort to 'levurage' – the natural yeasts and other wildlife on the crushed grapes are suppressed with sulphur, and then a briskly fermenting culture of the desired yeast is added. This is exactly what we do when we use a starter-culture.

When you come to make your starter, do not, for reasons of economy, divide your yeast in two and keep half for another day. It is easy to argue 'I'm starting a culture in a starter-bottle, so half the yeast will do, and I'll keep the rest in the fridge for the next batch'. The risk of contamination makes this a false economy. It is a pity to have to discard even a small amount of wine for the sake of a few pence worth of yeast.

Amateurs add, perhaps, ½ litre (1 pt) of starter to 50 litres (10 gal) of wine must, and this works satisfactorily. But the professionals are much more liberal, adding 20% of actively fermenting must to the remainder.

A starter can be made on a large scale by amateurs too. Suppose that grape concentrate figures in your recipe. You can make an effective starter by using all the grape concentrate, even though this may mean making 5 litres (1 gal) of grape concentrate wine to add to 50 litres (10 gal) made from the other ingredients.

And the concentrate can be worked into a recipe for this purpose. Since as little as a litre (2 pt) of concentrate in 50 litres (10 gal) of wine helps the speed and health of the fermentation, and the final quality of the wine, you can dissolve the concentrate in hot water in a 5 litre (1 gal) jar, add the yeast, wait until fermentation is well established and then add this brisk culture to the rest of the ingredients when they are prepared for pulp fermentation. This generous method is desirable but not essential. A bottle of starter will 'seed' many times its bulk of must.

There are many favoured recipes for starters. When using fresh fruit, one can boil up 100 gm (4 oz) of fruit or berries in 400 ml of water, strain the juice into a sterilised ½ litre (1 pt) bottle, dissolve 6 or 7 gm (heaped tsp) of sugar in the hot liquid and plug the bottle with a twist of cotton wool. When the liquid is cool (below blood heat) add the yeast and stand the bottle in a warm place. The reason for the head-space becomes obvious when the yeast starts to work.

Other bases for a starter include 15 gm (a tablespoonful) of malt or grape concentrate dissolved in 250 ml (½ pt) of water and brought through the boil. The exact amount is not critical. Adding a pinch each of citric acid and yeast nutrient helps to establish the yeast quickly.

When you add the starter to the bulk of the must, do not expect rising streams of bubbles to appear at once. Not only has the yeast to multiply up and get to work, but it has also to produce a great volume of carbon dioxide before any of the gas shows as bubbles. The gas is absorbed in the liquid to begin with, so only when the liquid has absorbed all that it will hold is free gas available to make the long-awaited plops in the fermentation lock.

If fermentation is to continue as it should, the yeast has to find in the must all the necessary ingredients. Gardeners will be familiar with the 'cask' analogy, when healthy soil is compared to a cask with many staves – one may be labelled nitrogen, one potash, one boron and so forth. The cask is only complete and useful if all the staves are present, and if one of the staves is short the cask's capacity is reduced. The same analogy can be applied to wine. Some of the staves are much broader than others (for instance, sugar and, of course, yeast), but even some of the thinner staves have their part to play (yeast nutrient and certain vitamins, for example).

A sound recipe is a description of the proportions of the 'staves' which will make a good sound wine 'cask'.

It takes a very well-balanced recipe to produce really high alcohol percentages, though this is not desirable in all types of wines. Bryan Acton, whose scientific approach to the craft has paved the way for many less scientifically minded winemakers to follow, has, by using grape concentrate and all the additives, obtained 22% by volume of alcohol – fractionally more than half the strength of pub whisky (36° proof as against 70° proof). One of these additives was vitamin B_1 – he uses Benerva tablets, which most chemists will supply, and he recommends not more than 15 mg per gallon (5 litres) of must, or 'In an emergency, with no tablets around, use a quarter of a teaspoonful [approx. 2 ml in 5 litres] of Marmite per gallon, which will assist matters considerably'.

In recent years, science has played an increasingly valuable part in home winemaking and brewing, although it is ironical that one of the ways that knowledge has been gathered has been by gas chromatography (the basis of the breathalyser). Such devices can produce very detailed analyses of wine or beer, but *only* the human palate can tell whether the resulting blend of organic and inorganic chemicals is pleasant to drink.

During fermentation, the sugary substances in the must are broken down by the enzymes in the yeast. (These enzymes can work outside the yeast cell – for instance, when a wine that has apparently completed its fermentation is left too long on its sediment, the yeast cells in the deposit may break down and release active enzymes into the wine to start a further fermentation.)

Even the definition of an enzyme as an organic catalyst does not carry the layman much further. Cedric Austin, in his *Whys and Wherefores of Winemaking*, explains what a catalyst does in neat parable: 'A good working idea of the position is to imagine a gang of navvies taking it easy; then the foreman, representing the catalyst, comes on the scene and the men start moving. The foreman takes no part in the actual labour, but his very presence *accelerates the reaction.*'

We cannot move a muscle without bringing enzymes into action. They occur in saliva – and there is a bizarre connection here with home winemaking and brewing. Columbus found the women of Venezuela making a crude but tasty beer by chewing kernels of corn and spitting them into a common vessel. The enzymes in the saliva broke down the starch of the kernels into molecules on which yeast could get to work. The romantic drink, kava, was produced from kava-root in a similar way, beautiful virgins with strong teeth providing the grinding action and the enzymes. There is no exact parallel with this process in modern winemaking and brewing! But other enzymes are essential.

Because almost exactly half the sugar broken down by the enzymes of the yeast becomes carbon dioxide gas (which disappears into thin air, leaving an almost equal weight of alcohol behind), the level falls in a vessel in which a brisk fermentation is taking place. This puzzles beginners – and more experienced people too – but is simply due to the fact that, when a pound of sugar is fermented out, the bulk of the liquid is reduced by half the volume of the sugar.

Before closing this chapter devoted to keeping yeast (the essential ingredient in any fermented drink) happy and hard at work, let us look at some of the well-established strains of wine yeast, remembering, however, that an *all-purpose yeast* from a good source will satisfy the unexperimental winemaker for almost every wine.

All-purpose yeast will make, for example, a very satisfactory sparkling wine, especially if the sediment is to be left in the bottle, as home-brewers do with the sediment in beer. If you intend to make a sparkling wine by the champagne process, as described in Chapter 13, and to get rid of the sediment by shaking it down into the bottle-neck and expelling it, then you will want a yeast that will not stick at the bottom of the bottle but will slide down the side of the bottle when it is tilted. A good *champagne yeast* does this – and many winemakers would add that it also gives a characteristic flavour to the wine itself.

If you set out to make a sherry with real sherry character, then invest in a *sherry* or *sherry-flor yeast* from a good source. But more about the sherry method later.

Some winemakers, finding that *Sauternes yeast* is more sensitive to sulphur dioxide than other yeasts, use it to make sweet table wines. They use less nutrient than usual, and rack the wine off the sediment at around a quarter of its starting gravity and again when the gravity has fallen far enough to leave a wine of the desired level of sweetness. Two Campden tablets per gallon are then added to 'stun' any remaining yeast cells. All being well, fermentation will stop (but it is safer to leave the wine to mature under an airlock). A further precaution to prevent refermentation is to filter the finished wine through a filter fine enough to remove even yeast cells. Sauternes yeast can be a slow worker, and sometimes has a disconcerting off-smell while it is working – there is no trace of the odour when the wine is mature.

Cereal yeasts, bought from good laboratories, have the ability to break down some starch in a must, so their obvious use is when making cereal wines. However, some fruits (particularly underripe bananas) and some vegetables can produce starch hazes which are stubborn to clear, and these can be avoided if cereal yeast (*Saccaromyces oryza*) is used.

Tokay yeast is unusual in preferring a higher working temperature than other wine yeasts. Given surroundings where the temperature can be maintained at 30°C (85°F) or even higher, Tokay yeast produces a very fast fermentation and, if fed with extra sugar, will (if the recipe is balanced) produce a very high alcohol content. The resulting wine has a characteristic flavour, marked by a fieriness due not entirely to the alcohol itself but also to the flavour of the yeast.

At the other end of the scale are the strains of yeast into which the 'blood' of the *Kaltgarhefe yeast* has been bred. These can ferment at temperatures almost as low as a lager yeast – 5°C (42°F), for example – once the initial fermentation is under way. Their most useful role is in the outhouse of the winemaker who simply cannot find a warm place in his home for his fermentations.

The above are useful yeasts. A useless one, which from the interest taken in it by the public and press would seem to be on the edge of a revival, in the 'ginger-beer plant' yeast, *Saccaromyces pyriformis*. This yeast, when placed in a weak sugar solution, produces clumps which drift slowly up through the cloudy liquid and then settle down again. After a fortnight or so, half the liquid is drunk (or thrown away) and the rest of the bees wine, beasty beer, Californian bees, Brazilian wine or Australian wine is made up with sugar solution and the clump-forming yeast gets busy again.

'Beasty beer', if ginger is included in the recipe, tastes marginally better than it sounds, but it does not compare with real wine, beer or ginger-beer – though the procession of crumbs has a hypnotic fascination!

In Asia they make a palatable drink from milk – it is described as leaving a taste behind it like almond milk, going down very pleasantly and intoxicating weak brains, for it is very heady and powerful. From mare's milk you get *koumiss*; from camel milk, *kephir*; and from yak's milk, *airan*. The necessary yeast does not seem to be available through the trade in this country yet, but doubtless if you have the ingenuity to obtain sufficient milk from mares, camels or yaks you will contrive to find a source of yeast that will ferment lactose.

11

A Matter of Gravity – the Hydrometer

The hydrometer is basically a very simple device, vital in making beer and sparkling wines and useful in making other wines. It has been made into a kind of fetish by some winemakers, eager to know to a fraction of a degree how strong their wine is – but it is certainly worth a page or two to itself.

Breweries and distilleries find accurate hydrometer readings are essential – they pay heavy duty on the results. We, happily, pay no duty.

A hydrometer (brass in breweries and distilleries, glass and high-impact polystyrene in home brewing and winemaking) floats high in a heavy liquid and sinks lower in a light liquid, thus exposing more or less of the calibrated scale on the high stem.

A litre of water at room temperature weighs 1 kg, but a litre of pure alcohol weighs 800 gm – proportionately, a gallon of water at room temperature weighs 10 lb, but a gallon of pure alcohol weighs only 8 lb. Float a hydrometer in water and you will find that the surface of the liquid cuts the stem at 1000 – put it in pure alcohol and it will sink to the bottom.

If you dissolve 500 g (1 lb) of sugar in water and make up the quantity to 5 litres (1 gal) the hydrometer will float at 1036. This figure is very close to the specific gravity of a fairly light home-brewed beer and represents about 4·8% alcohol when fermented out (or 5% for practical purposes).

A close approximation of the amount of alcohol in a beer or wine can be worked out by subtracting the original gravity from the final gravity and dividing by 7·4. A malt wine with an original gravity of 1090 might ferment no lower than 1016 because of unfermentable solids. The difference between the original gravity and the final gravity is 74, which – because this is an easy example – would give an alcohol content of 10%.

The hydrometer can also tell you the amount of sugar in your raw materials. Suppose you are using orange juice, and the tin contains 56 ml (40 fl oz). When you open the tin and float the hydrometer in the juice, it reads 1040. Diluted to a gallon, the juice would read 1010, representing a mere 56 gm (2 oz) of sugar in a gallon – fractionally less in 5 litres – which in practical terms can almost be ignored or, if you wish, can be allowed for by reducing the amount of sugar in the recipe.

Theoretically, if the original gravity of your must is 1115 or over, you are likely to have a sweet wine, since it takes an efficient yeast, well used, to produce more than 15% alcohol. In practice, you would have a very sweet wine, because yeast added to such a high-gravity must may refuse to work, or may work slowly and stop too soon.

The secret is to feed the sugar in gradually if you are making a sweet wine. You may start with a must of 1100 gravity, then take occasional hydrometer readings. When the gravity has dropped to, for example, 1030, you can add enough sugar to bring the reading up by 1015 – that is, 120 gm (4 oz).

It may be that the gravity will drop to 1015 and go no further, in which case you will have the sweet wine you desire. If the gravity drops to 1000, then add a further 120 gm (4 oz) of sugar. The gravity will rise to 1015 and fermentation may cease. By continuing to feed sugar into the wine in this way, one can obtain a social wine of high alcoholic content and the desired amount of sugar.

Dry wines, probably intended for drinking without long maturing, can be made with original gravities of 1085 or even lower, and these, depending on the basic ingredients, may ferment to below 1000 (zero).

How can gravity be less than nothing? But 1000 is not 'nothing', it is the gravity of pure water. A dry wine, or a dry beer, may contain a large enough proportion of alcohol to cause the hydrometer to float deeper than it would in water – remember the earlier comparison between the weight of equal volumes of water and of pure alcohol, and the effect the difference had on the hydrometer?

Many winemakers are well content to assess the alcohol content of their wine pragmatically – by its effect on them – or by rule of thumb, on the basis of the amount of sugar that has gone into the wine and fermented away. For example, in a 25 litre (5 gal) batch,

7·5 kg (15 lb) of sugar has been used in all. The hydrometer reading is 1015, representing 120 gm (4 oz) in 5 litres (1 gal). Of the original 1·5 kg in 5 litres (or 3 lb in each gallon), the remainder (1·38 kg or 2 lb 12 oz) has fermented away, representing 14% alcohol. A more exact assessment requires an allowance for unfermented solids in the fruit, and other considerations, but in practice a wine of 14% alcohol is indistinguishable from a wine of the corrected figure of 13·3%.

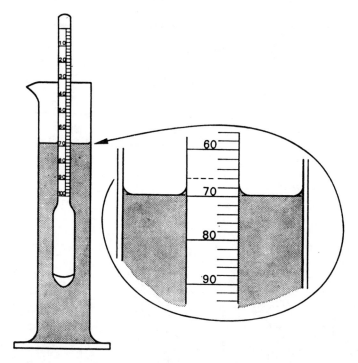

The hydrometer and trial jar. The reading is taken at the *bottom* of the meniscus, so the reading here (as in the enlarged diagram) is 70, not 66

Working on this rule-of-thumb basis, the sugar content of garden fruits and of flowers and vegetables can be ignored. Dried fruits such as elderberries and bilberries contain no significant amount of sugar, but figs, raisins, dates, etc. can be calculated on the basis that dried fruit represents half its weight of sugar. Similarly, honey, malt extract and grape concentrate can be used on the assumption that those ingredients represent their own weight in sugar. These assumptions can be checked with the hydrometer.

Having come to terms with the relation between a drop in gravity and a rise in alcohol content in terms of percentage alcohol – for example, a drop of 74 representing approximately 10% alcohol – the winemaker may be baffled by the question 'How does your wine compare in strength with whisky?' This would be simpler to answer if pure alcohol, mentioned earlier, was 100° proof. It is not – it is

Specific gravity	Degrees Brix or Balling	Potential % alcohol by volume	Amount of sugar in the gallon		Amount of sugar added to the gallon		Vol. of 1 gal with sugar added	
			lb	oz	lb	oz	gal	fl oz
1010	3·0	0·9		2		2	1	1
1015	4·3	1·6		4		5	1	3
1020	5·5	2·3		5		8	1	5
1025	6·8	3·0		7		10	1	7
1030	8·0	3·7		12		13	1	8
1035	9·2	4·4		15	1	0	1	10
1040	10·4	5·1	1	1	1	2	1	11
1045	11·6	5·8	1	3	1	4	1	13
1050	12·8	6·5	1	7	1	7	1	14
1055	14·0	7·2	1	9	1	9	1	16
1060	15·2	7·8	1	9	1	11	1	17
1065	16·4	8·6	1	11	1	14	1	19
1070	17·6	9·2	1	13	2	1	1	20
1075	18·7	9·9	1	15	2	4	1	22
1080	19·8	10·6	2	1	2	6	1	23
1085	20·9	11·3	2	4	2	9	1	25
1090	20·0	12·0	2	6	2	12	1	27
1095	23·1	12·7	2	8	2	15	1	28
1100	24·2	13·4	2	10	3	2	1	30
1105	25·3	14·1	2	12	3	5	1	32
1110	26·4	14·9	2	14	3	8	1	33
1115	27·5	15·6	3	0	3	11	1	35
1120	28·5	16·3	3	2	3	14	1	37
1125	29·6	17·0	3	4	4	1	1	38
1130	30·6	17·7	3	6	4	4	1	40
1135	31·6	18·4	3	8	4	7	1	42

175·1° proof. Proof is a purely arbitrary figure, containing 57·06% alcohol by volume.

Pub whisky, untampered with, is over 40% alcohol by volume, so your 14·1% wine is nearly a third of the strength of the whisky. And if that sounds disappointingly weak, console yourself by comparing the price of three glasses of your wine with the price of one glass of pub whisky.

The sugar content of the must, and the amount of sugar to be added to bring a must up to a desired figure, can be worked out from the table given opposite.

One final point to note about the use of hydrometers. Some winemakers are for ever 'taking the pulse' of their wines by racking a sample into the test-jar and taking a reading. Every time they do this they expose the wine to the risk (however small) of contamination and overaeration. As long as a fermentation is proceeding, leave well alone. When a fermentation ceases for more than a few days, take a test reading. The commonest cause of a stopped fermentation is that the sugar in the wine has been used up, or that the alcohol has built up to the highest level that the yeast can tolerate. Both are causes for congratulation! Only if fermentation stops completely at, say, 1030 and remains there for a week or two do you have to take the kind of remedial action indicated in the chapter on keeping yeast happy.

And remember – you may or may not choose to use a hydrometer when you are making wine. But if you do not use a hydrometer when making beer or sparkling wine, you are putting yourself in danger.

12

Step by Step – the Method

Keeping records

The first step in winemaking – and indeed in home brewing – has nothing to do with elderberries, sugar or malt but with paper and pen. Decide how you are going to keep a record of successive batches, and stick to the method you have chosen.

The more elaborate you make the records, the less likely you are (unless you are extremely methodical) to fill them in meticulously.

A spring-backed folder that can take A4 sheets is adequate. On the outside of the folder goes a neat intimation that this is your wine log. On the inside cover it is wise to record the capacity of your main containers – not what the maker says, but what you yourself have found them to hold by measuring water into them. Many gallon containers hold nearly 9 pt – or just on 5 litres – for example. You will be thankful many times in the future to be able to go to your log and check at once how much a vessel holds.

On the individual sheets can be recorded the name of the wine or beer and the date when you began work on it, then the ingredients (preferably tabulated in column form for easy reading), the yeast chosen, the method used, any extra sugar added, the dates of racking – all these can be noted down. Noted neatly by choice, but since the records are for your own eyes, as long as you can read the writing in a year's time, that suffices.

At each stage, note your opinion of the wine. It is surprising how often 'harsh, too fruity, too acid' at an early stage can gradually become more and more enthusiastic, until after a couple of years (in the case of a wine of that kind) the verdict can be summed up as 'Oh boy!'

To be able to note such details you have to taste and taste again. Only in this way can you educate your palate so that you know in what direction the wine is developing. No book, and no instrument, can replace that fund of knowledge, for it will tell you about your wine in relation to yourself, not in some abstract way. Only your own palate can tell you what you like.

Having made sure, by keeping careful records, that you will be able to recreate a successful wine as closely as possible, you start to make wine.

Methods of extracting juice and flavour

Some ingredients come ready-prepared. Fruit juices, grape concentrate, malt extract – they all come ready to make wine with the minimum of preparation. But how are you to extract the flavour from fruits, flowers and vegetables?

The flavour can be extracted in four ways, basically.

1 Pressing

The first – and this is the way in which the finest white grape wines are made – is by pressing. The fruit (grapes, apples, raspberries perhaps) is thoroughly broken up, put into a powerful and efficient winepress, and pressed until the juice flows out and the fibre remains behind. Related to this are the methods by which fruit juice is extracted, a cupful or two at a time, by domestic juicers and the like. With grapes, apples and pears, this gives a good sound juice which often needs a little adjustment before being fermented. It also works quite well with soft fruits like raspberries, although a great deal of the flavour is left behind in the pulp, but it is clearly hopeless for vegetables such as beetroots and parsnips.

2 Cold infusion

This is the second method of extracting flavour. You pulp your fruit, place it in a fermentation vessel and cover it with cold water in which one Campden tablet for every 5 litres (1 gal) of pulp volume has been dissolved (add a little water with the tablet in it first, then make up the amount needed just to cover the fruit). Left for a few days to soften in this way, the pulp yields more juice and more flavour, and the delicate fresh-fruit taste is retained. Cold infusion is used by many prize-winners.

3   Pulp fermentation

The third method is by pulp fermentation. The fruit is pulped, covered with water (usually boiling water) and left to cool. When the pulp is cool, a vigorously fermenting culture of wine yeast is added. The yeast establishes itself quickly and, as it breaks down the natural sugars in the fruit, also extracts colour and flavour.

The time you leave a pulp fermentation to proceed depends not only on the fruit but also on your personal tastes. The tendency nowadays is to reduce the long fermentations that were once so popular. Wines fermented on the pulp for, say, three days are likely to be lower in acid, tannin and fullness of flavour than those resulting from fermentations of a week or more. This has its parallel in commercial winemaking, where red wines become ready for drinking much earlier because the grape pulp has been fermented for a shorter time.

Because of the use of boiling water, or very hot water, in the first stage, Campden tablet treatment is not usually necessary, but the boiling water can extract a troublesome amount of pectin, so pectin degrading enzymes should be used in every case. They can be added, as a matter of routine, along with the yeast.

Some winemakers use Campden tablets with all three methods – direct pressing, cold infusion and fermentation on the pulp – arguing that even a low concentration of sulphite in the juice or the pulp helps to suppress any unwanted organisms. Obviously, the effectiveness of the sulphur dioxide varies according to the nature, the number and the vigour of the unwanted organisms, but it is also affected by the chemical composition of the liquid, being 'locked up' by sugars, aldehydes and other substances and thus leaving less free sulphur to deal with the bugs. If the liquid is acid, as it almost always is when fruit juice is being used, the sulphur dioxide works more effectively.

The maximum amount of sulphur dioxide allowed here, or in any reputable recipe, is far below the amount permitted in wine by law in Britain – 450 ppm (10 in 5 litres or 9 in a gallon). Most people would be aware of sulphurous fumes at that level – some people would be aware of a tang of sulphur at much lower concentrations – and many more would claim to be aware of it. The usual maximum of two tablets to the gallon is likely to be acceptable to all but a few. Campden tablets added at the cold-infusion stage have long since dispelled when the wine is drunk, but if for any reason two Campden tablets have been added to 5 litres (1 gal) at a later stage (perhaps to suppress an infection in the finished wine) and a detectable bottle-stink persists, then decant the wine an hour or two before drinking – the wine is likely to be all the better for decanting, anyway.

A point about pulp fermentations. The cap of fruit which rises to the top, if left undisturbed, is an ideal breeding-ground for the vinegar bug, so make a point of breaking up the cap and pushing it below the surface at least once a day. Ingenious winemakers have done what is practised on a larger scale in commercial wineries and have devised a perforated disk to hold the pulp below the level of the liquid. An oak board liberally perforated and held down by a large sterile stone would serve the purpose – but frequent stirring (especially in the early days, when every aspect of the craft is fascinating) is perfectly adequate.

4 Boiling

The fourth method of extracting juice and flavour is by boiling. This method is used with vegetables in particular. Theoretically, it would be possible to extract some juice from well-pulped parsnips (enthusiasts have even made a kind of cider from the juice of field turnips in this way), but in practice it is simpler to boil chunks of root and to drain off the resulting juice to make the basis for a root wine.

If the boiling method is used for fruit, it tends to liberate troublesome amounts of pectin, so plenty of pectin degrading enzyme should be added to the juice *when cool*. Boiling also, inevitably, alters the flavour of the wine, giving it a cooked flavour. But boiling has its place even with fruit – for instance, elderberries can be picked, roughly cleaned of the largest green stems, dropped into boiling water and heated until boiling-point is reached again. The contents of the boiler can then be ladled into the press and pressed steaming-hot. The juice that results is high coloured but does not contain an excess of tannin or acid, and can be made into a quickly maturing red wine.

To recapitulate: direct pressing is useful chiefly when large quantities of apples are available; cold infusion gives a wine that tends to preserve the original taste of the ingredients but has the snag that too much of the flavour is left behind in the pulp; boiling is used, of necessity, for root vegetables and can be experimented with using fruits plus plenty of pectin degrading enzymes. But pulp fermentations are probably the most popular with those winemakers who do not take a short-cut to the next stage by using juices and concentrates.

By the way, it can be disconcerting to put what you think is an almost air-tight lid on a fermentation vessel full of pulp, then look in next day and see an earwig taking a stroll on the top of the cap. The earwig may do little harm, but it is an indication that a dustbin lid is not as insect-proof as it seems. Even if the lid is a close fit, what is an even better protection is a sheet of clear polythene, which is allowed to sag onto the surface of the wine and is then secured round the rim with a big rubber band. The film helps to seal the surface against air – and earwigs – and the carbon dioxide which is formed is free to billow up underneath the film. The polythene, too, is easily rolled back to allow the cap on the 'mush' to be pushed under daily.

Pressing the pulp

When you judge that the pulp is ready to be pressed – after it has fermented on the pulp or infused, protected by Campden tablet solution, for between three days and a week – you prepare the winepress, washing it down with hot water and then giving it a thorough damping with sulphite solution to discourage any bugs in the crannies of the woodwork.

The pulp can be put in the barrel of the press in a coarse bag, but pressing is quicker and easier if you put the fruit directly into the barrel. Some pulp and pieces of fruit will be squeezed out between the bars, but these can be trapped in a coarse strainer or piece of netting as they run from the press in the juice.

Slow and steady – that is the motto to remember when operating a winepress, small or large. Take up the strain regularly, as the pulp settles, but never force the screw round brutally – if you do, you may burst the spars or strain the frame.

And if you have no press? Then put the pulp in a piece of nylon or terylene netting and squeeze as much juice from it as you can, or indulge your ingenuity to contrive a press with planks and cramps. And if you feel that you do not succeed in getting as much juice in this way, console yourself by remembering that some winemakers blame overenthusiastic pressing for a particularly stubborn type of haze. Pressing *may* be the cause (it would be difficult to prove experimentally), but other winemakers, with efficient presses capable of exerting a force of tons on the pulp, have never seen this particular haze.

What is less disputable is that overenthusiastic pressing may give the wine a coarse flavour, since only at the end of the rigorous process do some of the more stubborn cells (those in unripe berries or pieces of green stem) burst open and contribute their unwanted flavour to the juice. In commercial winemaking the best and most delicately flavoured wine is made from the juice that runs from the press under the weight of the grapes alone before pressure is applied with the screw.

The answer to the question 'How hard should I press the pulp?' is 'Keep pressing until you no longer get a worthwhile trickle of juice, or until you notice the flow becoming turgid with pulp; or until you find, on tasting the juice, that it is becoming harsh or "grassy" in flavour.' Usually the reason for stopping is that you have squeezed out all the juice worth extracting.

The juice from the press at this stage is likely to contain solid matter-pulp particles, seeds and the like. Some commercial wine-makers, after pressing out the grape juice, introduce an intermediate stage, *debourbage*, letting the pressed juice stand, lightly sulphited, in a container while the solid matter settles out. If you have the space, the time and the spare containers to make this possible, it is worth doing, especially with juices that throw a heavy sediment, such as the liquid pressed from figs or strained from boiled bananas. With hedgerow fruit like rosehips and elderberries, some dust and grit will be among the material that settles out. With dried elderberries, you may find that the strained juice has contained a little of the soil of Middle Europe or Portugal.

Sweetening and adjusting the juice

It is at this stage that the juice is sweetened and adjusted, and becomes *must* (must is wine in the making, just as wort is beer in the making).

The additions at this stage may be acid (citric acid usually, or some of the others singly or in blends), tannin, yeast nutrient, Benerva tablet if used and, by far the bulkiest, sugar.

Most of the additions, if put straight into the juice, will dissolve satisfactorily. But if you put dry sugar into the wort, it sinks to the bottom and lies in a grey sludgy layer which discourages the yeast. Even if you make up a syrup as recommended and pour this in, it may lie undissolved for days until thermal movement, and the stir caused by the rising bubbles of carbon dioxide, helps to diffuse it through the wort. Sugar lying undissolved in this way not only discourages the yeast but also makes nonsense of any hydrometer readings. If the sample is taken from the top, it is far too low, if drawn from below, it is far too high. Therefore, stir the sugar into the wine very thoroughly.

Racking the wine

The wine is now almost made. If you now put the sweetened must in a suitable container, fitted a fermentation lock and left it in a warm place, it would end up as wine. It would probably be a dry wine, since the sugar you added at the beginning would be insufficient to make a sweet wine, and there would be a risk that the thick layer of sediment which would form in the course of the months might begin to break down if left. It is mainly to get rid of this sediment that we rack the wine from time to time. The first racking may be from a bulk fermentation vessel, holding perhaps 25 litres (5 gal), into 5 litre (1 gal) jars and then from these jars into others as more sediment forms.

Racking is easy to do. The full vessel is placed somewhere high – on a chair on the draining board beside the sink, for example – and the empty vessel is put at a lower level – perhaps in the sink itself. One end of the rubber siphon is placed in the wine in the high vessel. A suck on the other end of the tube, at the level of the neck of the lower vessel, will fill the siphon and start the liquid flowing. It is then a matter of making sure that the high end of the tube is kept just below the surface of the liquid. As soon as it can be seen that the siphon is drawing up sediment, you stop racking. This means that, if you are racking from one jar into another the same size, the second will not be full because of the bulk of sediment left behind. Not only this, but the process of fermentation reduces the bulk of the wine by the amount of sugar that dispels as carbon dioxide.

How can you make up the ullage, the air-space over the wine? You can drop in sterilised pebbles – as is done in some parts of France – or marbles. Or you can top up, either with sugar syrup (at the early stages), with boiled water which has been allowed to cool or with another wine of a similar type. Sometimes the addition of a little mature wine to a new wine results in the rapid clearing of the bulk, sometimes, too, a little of a fermenting new wine added to an older wine with a stubborn haze will, for some reason, clear that as well.

Blending

Some winemakers feel strongly that it is a disgrace, a confession of failure or perhaps even cheating a little, to blend two or more wines at any stage into a satisfactory mixture. Port, sherry, almost all champagnes, cognac, whisky – all these are blended, as are many of the table wines sold under brand names. Theophrastus summed it up when he said that wines were blended by the Ancient Greeks so that 'the effect is that they may simultaneously destroy one another's inferior qualities'.

Blending can be done at any stage – the fruits can be blended in the original recipe, two fermenting musts may be blended or two wines while still raw may be united. Perhaps the best time is when the wines are still young but beginning to show their quality. One is thin and acid, another is fruity and rather flabby. How would they taste together? Take a dram glass, or even a test-tube, of each wine and mix them. If the result is pleasing, you can be pretty sure that the blended wine, after a few days' honeymoon, will be better, and much better still after longer maturation.

Remember, though, the cautionary proverb in the dairy industry: 'If you put a gallon of bad milk in 100 gallons of good milk, you get 101 gallons of bad milk.' The same principle applies to winemaking. Never try to lose an unsound wine (infected with vinegar, ropiness or the like) by mixing it, untreated, with a large bulk of sound wine. You stand a very good chance of infecting it all.

For those who do not like even country wines to taste recognisably of one fruit, blending has the added advantage of producing an 'anonymous' wine, which does not declare its ingredients at first taste. Single raspberry and single gooseberry wines tend to boast of their origins in this way – more acceptable in a social wine than in a table wine.

Fermentation period

How long should it take, from winepress to wine bottle? It is impossible to guess, for there are so many imponderables.

Some winemakers prefer to keep a fermenting wine in a really warm place until fermentation is complete as this speeds up the process. Others say that, after the first rapid fermentation, the wine should be moved into cooler surroundings and left to work slowly and steadily to achieve the best quality. Again, every time the wine is racked the process is slowed until the yeast can multiply up and carry on the work. There is in winemaking, as in brewing and all processes involving living organisms, an element of unpredictability – a wine that fermented to perfect clarity last year inside five weeks may take five months this year. We must believe that there is a good reason for this, but finding it is difficult.

This element of unpredictability applies very obviously to the speed with which wines fall clear. Usually, for example, banana wine is a quick clearer and helps other wines to clear when blended, but once in a while one encounters a stubborn haze.

Time, and a thorough chilling, will clear most wines. Before resorting to filtration – unless for special occasions, for instance preparing a wine for a show – give your wine plenty of time to clear of its own accord.

Fining and filtering

When you start to make wine, every part of the process brings its own pleasure, but when you are established in the craft and making a realistic quantity, any way in which you can simplify the process and save unnecessary work, and yet keep up quality and quantity, is welcome. Being overelaborate in recipes and methods is one of the prime reasons why people become discouraged with winemaking and home brewing.

There is no doubt, though, that filtration – a process that a generation of winemakers had dismissed as unnecessary – is becoming more and more popular. One reason is obvious – if you want to drink your wine young, and object to drinking it milky or hazy, then you must fine and filter it – do for yourself what time would have done for you. The second reason is that there is now on the market a selection of good filters, not too difficult to use and supplied with detailed instructions. We have come a long way from filter-paper in a funnel, dripping slowly and aerating the wine drastically.

Basically, the process of filtration consists of straining out large particles and letting the rest pass through – a builder could be said to filter his aggregate when he shakes it through a sieve.

The key to the matter is the question 'How big is big?' If you are straining wine to get rid of visible floaters or particles of Campden tablet filler, then a paper handkerchief or tissue laid in a colander in the mouth of a large funnel works very well.

However, although this will trap most of the visible particles, it will not hold back all the causes of cloudiness and hazing – some of them, like the tiny blobs of jelly in a pectin haze, will ooze through the holes, given time. If you multiply the number of layers of paper tissue, you multiply your chances of catching the particles, but you also slow down the process.

But if paper tissues will filter all the particles we can see floating in the wine, why filter out the particles that are too small to see? Because, in mass, these microscopic particles *do* cloud the wine, just as a chimney which is discharging no visible smuts can still pollute the atmosphere by belching out masses of microscopic particles.

Some of the filters obtainable from winemakers' suppliers are designed to remove particles well below visible size – even yeast cells. In their case, the answer to the question 'How big is big?' might be 'You would need to range 100 000 of the particles side by side to span 25mm – an inch.'

If there are visible particles in the wine, either strain them out first or give them time to settle out before resorting to fine filtration.

It is, in any case, better to fine the wine that you intend to filter. This gets rid of a great deal of material which might block the fine pores of the filter, and it may well be that, after using finings, you will find that you no longer need to filter.

Modern filters have made the process much simpler. Winemakers who used to say 'Life's too short to watch wine dripping through laboratory blotting-paper' can now set up the filter and leave it to do its work. But those who say 'Fining and filtration take more out of a wine than merely suspended particles – they take freshness and some flavour out of it too' will be harder to convert.

But although successful fining clears a wine and helps to stabilise it, and may also correct overhigh tannin where this is a fault, it does affect the balance of a wine. If you like your wine as it is, do not fine it unless it is absolutely necessary.

You will also lose a certain amount of wine through fining and filtering.

Many substances have been used to fine wine, from gelatine to isinglass and from bull's blood to the white of an egg. The mental picture of a fine net falling through the liquid and trapping the particles is not the whole story, for these substances act like magnets, drawing the particles (with their opposite electric charges) towards them and making them into tiny clumps, which settle out. If the haze has the same electric charge as the fining agent, you will make bad worse, and the amount of finings can be crucial.

Happily, there is one form of fining that, though it has its shortcomings, is more satisfactory than the others. This is Bentonite, which takes its name from Fort Benton in Wyoming, where the clay from which it is prepared is mined. Although it does not extract the tannin from the wine, with the risk of leaving it flabby, and although there is no risk of permanent hazing if you miscalculate, Bentonite does leave a thick sediment, and there is the risk of an earthy off-taste if you leave the wine too long on this sediment.

Some winemakers have found Bentonite stubborn to liquidise. The secret is not to rush the job. The little plates of Bentonite will absorb a remarkable amount of water – given time.

If you pour 400 ml (12 fl oz) of water into a sterilised wine bottle, then add 30 gm (1 oz) of Bentonite and stopper the bottle, the Bentonite will lie in a sludgy layer, looking just like clay. Give the bottle a shake from time to time, just as you remember, and in a couple of days you will find that the bottle contains a homogeneous creamy substance. 50 ml (1½ fl oz) to 5 litres (1 gal) of wine should be sufficient – do not add it direct to the wine but take 500 ml (1 pt) of wine, stir the Bentonite cream into it, then return the pint to the bulk, stir it in and leave it to settle.

Bentonite is also available from winemakers' suppliers in the form of a gel, which solves the problem of wetting the clay.

Treated wines can be left for up to a month on the Bentonite sediment. If the clarification is not as good as you had hoped, you can give the jar a swirl to disperse the Bentonite through the bulk, which should become brighter as the Bentonite settles again.

13

Stars in the Glass – Sparkling Wines

'I am drinking stars!' said Dom Perignon when he first tasted sparkling wine. The Swiss still call them 'starry wines', which sounds much more romantic than the English 'brisk' and the American 'crackling'.

It is more honest to invite a friend to have a glass of your 'Brisk and Starry' than your champagne, for real champagne comes only from the fields of La Champagne in northern France. There, 1 tonne of grapes yield 500 litres of juice at the first gentle pressing, to give the wine that almost everyone regards as the mark of a special occasion.

We may not be able to make something exactly like vintage champagne, but we can make very acceptable wines with authentic bubbles.

The bubbles in a sparkling wine are not like those in, for instance, lemonade. The wine is not merely saturated with the gas but holds it locked up chemically in an unstable compound, ethyl pyrocarbonate. The gas is slowly released from this compound – unlike the bubbles in pop or carbonated wines, which escape much more quickly.

Considering the range of basic materials available to the home winemaker, there is no need to restrict yourself to sparkling *white* wines – even though wine-lovers tend to look down their noses at sparkling red commercial wines. One word of warning – a really brisk sparkling red wine can give a white tablecloth an impressive 'measles' rash for an inch or two round the glass!

Most sparkling home-made wines occur by accident. A wine is bottled a shade too soon and fermentation continues in the bottle to give the wine its locked-in starry bubbles waiting for the cork to be drawn. More rarely, a malolactic fermentation, reducing the malic acid to lactic acid, creates some carbon dioxide.

To make 'brisk and starry' wine deliberately, you start with a light-flavoured wine, ferment it to dryness, wait until it clears, prime it with sugar (as in beer-making) and a fresh yeast culture, and bottle it in strong bottles. The enthusiasts go on to complete the champagne method by persuading the yeast down onto the corks, by gradually turning the bottles, and then by expelling the sediment in a frozen plug and recorking. Many winemakers, however, are content to make their sparkling wine by home-brewing methods and to pour the wine carefully, leaving the sediment behind in the base of the bottle.

Sometimes you can produce the basis of a sparkling wine by diluting a table wine or social wine. A sweet social wine may need to be broken by dilution with an equal quantity of water, and this will knock it well out of balance. Lack of acidity is likely to be the most noticeable defect, but acid crystals can be dissolved in the wine until it is distinctly tangy to the taste. A sparkling wine lacking in acidity is likely to taste flat and uninteresting. Tannin may also need to be discreetly added.

As a rule of thumb, the basic wine (whether made specially or contrived from an already completed wine) should contain not more than 1 kg (2 lb) of fermentable substances – that is, fruit sugars, added sugar, malt, wheat syrup and the like – in 5 litres (1 gal). If you wish to step up the gravity of the basic wine, 60 gm (2 oz) of sugar makes a difference of 5° on the hydrometer.

One important difference between the basic wine for a sparkling wine and that for other wines is this – with most wines, one that tastes dry *is* dry, since your palate is the final arbiter. When you make a sparkling wine, however, you cannot merely assume that, if it tastes dry, it is dry, because, masked by acidity, tannin and fruit flavours, enough sugar may remain to produce a dangerous pressure in the bottle.

So you must check the amount of sugar in the finished wine before bottling it. The most convenient way is to use the Clinitest, which was devised for diabetics. It is a chemical test, which includes a colour comparison chart. The wine, before extra sugar is added, should contain no more than 15 gm (½ oz) residual sugar. Incidentally, the test is not accurate if sugar has been recently added to the wine – it registers only inverted sugars, and even when a wine is fermenting briskly the yeast takes a little time to invert the sugar that is added. This is an important point, because a misreading of the Clinitest or the similar commercially marketed sugar-testing kit may mean that sugar, passing undetected into the bottles, may once again build up a dangerous pressure in the bottles.

Because of the dryness of the wine, acidity and high tannin show up sharply on the palate. This can be muted and a trace of roundness given to what otherwise might be a thin wine by adding a little glycerine, itself produced as a side-product of fermentation. 10 ml (2 tsps) in 5 litres (1 gal) may be enough – try a sample bottle first before you commit yourself to blending glycerine into the bulk of the wine.

A dropper seems the obvious thing to use to measure out a small amount into each bottle, but glycerine, being an oily viscous liquid, will not readily draw into the dropper.

Having made a suitable basic wine, given it time to clear perfectly, fined it if necessary and balanced it if acid, tannin or glycerine were needed, make sure that you have enough strong bottles. Bottles that have held champagne and other sparkling wines are ideal, and easily obtained – hotels throw out scores of them after wedding receptions. Some labels and foil can be very stubborn to remove, but avoid scratching heavily at the bottles if you can, since even small scores on the surface of glass weaken it greatly – there is little point in selecting strong bottles able to stand pressure if you then weaken them by scraping.

Pressure in a commercial champagne bottle can rise to over 8 kg per sq cm (120 lb per sq in) – contrast that with the 0·7 kg/cm^2 (10 lb/in^2) regarded as sufficient to give home-brewed beer in a keg its proper liveliness. Amateurs must certainly not aim at the commercial champagne pressures, but, on the other hand, pressure in beer kegs would only be sufficient to give the wine a little briskness.

Plastic stoppers specially designed to fit sparkling wine bottles are now on the market. They are a tight drive-home fit for the average champagne bottle and should be softened in hot water if they will not push home with the heel of the hand. Hollow-headed fitting tools are available to fit over the domed head of these stoppers – and such a tool should be used, for the plastic stoppers are too expensive to risk damaging with a mallet.

Some winemakers successfully add the blend of priming sugar and actively fermenting yeast direct to each bottle in a measured dosage, but it is better to add them to the bulk of the basic wine and to delay bottling until the secondary fermentation has started. If you add the yeast and sugar, and immediately fill the bottles with the still wine, a fermentation may not start at all or, more likely, will start in some bottles and not in others, and you will not know whether you are going to serve still wine or 'stars' until you cut the ties and draw the cork.

If you do not wish to go to all the considerable trouble of remuage – that is, of disgorging the yeast – you can cheat a little by decanting the wine instead. Wine reduced to just below freezing-point, by standing it in the fridge for an hour or so, can be decanted into clean bottles, leaving the sediment behind, without too much loss of effervescence.

If you mean to go the whole way, by following the method devised by the Widow Cliquot of gently shaking the sediment down on to the cork and disgorging it, remember that it does take some natural deftness and some forward planning.

The sediment has first of all to be moved down the bottle gradually. Obviously, the easiest way to do this is to up-end the bottles on their corks in one swoop, but if you can persuade the yeast to slide down the glass and on to the cork it will not be dispersed through the wine, which by now should be starbright.

A special rack or pulpit is used in champagne-making, so that the bottle can be moved by degrees from its side to its cork without disturbance, and any winemaker who is prepared to go to this trouble will contrive to devise similar apparatus, perhaps from crates and from varying shapes of blocks to hold the crates at different angles.

When giving the bottles their regular twist to move the yeast downwards, it is wiser to wear a heavy glove in case of mishap – the glove should be left lying close to the wine to encourage its use. When handling sparkling wines – or, for that matter, bottles of beer that you suspect may have built up too much pressure – grasp the bottles in a thick piece of towelling. The rough surface of the fabric grips the glass, and the thickness of the towelling gives some protection if the bottle splits.

The chance of a burst bottle may be small but the penalties can be great. That is why, although it is not difficult to make sparkling wine, it is advisable for beginners to acquire a fair amount of experience in making other wines before trying sparkling ones. You have, for instance, to be sure you can read a hydrometer accurately ten times out of ten.

When the Widow Cliquot devised her method of ridding her champagne of the yeast, the workers depended on their skill and quickness to open the bottle, release the yeast and cloudy wine, put the bottle back on its base, dose it with sugar and alcohol to make up the loss, cork it and tie the cork down, all with the minimum loss of champagne.

Fortunately, the amateur can adapt the professional method of cutting down the loss by using a mixture of salt and ice. A mixture of salt and ice is much colder than ice alone – a fact that needs little proof to anyone who has had to stand around on a snowy road after it has been gritted with salt.

If you immerse the neck of your bottle in 2 parts of crushed ice and 1 part of coarse salt, the liquid in the neck of the bottle will quickly freeze, locking the sediment in a plug of ice. When the cork is eased out, the sediment will be blown out, with greater or lesser force depending on the liveliness of the wine. The neck of the bottle should then be given a quick but careful wipe (outside to remove the salt, inside to remove any last traces of yeast) and the loss made up with a little of the wine. The bottle can then be corked, without any unnecessary waste of time during which the precious 'stars' are disappearing into thin air.

The most professional-looking way to keep the cork in place is to fit a special metal cap over the cork, and to hold cap and cork in place with wire ties, which can also be bought from specialist suppliers. But for wine intended for household use, the cork can be tied down with strong string – some of the synthetic cords are practically unbreakable and can be knotted tightly.

When disgorging the wine, or when you come to serve it, you will find that you have more control over the cork if you hold it firmly in your left hand and gently turn and pull the bottle – this is because of the much greater diameter of the bottle.

When you come to serve your sparkling wines, do not make them too cold. Cellar temperature – 7°C–10°C (45°F–50°F) – is cold enough, unless the wine is not too satisfactory, in which case you can chill it to render it dumb so that its imperfections will be less apparent! Another reason for not serving sparkling wine too cold is a physiological one – you may embarrass your guests as gas is released from the warming wine in their cosy innards! (For the same reason, don't drink sparkling wine in the airport just before you take off – the bubbles locked up in the liquid are quickly released as pressure falls, with embarrassing results.)

Chilled wine warms up surprisingly quickly in any case, and even faster if it is lying in a flat puddle in the 'traditional' champagne glass, so well adapted for holding ice-cream. However, an ordinary

Paris goblet, or a tall fluted glass, will show the wine off better and hold the sparkle longer.

Having read the description of the champagne method, it is tempting to ask 'Are there no short cuts to simpler sparkling wines?' This question has been asked by the commercial producers for years, and the answer has been the 'tank method' (*charmat* or *chaussepied*) in which the final fermentation is carried out under pressure in a closed vessel. The process was invented in France in the nineteenth century and is now used in many parts of the world to produce the less expensive sparkling wines.

Amateurs can adapt this method by making a low-fruit and low-sugar wine and, when it has fermented down to below zero and is satisfactorily clear, by racking it into one of the plastic kegs sold to home-brewers for draught beer, then adding ½ litre (1 pt) of briskly fermenting champagne yeast culture and priming sugar at around 90 gm (3 oz) to 5 gal. Pressure can then be maintained, as for beer, by using carbon dioxide injection.

Sparkling wine on draught, starry to the last glass. As the saying goes, 'There's posh for you!'

14

Exceptional Wines

Sherry

'Have a glass of my sherry.' We have all had that offer, and received a wine which, though pleasant enough, had nothing of sherry character about it at all.

Sherry is made by a method that contradicts all the previous advice about keeping vessels full and preventing air from getting at the fermenting wine. After the first tumultuous fermentation, the wine is racked into vessels which are left with a considerable air-space. There it lies on its yeast, exposed to the air, with the result that it oxidises and acquires that characteristic hot tang.

Commercial sherry is also fortified by the addition of grape spirit. Since home-made sherries, if well made, may be three-quarters of the strength of commercial fortified sherry, fortification is not really necessary for home-made wines – the alternative is to fill the glass a little fuller.

Commercial sherry, too, is always uniform, being blended on the solera system – 'progressive fractional blending' sums it up. This process is imitated by some winemakers, but it requires a good supply of uniform sherries, a good palate – and patience. The commercial blender stores his casks row on row. In the bottom row are the most mature wines. When wine is drawn from the lower tier of casks, the bulk is made up from the next oldest, in the row above. In turn, these casks are refreshed from the casks above them, and so on – perhaps for a dozen rows of casks.

Because of this 'nursery' system, there are no vintage sherries. The amateur is well advised to forget about establishing his own criadera and instead make every sherry a unique vintage wine.

Tied into the mystique of sherry-making is the sherry-flor, a combination of yeasts which forms a heavy film on the surface of the sherry and which contributes greatly to the character of the finished wine (it has a disconcerting resemblance in the early stages to the common disease, flowers of wine, which is also a surface-forming yeast). Commercially, the sherry flor is becoming better understood, and in countries such as Cyprus, where sherry is imitated, batches are inoculated with sherry-flor cultures. Sherry-flor yeasts are also available to the home winemakers, but they do not always form that surface film – over-lavish use of sulphur can discourage them, for instance. Even when the film does not form, the yeast ferments the wine satisfactorily, and if the wine is matured in the right conditions (say, in gallon jars filled to the shoulders and plugged with cotton wool) the result will have a recognisable sherry character – which is more than can be said for the results of some of the old country sherry recipes.

Port

Real port is more difficult to approach. Commercially, port is made by stopping the natural fermentation of the grape must in its tracks by the addition of massive quantities of spirit. The result is that the wine retains much of its fruit sugars and fruity body and flavour. This process, for financial reasons, is beyond the scope of most amateurs. The way round the difficulty is to make a full-fruit red wine, pushing the fermentation along to achieve as high an alcohol content as possible, and then, if you wish, fortifying the wine with brandy or a neutral spirit. The result will be a fruity, strong social wine. But although it is not uncommon to taste sherries that could pass for the produce of South Africa, if not Spain, it is unusual to taste a home-made port that might have been shipped down the Douro to Oporto.

Fortified wines

Some winemakers' motto might be 'strong is good, so stronger is better', and to them fortifying their wines has a great attraction. Before you fortify a wine, make sure it is absolutely star-bright, for the addition of the spirit may stabilise any cloudiness or haze, making it impossible to clear later.

If you know the exact strength of the wine you have made and you wish to fortify it to an exact percentage of alcohol, you can work out the addition of alcohol mathematically, but the chances are that, even if you take a succession of careful hydrometer readings during the fermentation, the best you can achieve without laboratory techniques is a close approximation.

Fortification can be undertaken on a rule-of-thumb basis much more simply, by assuming that the well-made wine you wish to fortify has reached 15% alcohol. Using Polish White Spirit of 140° proof and putting 30 ml (1 fl oz) in each wine bottle before filling it with sherry or port, will result in a wine (give or take a little) of around the right strength. If you wish to use whisky or brandy, because you feel they will better complement the nature of the basic wine, then 2 fl oz is the capacity of the popular miniature bottles of spirit, so you can fortify one trial bottle and see if you wish to do the rest.

Tokay wine

A wine with a marked character of its own is Tokay. Made from a very high-gravity grape pulp, it can ferment for years to yield at last a very sweet, powerful wine reputed to be a cure for every ill except death itself. Home winemakers can use Tokay yeast to achieve high-alcohol wines very quickly. With a well-balanced recipe, a Tokay yeast and a hot place, you can sometimes complete fermentation inside a fortnight. A shaded corner of a greenhouse in summer is the sort of place for this, but do keep the wine out of direct sunlight, not only to avoid wide swings in temperature but also to guard the must from ultra-violet radiation, which is harmful to the yeast.

The Tokay high-temperature fermentation is over so quickly that some winemakers do not trouble to fit a fermentation lock, simply covering the top of the vessel to prevent insects falling in. And the concentration of alcohol soars so rapidly that the wine is beyond the worst risks of disease in a day or two.

So why doesn't everyone use Tokay yeast? One reason is that the resulting wine is so strong and fiery, with a characteristic hot taste all its own, that it takes long maturing to be at its best – the time saved in the fermentation is more than lost in the cellar.

Mead

Making mead is almost as much a craft in its own right as brewing – but no one expects beer to taste like wine. Not everyone likes mead.

People face a glass of mead with preconceived opinions, thinking 'I like honey, so I'm bound to like mead'. But this is misleading, for although mead may have some of the taste and smell of fresh honey this is transmuted by fermentation and maturation into something much more spirituous. (Some commercial meads seem to be blended to match up to customers' preconceptions of what mead *should* taste like and thus can taste as if they had been compounded from honey caramel toffees.)

Mead has been around for thousands of years, for honey is one of the earliest forms of food known to man – cave paintings show primitive man braving the bee-stings to harvest honey from a hole in a cliff.

It is a safe assumption that man, or his successors, would not be slow to learn that a mixture of honey and water would ferment agreeably. Honey (like dates, an early source of sweetness, and of wine) is very high in energy value – 1600 calories to the pound. You might call it the first 'concentrate' to be used by winemakers, for the pollen of a myriad flowers is concentrated in it.

Mead could easily have been discovered by accident. Perhaps someone left a honeycomb soaking in water to recover the last traces of sweetness and it fermented, making a very light refreshing drink.

Not all the meads of history have been like our present-day heavy meads. Many were light enough to be swigged like ale – these can still be made today, though they are out of favour with mead enthusiasts.

Honey can be substituted for sugar (weight for weight) in many wines (the honey contains fractionally less sweetness than the sugar).

Although the ingredients of a jar of mead may contain the plunder from a quarter of a million flowers, fermentation may be slow and may stop too soon if yeast nutrient is not added generously. It is safer to double the amount you use in a fruit wine, and to make sure that the optional additives such as vitamin B and a pinch of Epsom salts are also included.

One way to ensure a quicker fermentation (though it disqualifies the wine from being mead – it is, in fact, melomel) is to incorporate grape concentrate in the recipe. The resulting drink is quicker to mature, and often more acceptable except to the purists.

Grape concentrate does alter the flavour. But an alteration is also made to the flavour if the choice of method is to sterilise the honey, which, in addition to a complex blend of sugars, minerals and other healthful and flavourable substances, may contain wild yeasts and other organisms. The honey is sterilised by boiling it in a little water and skimming off any scum that rises. If you do this you are left with sterile honey, but honey that has lost some of its more delicate flavour. If, however, the must for the mead or melomel is made up and two Campden tablets are added to 5 litres (1 gal) of liquid, any unwanted organisms will be suppressed. The yeast starter can be added next day.

Any wine yeast can be used. All-purpose yeast is, as with so many wines, perfectly satisfactory and has the advantage of sedimenting well. Maury yeast, which has become accepted as the traditional yeast for mead, seems to have no clear advantage in flavour and certainly does not sediment as well as other more common yeasts.

Mead, then, can be anything from a full-bodied wine fermented in the sherry way with a sherry yeast to a light, effervescent brew flavoured discreetly with hops.

Try to taste several types, made by enthusiastic experts, before you commit yourself to making a big batch of mead, for honey, like other concentrates, is not cheap.

Cider

For those who have plenty of apples cider can be made for next to nothing. Old-fashioned English scrumpy (like thin pea soup with pieces of apples floating in it and more than a hint of vinegar in its bouquet) is not too difficult to equal, or surpass. In spite of its failings, scrumpy was cheap and refreshing, and you acquired a taste for it after the first mouth-shrinking priming of the pump.

Despite its crunchy solidity, more than three-quarters of an apple is liquid, and to extract this the ripe fruit has to be broken up finely. You can tell when an apple is ripe literally by rule of thumb, for it can then be dented by the thumb.

There are various ways of breaking up the fruit – one wonders if those who recommended using a mincer have tried to mince even a couple of pounds of apples. The simplest and quickest way for the amateur, however, is to smash the apples in the bottom of a plastic bucket with the butt-end of a heavy piece of timber – do not do this in the living room, for occasional splashes of juice can be driven quite a distance.

As the fruit is smashed up, it can be put into the winepress, but if there is any delay the apples will start to discolour through oxidation. It is therefore better, and no more difficult, to put the pulp into a plastic vessel and cover it with a minimum of water in which Campden tablets have been dissolved (around one tablet to 5 litres (1 gal) of pulp, but the exact amount is not critical).

When the crushing process has been completed, the pulp can be pressed right away or, if it is more convenient, left overnight protected by the sulphite.

As with pressing fruit for wine, the pressing process should not be hurried. Screw down the press when the juice ceases to flow freely, but do not strain yourself, or the press, by using too much force.

When the pressing is complete, break up the cake of apple and press it again, to extract what juice was not expressed the first time.

The juice you have obtained can be yeasted straight away, but it does contain a fair amount of coarse pulp in suspension and so it is probably better to give it a day to settle. Once again, the juice must be protected against oxidation and disease by dissolving one Campden tablet to 5 litres (1 gal).

When the juice has settled, pour or rack the clear liquid off, leaving the pulp behind.

Put the liquid in a suitable fermentation vessel, add the yeast and leave it to work, and you have made cider – for cider is the fermented juice of apples. Once you start adjusting the gravity with sugar, diluting the juice and adding tannin or acid, you are making apple wine instead – and very good it can be.

Cider made from a blend of cooking apples, dessert apples and crab apples has every chance of being refreshing and palatable, though thin. It is more acceptable to most palates if made sparkling. Once it has fermented out, bottle it in the same way as beer, with half a teaspoonful of priming sugar to the pint bottle. Like home-brewed beer, cider may need to be poured with care to avoid disturbing the sediment, and there will be a small amount of waste at the bottom of each bottle or flagon, but since it has cost nothing but your apples, your labour, the yeast and a half-teaspoonful of sugar, a little waste can be overlooked.

A small amount of cider (which in cider-making terms is 25–50 litres (5–10 gal) can be made by following the simple instructions given above. For even smaller amounts, you can contrive to do without a press by squeezing the pulp in terylene netting instead.

Cider, being cheap, is distilled in many countries. In France it makes Calvados and in America it can become a moonshine called 'essence of lockjaw'. In Britain cider is not distilled commercially on any scale, and there are rigorous legal penalties for any amateur who attempts it.

15

Liquid Sweetmeats – Liqueurs

Liqueurs, 'those pretty little liquid sweetmeats, glowing with colour like slivers of stained glass' as Cyril Ray called them, are not easy to duplicate, and their imitation is almost a separate branch of the winemaker's art.

Although home-made liqueurs are not expensive when compared with the originals, they are substantially more expensive than other home-made drinks, chiefly because of the cost of the fortifying spirit.

A basic method of making a liqueur is to put 120 ml (4 fl oz) of spirit – whisky, brandy, rum or vodka, according to choice and the type of liqueur – into a wine bottle, add 120 ml (4 fl oz) of standard sugar syrup and the purchased liqueur flavouring, and fill up the bottle with suitable wine.

The flavourings of commercial liqueurs are very complex: Green Chartreuse and Yellow Chartreuse are said each to consist of over 100 ingredients, including herbs and flowers; Grand Marnier is flavoured with a spirit produced by steeping the peel of Haiti bitter oranges with sugar in alcohol for two months (in France it is not only drunk as a liqueur but also used for flavouring ice-cream and yoghurt); and Advocaat, the well-known egg-flip which looks so easy to simulate with sweetened brandy or strong wine, egg yolk, vanilla and coffee flavouring, has its own secrets – not even an *advocaat* (a Dutch lawyer) could advance a case for some of the alleged advocaats one is offered.

Commercial liqueurs are made by three processes: distillation, in which the fruits, herbs and other ingredients are macerated in spirit and the mixture is then distilled; infusion, in which the ingredients are added to spirit, which is then filtered and sweetened; and the addition of essence, which involves adding natural or synthetic materials to spirit, which is then sweetened and coloured.

The last process is the commonest for amateurs, and although one authority sums it up as being used 'chiefly but not entirely for the production of cheap and inferior liqueurs' some pleasant drinks can result.

Ferins offer a variety of liqueur flavourings, with detailed instructions on how to use them for making liqueurs (in which case one bottle of flavouring is required to make one bottle of liqueur), for flavouring wines (one bottle of flavouring to three to six bottles of wine) or for flavouring cooked dishes and sweets.

Some liqueur names (Drambuie and Glayva, for example) are copyright trade names and should be used with discretion, if at all, no matter how closely you think your liqueur matches its commercial equivalent.

When making liqueurs the amateur can give full rein to his imagination and need not be limited to the flavour or the strength of commercial liqueurs, the strengths of which can vary from 40° proof Apricot Brandy to 75° proof Chartreuse. By using ginger and other spices, grated peel, herbs and flowers (fresh or dry) in conjunction with his own strong wine, and by using fortifying spirit such as 140° proof Polish White Spirit, which is neutral in flavour, he is able to achieve results that not even the ingenious monks and even more ingenious chemists have matched.

But first of all, buy a liqueur flavouring (of a type you know you like – Cherry Brandy or Crème de Menthe, for instance) and make a bottle or two, following the instructions carefully. It may be that you will discover that you prefer your wine as it is rather than pepped up with spirit and flavoured with essence. If not, a wide field of experimentation is open to you.

16

Cork and Bottle

Some winemakers do not bottle their wine, except perhaps a little which they give as presents to friends. Instead, they mature their wine in the jars and, when the time comes to use it, pour some into a decanter, refilling the decanter as necessary until all that gallon of wine has been used. Because the jar of wine is disposed of in a week or two and is kept close-covered during that time, the last decanter-ful may be almost as good as the first.

Most people, however, prefer to give their wines a period of maturing in a bottle, corked with a real cork.

Corks and plastic stoppers

Real corks are very suitable for our purpose. Natural cork is the outer bark of the cork oak, which is harvested every ten years or so. It has many uses, from the heels of ladies' shoes to fishing-net floats and from insulation to . . . wine-bottle corks.

50% of a cork is air – millions of bubbles imprisoned in tiny cells. This cellular structure gives cork its resilience, so that the little irregularities in bottle necks are taken up by its springiness. When dampened by wine, the cork swells and fits the neck even more closely, yet, perhaps years later, it will yield almost always without trouble to the pull of a corkscrew.

Winemakers tend to grudge the cost of corks and stoppers, yet the French (not notorious for their spendthrift natures) buy the very best of corks for their quality wines – a champagne cork may cost the bottler more than we lay out on a bottle, and its cork, *and* its contents!

A good wine – one that you intend to lay down for some years' maturing – deserves a good cork, which is firm, even-grained and not crumbly or spoiled by large flaws or cracks. Remember that the work of making the wine, and the long waiting-time, may be wasted if the cork fails. For big wines, it is worth finding long corks – 1¾ in (44 mm) is the trade length, known as short longs, but even longer and better corks can be found.

It *is* possible to sterilise corks and cork stoppers that have been used already – they can be soaked for days in strong sterilant solution – but it is certainly not worth the risk, whether the corks come from commercial wine bottles or from other bottles of your own wine. They are not only suspect from the point of view of hygiene but are also likely to be marred by corkscrew holes.

Corks should be stored in a perfectly dry place, because damp corks provide a ready home for moulds and other unpleasantnesses, and a wash and a brief soak in sulphite solution may not be enough to kill off the infections, which may have established themselves deep in the cells of the cork.

When you come to use the corks, you can soak them in cold water for twelve hours, or in warm water for four hours, and then steep them in the wine to be bottled for a further four hours – this is the process followed by commercial winemakers bottling a particularly fine wine. Most winemakers find that a couple of hours steeping in a bowl of warm water, held down by a weighted plate, is adequate, followed by a rinse in sulphite solution.

If, from past experience, you have found that the corks are a very tight fit, you can add a little glycerine to the soaking water in order to help the corks to slide home.

A well-driven cork, in a bottle laid on its side so that the wine keeps the cork damp, is such a firm seal that it seems frankly impossible that it could admit any air to the wine – yet it is the opinion of generations of commercial winemakers that a corked bottle admits just enough air to bring out the full potential of the wine's bouquet.

Plastic stoppers are readily available through the trade and have a valuable place as short-term closures. However, the virtues of natural cork make most winemakers prefer it for prolonged cellarage. Besides, as you work with natural corks, you can imagine the oakwoods from which the bark was stripped, with the lean porkers snuffling for acorns. It takes a vivid imagination to conjure anything like that from a white plastic stopper.

Good-quality plastic stoppers should be used in bottles containing fortified wines or wines that have been 'pushed along' to a high

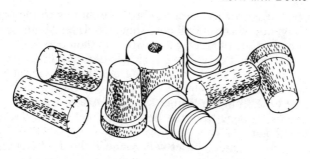

Various types of corks and bungs

alcohol content, and the bottles should be stored upright. This is because 70% of the substance of a cork is suberine, which is soluble in alcohol. A strong wine will certainly not etch its way through the cork to freedom, but it will absorb too much of the cellular walls of the cork itself.

If we could be sure that our wine was perfectly stable, we could bottle it in crown-corked bottles, as is done with millions of gallons of sterilised commercial wines. But a cork, which can, if the worst comes to the worst, fly free and release the pressure, acts as a safety-valve. Better a started cork, and some wasted wine, than burst bottle and flying glass shrapnel.

Corks designed to release any build-up of pressure can now be bought for both single bottles and gallon jars. Although more expensive than more ordinary forms of closure, the safety corks are a good insurance when there is a danger of the wine refermenting, perhaps because of fluctuating temperatures in store.

Wine bottles

Wine bottles have a long history, the shaft-and-globe, which has a long neck and a round body, being one of the most primitive types (the Chianti bottle is its modern successor).

There are many kinds to choose from, but, whatever your choice, do not bottle wine in thin-walled screwtops (whisky bottles, for example), which may easily explode. And it is also safer to avoid thick-walled screwtops, like lemonade bottles or cider flagons, unless you are making a sparkling wine under carefully controlled conditions.

The purists prefer to select the bottle according to the type of wine. Burgundy will go into sloping-shouldered green bottles; claret into a simple bottle of green glass, with high shoulders and parallel sides which make it easy to stack in a cellar; sparkling wines will have the thick and heavy champagne bottle; light German-type wines will be bottled in long, elegant green or brown bottles, which have held wine from the Rhine, Mosel or Alsace – and there are many others, ranging from the Beaujolais 'pot' to the Australian Burgundy flagon.

Clear, white, punted bottles with rounded shoulders, as recommended for showing wine, are very suitable for most home-made wines.

Wine bottles can usually be bought from suppliers to the craft, but they can in any case be obtained at the back door of hotels and restaurants for the carrying away, or for a small 'sweetener' to the lad who would otherwise have to dispose of them. However fresh they seem, do not be tempted to use them without scrupulous washing and sterilising with sulphite solution.

Wine in clear bottles should, of course, be protected from the light by being stored in the dark. Such bottles have the advantage that you can readily see what is happening in them – sediment, ropiness or other disorders are immediately noticeable. More commonly, and more happily, you can admire the starbright clarity of the contents.

Corkers

The corks are ready-soaked and *can* be flogged in. Some amateurs are still back in the 'boot and flogger' days – the boot was a small bucket which held the base of the bottle and was padded in the bottom with soft cork or leather so that, when the cork was flogged home with the wooden flogger or a heavy leather thong, the bottle would not break.

This method does work, but the simple plunger-type corkers, which compress the cork as it is forced down the bore, work much better. And if you are going to commit yourself seriously to the craft, then buy a real corker (or, better still, drop hints until someone else buys it for you). When the handles are brought together the cork is compressed, and when the lever is pushed firmly down the cork pops into the neck of the bottle with the minimum of fuss.

Before putting the cork into the corker, glance at both ends and

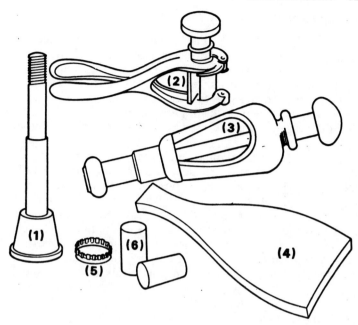

(1) A tool for applying crown caps (5); (2) and (3) corkers for inserting cylindrical wine corks (6); and (4) a 'flogger' for the same purpose

arrange it in the cylinder so that the best end will be next to the wine.

Squeeze the cork tightly in the corker *before* placing the mouth of the machine over the open bottle-neck – by doing this you help to prevent a drop or two of discoloured water from the cork running into the wine.

It takes a strong downward thrust of the handle to push the cork home, and you may have the rather precarious feeling that the bottle is going to topple sideways, however firm and level the surface on which the bottle is standing. If this troubles you, persuade a friend to hold the bottle firm (but advise him to wrap a heavy cloth round the bottle in case, by a chance in a million, it should split with the pressure), or adapt the idea of the old-fashioned professional boot and cut a socket the size of the base of the bottle in a very heavy piece of wood.

Bottling your wine

Is there a right and a wrong time to bottle wine? One of the most persistent superstitions (so persistent that one is left wondering whether it may not have a basis of fact) is that wine should only be racked or bottled in dry, brisk weather, not in damp, close weather.

A simple way to transfer wine from the bulk container to the bottle is to stand a chair on the draining board beside the sink, with the bottles ranged in the sink, then fill the bottles methodically with the siphon.

The 'head' between the container on a chair on the draining board and the bottle in the sink is just ideal. It is tempting, to save time, to place the bulk container as high as possible, so that the wine comes jetting from the siphon like water from a fire-hose. This, however, aerates the wine so thoroughly that any yeast cells left in it may be jogged into life and encouraged to start to multiply, producing blown corks or burst bottles, or the wine itself may be oxidised.

So allow the wine to flow into the bottles gently, without bubbles or whirlpools. The ideal accompaniment to this job, which should be tackled at a leisurely pace, is a radio programme interesting enough to hold your attention but not so enthralling that you allow the siphon to run unheeded and the wine to spill to waste.

So far, no ingenious firm has marketed an adaption of the commercial process by which wine being bottled is saturated with nitrogen and the last of the air in the bottle is expelled and replaced by the inert gas. Some winemakers go to considerable trouble to pipe carbon dioxide from a rapidly fermenting wort down onto the wine as it is bottled in order to replace the ullage of air with carbon dioxide, but the amount of air in the small space between the cork and the surface of the wine is likely to be helpful in speeding up the maturation of the wine rather than harmful and a source of disease at this stage.

Wine (or cider) can be pasteurised. The bottles are placed in a tank of water and brought to a temperature of 66°C–69°C (150°F–155°F) – the temperature so familiar to brewers of mashed beer. This temperature is sustained for twenty minutes, then the bottles are left in the tank to cool.

Three points should be noted:

1 An air space of about 1 in should be left in the bottles to allow for expansion.
2 In this case, screwtopped bottles are more suitable than those that take natural corks.

3 The water should be kept stirred during heating, to avoid hot-spots and cool patches.

This is *not* a process that the average amateur needs to carry out and, though it may stabilise the wine, is unlikely to improve it.

The wine, well corked and fitted perhaps with a capsule or Viscap and a neat label, should now be laid 'in cellar cool', where, without further help from its maker, it will undergo the complex process of maturing, to end, all being well, a much better and more subtle wine than before.

17

Give the Wine Time

The saying in the wine trade that more wine has been spoiled by being drunk too late than by being drunk too soon does not yet apply to home-made wine, but it is as well at the outset to remember that there are many wines that do not deserve long maturing and would not benefit from it.

The poet's wine that had 'sucked the fire from some forgotten sun, And kept it through a hundred years of gloom' obviously deserved the respect shown to it, but when it comes to our rosehip-and-fig and elderberry wines there is no need to think in terms of centuries. We can content ourselves with drinking the half-forgotten suns of two or three years ago.

How long will a home-made wine keep? The answer to that question depends on the surroundings as well as on the wine. Laid away in a dark, cold cellar, a wine will slumber on, long after wines that have been stored in racks in a warm corridor under the glare of strong lighting will have not only aged but spoiled too.

Raymond Postgate, writing of commerical wines, has said that 'Wine is like a baby – it's a lot tougher than anxious parents think' and has backed this up with the story of the Jurade of St Emilion who found a hoard of really old St Emilion which had been covered for years by coke. They were about to get rid of it at bargain prices when one of the vignerons drew the corks from some specimen bottles and found they were superb. And one wine-shipper tested the stability of Lutomer Riesling by subjecting it to temperatures ranging from 60°C (hotter than the tropics) to −60°C, colder than the Arctic.

Nevertheless, there is no excuse for trading on the hardiness of your best wines. As in other aspects of winemaking and brewing, a little ingenuity goes a long way. We cannot all be as lucky as the man in Leeds who, some time after buying a new house, investigated a door he had never opened before and found it led down into a large cellar ready-stocked with scores of bottles of home-made wine left there by some forgotten occupant of the house. He resolved to begin to make wine himself, so that he could replace each bottle as it was emptied and in turn leave a fully stocked cellar to his successor.

A cellar like that is ideal. Sometimes the space under the stairs, if not already in use as a fermentation box, can be turned into a small cellar (since a cellar is simply, by definition, a storeroom – it does not have to be underground).

The basic needs are an even temperature, darkness, humidity and cleanliness, and these needs can be met under the stairs, in the dead-end of a corridor or in a converted shed in the garden.

If you make your cellar under the stairs, do not make the mistake of fixing the racks to the underside of the treads of the stairs themselves, otherwise the bottles will bounce and jingle every time someone walks up or downstairs.

Be lavish with expanded polystyrene tiles or slabs when insulating the cellar, and this will help to prevent rapid swings in temperature. Cellar temperature can be around 7°C–10°C (45°F–50°F) for white wines and sparkling wines, and 10°C–13°C (50°F–55°F) for red wines and heavy social wines. Since warm air rises, it is better to store the white wines at floor level and the red ones above them if you wish to make the most of the temperature differential.

A cellar should certainly be dark, because sunlight bleaches the colour of wines and, by artificially ageing them, renders them unbalanced and off-flavoured.

Not everyone likes to see the characteristic cellar mould on the inside of their cellar and over the bottles which have been maturing for years, but it is regarded by commercial winemakers as a sign of ideal conditions and is reputed to have the ability to absorb taints and smells in the air which might otherwise have affected the wine.

If your improvised cellar is so placed that the bottles jump every time a heavy lorry passes on the road outside, stand the crates on a pad of sponge rubber or plastic foam. This certainly damps down the vibrations.

'Bad vibrations' of another kind were once reputed to harm wine, for it was said that cursing in a cellar disturbed the wine's rest. There is no scientific evidence for this and, in any case, it is not the kind of behaviour we associate with the cloistered calm of a cellar!

The binning of the wine also lends itself to ingenuity. There are fine commercial racks, big and small, plastic, metal and wood, to be bought, and racks can be contrived from strips of wood nailed across each other trellis-fashion.

Wine cartons, being compact units, have their advantages, and your grocer will be glad to give you the cartons in which wine is supplied to him. The sections are exactly the right size, whereas the sections in a soft-drinks crate are sometimes too small. Although made only of cardboard, these cartons last indefinitely in a dry place – and for a surprisingly long time even in a fairly damp cellar, provided that they are kept off the ground.

They can safely be stacked, open end outwards, two or three cartons high, but remember to raise the front of the bottom carton about 50 mm (2 in) with a strip of batten. This tilts the stack back a little so that there is no risk of the bottles sliding forwards and breaking, or of the whole stack falling outwards if you have to pull on a stubborn bottle.

The tradition of laying bottles on their sides has a practical basis. Treated like this, the corks in the bottles will not dry out, shrink, and admit air and airborne organisms. (Because natural corks do shrink in this way, it is prudent to avoid shops and restaurants where wine is displayed, standing upright and sometimes in strong sunlight, for weeks at a time. The wine, to say the least, will be none the better for this.)

One advantage of plastic corks is that the bottles can be stored upright. This takes slightly more shelf-space than stacking them horizontally, but if the wine throws a little deposit, this falls to the bottom and settles in the groove round the punt, being left behind when the wine is carefully poured.

Although bottles corked with natural cork must be laid on their sides for long storage, there is no reason why you should not, if you know you are going to drink a wine soon, lift the bottle and set it upright with a slight bump to move any small amount of sediment downwards into the groove. The bottle can be left upright like that for a week or two – cork shrinkage does not normally occur as quickly as that, especially if it is fitted with a capsule.

When laying wine down for really long maturing, put a tiny spot of white paint on the upper side of the bottle, on the shoulder, so that when you come to enjoy the wine you can carry the bottle, spot uppermost, and decant it carefully without disturbing any sediment which may have formed along the lower side.

Why should wine be left to mature like this? Not because it will contain more alcohol after prolonged storage – it will not, though it is the experience of winemakers and drinkers over many centuries that an old wine is undoubtedly more potent and should be drunk with extra prudence. No, wine is allowed time to mature because, in cask or bottle, a complex chemical and biological process reduces the harshness of the tannin and the sourness of the acid, creating delicate esters to delight the drinker when he comes to inhale the bouquet.

There is no doubt that the ideal container in which to mature wine, at least for the first year, is a sound oak cask. The commercial winemakers would not go to endless trouble to secure good casks if this were not so. Champagne casks of the highest quality are made from staves shaped by an axe, because a saw tears open the grain and releases taints into the fine wine. Cognac casks are made from oak from selected forests where the individual trees have their own names.

There is a certain amount of loss from even the soundest cask – the level in a wine cask may drop 12 mm (½ in) in a month. Some of this is the poetic 'angel's share', the alcohol that evaporates through the pores of the cask. In a dry cellar, more water is lost and less alcohol; in a damp cellar, more strength and less water.

If the level of a cask falls faster than that, examine it carefully in case it is a 'weeper'. Sometimes the small leak is between the staves, but sometimes the liquid weeps through a porous patch in the wood itself. It will depend on how near your nearest cooper is, on how good terms you are with him and on how much you value that cask as to whether you will be prepared to lay out cash to have the weeper tightened up or put right.

The ends of small casks are sometimes painted to reduce evaporation and oxidation. Louis Pasteur, the father of scientific winemaking, used to quote the example of the wine from a painted cask in the Clos de Vougeot which always tasted a year or two younger than that from the casks that had been left unpainted.

'To cask or not to cask' is a matter for individual judgement. If you make 150 litres (30 gal) of red wine every year, and it is fruity and high in acid and tannin, it will be improved immensely by a year in a good cask. Small quantities are much more speculative.

And do not indiscriminately put every wine down to mature for years. Some may need it, others are better drunk young. Our apple wines, like the German 'federweisser' and the Austrian 'heurigen' wines, can be enjoyed while they are so new that they are still prickly with fermentation. Others can be relished when the winter cold has cleared them, and very many home-made wines are nearing their best at one year old.

But the big ones, raw and harsh at one year old, may be smooth and harmonious at five years, and still a wine to remember at twenty years old.

And it is possible that some wines (heather-honey mead, perhaps, made with no sugar, only honey, and fermented with a Tokay yeast) would still, after 100 years of gloom, recall not the fire from some forgotten sun but the fragrance of the flowers of a century before. Surely it would be a kindly winemaker who would lay down a legacy like that for his great-great-grandchildren when they grew up?

18

Serving Your Wine

Wine can be drunk in many different surroundings, and it will taste quite different when swigged out of a mess-tin than when served in a thin Baccarat glass which has been washed in distilled water and then hung to dry so that not even a fine linen cloth may taint it.

One of the first considerations is temperature. A bottle of strong social wine or a strong red wine brought straight from the cold cellar may taste dumb and disappointing, whereas a light and slightly acid wine may taste at its best when served cold.

Ideally, wine that should be raised to room temperature before being served should be brought into the house the day before and left to rise naturally a degree at a time, but this is not always possible if an occasion arises to drink your social wines.

There is no need, in such a case, to hold the bottle under the hot tap, or to set it in front of the gas fire or on a radiator. Wrap it in newspaper, to avoid thermal shock, and stand it in a basin of water no hotter than 26°C (80°F) – which is just perceptibly warm to the bare hand.

If the wine has thrown a sediment it is wiser to decant it first, but, since you may not wish to wrap the decanter in wet newspaper and stand it in a basin of warm water, you can introduce a halfway stage and decant the wine into an empty wine bottle first (for the warming-up process), then into that cut-crystal decanter.

Wet newspapers can be used for the opposite purpose – to cool wine down. A bottle of wine, wrapped in wet newspaper and placed in a breezy spot before a picnic, will grow colder as the day grows warmer, as long as the paper is kept wet (the heat needed to evaporate the water is drawn in part from the wine itself).

The wine, at the right temperature and in a clean glass (in which it will not be subtly nobbled by a film of lightly scented detergent), now comes to the stage for which it was made – to be enjoyed.

'How does it taste?' we ask, but in fact our taste-buds can only signal four basic facts: the sweetness, saltiness, acidity and bitterness of what we drink. Beyond this we depend on our sense of smell.

To taste and appreciate a sip of elderberry wine is a task well beyond the most complex computer, for we not only assess hundreds of variables but also, simultaneously, flip through our memory-bank of associated feelings, memories and sensations.

In contrast to 200 or 300 taste-buds scattered right down into the throat, we have hundreds of thousands of special cells connected to an area high up in the nose, and it is through this tiny area that we assess the bouquet of our wines. It takes only a minute amount of any substance, a mere billion molecules or so, dissolved in the moist mucus on that layer to tell us what is present.

Some years ago it was discovered that this ability varies during the day. The sense is sharpest in the late morning and again in the afternoon, and scientists can tell if you are in good wine-judging fettle by checking the sugar content of your blood.

Smell has been well described as 'taste at a distance'. The part it plays in wine-tasting can be tested by taking a sip of your best wine while holding your nose. It will probably taste like vinegar, and weak vinegar at that. This is purely an experiment – few wines are so bad as to require that treatment.

We may envy dogs, who can identify a man from the scent of his fingerprint – but no dog has yet qualified for the Guild of Wine Judges.

If you are sampling a series of wines, you very soon discover that you need to clean your palate. Some favour a plain biscuit (a Bath Oliver, perhaps); others prefer the traditional bread-and-cheese. In the wine trade it is sometimes said that one should sell wine on cheese but buy it on apple – and certainly a piece of apple does make a clean sweep of stale tastes and aromas. Apple is even used by the Metropolitan Water Board's official water-taster, whose palate has to be in trim for eighty samples a day of water from many sources.

Aroma and bouquet, as used by wine-tasters, are not really interchangeable words. The aroma is the fresh-fruit smell of wine in its early stages. As the wine matures, this smell changes, becoming more subtle and vinous, and is described as the bouquet. Although a good bouquet is the climax of a very complex chemical process, it is worth remembering that great wines with great bouquets have been made by traditional methods by men who knew nothing of esters, aldehydes, fruity acids and higher alcohols.

To appreciate aroma and bouquet we need a 'good nose', and there is no doubt that everyone can improve their ability by 'listening' to what their nose tells them as it processes its 500 cubic feet of air a day. Uneducated noses can detect 4000 scents, but trained noses can recognise more than 10000.

The bouquet and the taste of a wine often improve as you get to the bottom of the glass. You have given it time to absorb oxygen – to breathe – and the empty space over the surface fills with the bouquet of the wine. Civilised, leisurely drinking is justified.

It is surprisingly difficult to separate what your eye tells you from what you taste. One firm of wine merchants, when assessing wines, serves them in blue glasses so that the taster can concentrate on the taste and bouquet. Using these blue glasses, or tasting blindfold, it would be very difficult to tell whether you were drinking a red country wine or a white one, since (unlike commercial wines) our red wines are not consistently higher in tannin than white wines.

To assess the clarity and colour of a wine, a clear grey sky is the ideal background. But assessment of this kind is moving out of the realms of social drinking and into those of wine-judging.

19

Troubles to Avoid

Winemakers are not likely to encounter too much trouble if their wines are adequate in acidity, are not subjected to fluctuating temperatures or sustained high temperatures, are not brought into contact with contaminated containers or equipment and are protected by the use of Campden tablets or sulphite solution.

A 'sick' wine may contain micro-organisms of several different kinds, the most notorious being the vinegar bug, which turns alcohol into acetaldehyde and then into acetic acid, giving the wine a very characteristic chip-shop smell.

It is worth stressing that this infection, though frustrating to the winemaker, is not harmful to the drinker, and an incredible gallon-age of acetified or 'pricked' wine must be drunk annually through-out the world, mainly wines that are not yet a year old and would otherwise be vinegar before their next birthday.

The little fruit-fly is sometimes called the vinegar bug too, because when it visits the young wine after feeding on bruised and rotten fruit it passes on the infection.

Since acetobacter bacteria thrive where they can find plenty of air and heat, they are much less likely to infect a must, a wort, or a wine or beer which has been kept in a well-filled container in a warm place rather than a hot one. The damage done by the bacteria is irreversible, but they can be checked by the addition of two or more Campden tablets to the gallon. This serves some purpose once fermentation has finished, but in the early stages of a wine it may lead to a very slow or stuck fermentation.

The surface-forming yeasts, particularly *Candida mycoderma*, also thrive in the presence of air and heat. The surface of the wine at first looks as if it has been lightly dredged over with fine flour, then the film thickens and can become an unbroken skin if left untended. These organisms can sometimes produce small quantities of alcohol, but more characteristically the result of their presence is that the alcohol the winemaker has striven to produce is broken down into water, carbon dioxide and a little acetaldehyde.

Once again, the best prevention is cleanliness, plus full vessels. It is no wonder that flowers of wine is one of the commonest maladies of home brewing and winemaking, for the organisms that cause the disease occur widely – they have even been isolated from human spittle (surely a rare source of infection, though it is just possible that the bugs might find a foothold in the wine from a sucked siphon tube!).

If, on opening a wide-mouthed fermentation vessel, you find that there is a layer of flowers of wine on the surface, do not disturb it. Instead, take a tissue (an unscented paper handkerchief, for example) and allow it to float gently down onto the surface of the liquid. Let it lie there for a moment, then lift it very gently by the centre and you will find that most of the surface film has come away with it. However, there are more than ample organisms left to reinfect the wine, so treat it liberally with Campden tablets or sulphite solution, allow it to stand overnight and then very gently rack the wine into other containers which can be filled up into the neck. Any fragments of film will be left behind in the first vessel.

Both the vinegar bug and flowers of wine are diseases of weak wine, so if you can establish an early quick fermentation you do much to avoid future trouble.

Moulds of various kinds can infect wine. Sometimes the infection looks much worse than it is – a heavy layer of mould on a pulp fermentation or on the surface of juice before fermentation is well established is an unwelcome sight, but there is no immediate cause for panic. Do not flush the batch away in anger and disgust.

Old books on winemaking used to describe, as a matter of course, how one was to roll the skin of mould off the surface before straining. Revolting? Certainly, but many a good wine was made in spite of the mould – or perhaps because of it, for little is known of the *good* effects of moulds except in the making of such wines as Sauternes.

So, unless your stomach revolts at the thought, remove the mould, add a Campden tablet to the gallon and go hopefully ahead.

Less dramatic, but usually much more serious, are infections by slime-forming bacteria, which can turn wines and beers ropy or oily. Although it *is* possible to break up the slimy chains by beating the liquid furiously, adding Campden tablets and straining, most wine-makers will prefer to pour the wine away and then sterilise the vessels very thoroughly, possibly with a combination of heat, then bleach, then sulphite.

Some bacteria produce not only changes in texture in the affected wine but also changes in smell. Some are reasonably pleasant, like that of overripe bananas, but others are sour or rank and offensive.

Many infections are combined with hazes, which can prove stubborn even when the organism causing the haze has been disposed of.

Other hazes occur for chemical reasons – though the chemistry of metallic hazes can be, to the layman, a complicated matter. Iron contamination in a wine with a high tannin content produces a dilute solution of ink! Other metals may tinge the wines with other off-colours, and if your wine turns grey, brown or blue, and you suspect metallic contamination, the safest course is to jettison it.

It is easy to exaggerate the risk of lead-poisoning from home winemaking and brewing – it is, in fact, very rare – but it is not so easy to exaggerate its seriousness when it does occur.

How easily a whole family can fall victim is shown by the case of a family in South London who used a little brown jug to hold their cider. The cider dissolved lead from the glaze. The man of the house was the worst affected and was treated in hospital for weakness, depression, sickness and aching muscles. It took medical detective work to trace the family's ailments to the little jug.

There are those who say that the Romans lost their empire not from loose-living but from lead-poisoning – lead from the new-fangled water pipes, from cooking vessels and from wine that contained a preservative made by long boiling in leaden vessels. (Among the Romans' symptoms were loss of appetite and a metallic taste in the mouth – but winemakers and home-brewers may encounter similar symptoms the 'morning after'.)

Containers brought back as souvenirs from abroad should be treated particularly suspiciously. If lead-glazed, they may give you what the cider-drinkers used to call 'Devonshire colic' and the American colonists labelled 'the dry belly-ache'.

Keep wine and beer from long contact with metals, other than stainless steel, and you should never be troubled by metallic hazes.

Pectin hazes should not occur either if you are careful to use pectin degrading enzymes whenever it may seem necessary, and pectin hazes in a mature wine can be dispersed with the same enzyme.

Starch hazes are rarer, except in grain and vegetable wines, and do sometimes clear, given time. If they do not, fungal amylase, used according to instructions, should dispel a starch haze.

The presence of sulphur in the wine can lead to some offputting smells. Aeration and maturity sometimes mute the odour, which is usually caused by organisms breaking down the sulphur compounds into the familiar stink-bomb chemical, sulphuretted hydrogen.

Oxidation, the process that turns a cut apple brown, is sometimes listed as a disease. Overexpose a young wine to air and the characteristic hot tangy taste which oxidation gives the wine results. Oxidation plays a large part in the taste and bouquet of sherry, and has also an important part to play in the maturing of most wines. Once again, keeping fermentation containers full, fitting efficient locks and racking gently without splashing keep trouble away. Once a wine has been affected, the taste remains, though it is often muted by time. But although oxidation is a fault which will down-point your wine at a big show, it confers a flavour that is not disliked by everyone. 'Now that wine's got a bit of a bite to it' they will say, approvingly.

Some of the other troubles of wine are dealt with in Chapters 4, 10 and 12, and home-brewed beer has its own rogue's gallery, but common to them all is the old, tried but true, advice that prevention is better than cure.

20

Wine Recipes

Notes on the wine recipes

There are millions of recipes and permutations of recipes for wines made from scores of ingredients. Those which follow are a few representative examples, and winemakers who have absorbed the basic principles are unlikely to come to harm by experimenting a little.

Experimentation is part of the pleasure of the craft.

Where no specific yeast is named, a good all-purpose yeast is suggested.

Benerva tablets and a pinch of magnesium sulphate (Epsom salts) help to promote fermentation and can be added to any recipe.

Please note that the metric and imperial quantities in the recipes are not, strictly speaking, interchangeable, though it is most unlikely that any wine will be spoiled by the small variation which would occur if a winemaker used some ingredients from the metric and some from the imperial scales.

The teaspoon of the recipes is the 5 ml teaspoon which is now common. Some domestic teaspoons are fractionally bigger. Once again, the variation caused by using one instead of the other is likely to be minimal.

The procedure for preparing yeast as a starter is described on pages 87–8.

Apple wine (basic)

3·5 kg (7 lb) apples (a mixture of dessert, cookers and crabs if possible)
1·5 kg (3 lb) sugar
3·5 g (1 tsp) citric acid
Yeast nutrient
Pectin degrading enzyme
All-purpose yeast, prepared as starter

Dissolve a Campden tablet in 1 litre (2 pt) of water, and place the solution in a plastic bucket.

Smash the apples up as thoroughly as possible. As you proceed, drop the pulp in the Campden tablet solution to prevent browning. Leave the bucket of pulp overnight, covered. Next day, stir thoroughly, then add the yeast, made up previously as a starter. Add the nutrient (3·7 g, or a teaspoonful, or according to instructions) the pectin degrading enzyme, according to the instructions on the packet, and 500 g (1 lb) of sugar. Stir thoroughly again.

Keep the bucket in a warm place, closely covered, for a week, stirring at least once daily.

Press the liquid from the pulp as thoroughly as possible, with a wine-press if you have one, or in strong netting, such as terylene. Taste the juice. If it is not distinctly acid, add the citric acid crystals. Pour the liquid into a 5 litre (1 gal) jar, and add the remaining kg (2 lb) of sugar as sugar syrup (as described on page 70) and swirl to mix thoroughly. Fit a fermentation lock. After any vigorous frothy fermentation is over, top up the jar with water.

This wine can be drunk with pleasure at any stage, being regarded as a health drink when actively fermenting. It is, like most wines, much the better if given time to mature.

Pears can be incorporated into this recipe, though in large quantities their skins can give a hard harsh taste, due to tannin. Very ripe (sleepy) pears should be used with caution because they can give a bland over-ripe taste.

Rack into another jar only when a noticeable sediment forms. Do not rack for racking's sake! Crush a Campden tablet, dissolve it in a little wine or warm water, and put this solution in the jar into which you rack the wine, to prevent oxidation.

Bottle only when you are sure that fermentation has ceased, and the wine in bulk is star-bright.

Apricot wine (dried) – as Fig

Beetroot wine (old)

    2 kg (4 lb) old beetroot, well scrubbed but not peeled
    1·5 kg (3 lb) sugar
    3·5 g (1 tsp) citric acid crystals
    3·7 g (1 tsp) yeast nutrient, or one nutrient tablet
    250 ml (½ pt) strong tea, or 0·5 g (¼ tsp) grape tannin
    Wine yeast, prepared as a starter
    30 g (1 oz) root ginger

Prepare the yeast as a starter.

Cut the roots into even-sized chunks and put them in a panful of water with the root ginger, which should be bruised or crushed. Bring through the boil and simmer until a fork pierces the pieces of beetroot easily, without breaking them up.

Strain the juice – without pressing the beetroot pieces, which can be then used for pickling – into a plastic bucket containing 1 kg (2 lb) of sugar, the acid, the nutrient, and the tannin or tea, and stir very thoroughly. Leave, covered, until cool, then pour the juice gently into a 5 litre (1 gal) jar, leaving any sediment in the bucket. The jar should not be filled above shoulder level. Add the yeast starter and fit a fermentation lock.

When the first vigorous fermentation is over, add the remaining sugar as sugar syrup, made as described on page 70, making sure the syrup is thoroughly mixed with the wine.

Rack into another jar when a noticeable sediment forms, and again as necessary.

Some time before bottling, check for acidity by tasting the new wine. If the flavour is bland, add further citric acid crystals (perhaps 2 g or ½ tsp). Since this wine is likely to take a year or more to mature, a little over-acidity at this stage is indicated.

Bottle when fermentation is complete, and the wine is star-bright.

When new, this wine has a raw-meat redness, but this mellows with time to a tawny colour.

The ginger – or cinnamon, mixed spice, etc. can be used if preferred – helps to mask the 'rooty' taste common in beetroot wines.

Beetroot wine (young)

2 kg (4 lb) well-scrubbed young beetroot
1·250 kg (2½ lb) sugar
0·5 g (¼ tsp) grape tannin
3·5 g (1 tsp) citric acid
3·7 g (1 tsp) yeast nutrient, or one nutrient tablet
Wine yeast, prepared as starter

Prepare the yeast starter.

Slice up the young beets, place them in a polythene bucket, and pour over them a scalding syrup made by boiling up 1 kg (2 lb) of sugar in 2 litres (4 pt) of water. Cover the bucket closely, and stir two or three times a day for four days.

Strain off the juice, and wash the sliced beet in 500 ml (1 pt) of hot water and add the washings to the juice.

Bring the juice through the boil. When it is cool, pour it into a 5 litre (1 gal) jar which it should fill to the shoulder. Add the tannin, acid, nutrient and yeast starter, fit a fermentation lock, and put the jar in a warm place. When fermentation has died down, after a week or two, add the rest of the sugar as syrup (prepared as described on page 70).

Rack into another jar when a noticeable sediment forms, and again as necessary, topping up the jar every time.

When the wine is nearly clear, taste it to check that it is sufficiently acid. If there is no distinct acidity, stir in a small amount – perhaps 2 g or ½ tsp – of citric acid crystals, and check again.

This wine is lighter in colour and flavour than beetroot wine made by more conventional methods, and will be ready to drink much sooner.

Birch sap wine

2·5 litres (approx) or 5 pt of birch sap, collected as described on
    pages 32–3
1 kg (2 lb) white sugar
250 ml (½ pt) white grape concentrate
3·5 g (1 tsp) citric acid crystals
Yeast nutrient
Wine yeast, prepared as a starter

Prepare the yeast starter.

Dissolve the grape concentrate, the sugar, citric acid and nutrient in the sap, pour into a 5 litre (1 gal) jar, add a well-crushed Campden tablet, and plug the neck of the jar with cotton wool. Next day, swirl the jar to make sure the ingredients are well mixed. Add the yeast and fit the fermentation lock.

The speed of fermentation and of maturity varies from wine to wine, but the use of grape concentrate helps to encourage the yeast.

Rack when a noticeable sediment forms, and again as necessary, topping up the jar each time.

Bottle only when fermentation has ceased, and the wine is star-bright.

Birch sap is an attractive wine, the unusualness of the main ingredient adding to its attraction.

Try to collect the sap over as few days as possible, and if the sap has to be left for a day or so, remember to protect it from infection by adding a Campden tablet per 5 litres (1 gal). Other saps – walnut and sycamore for example – can be used with this recipe.

Blackberry wine (bramble) – see raspberry wine   (sweet)

Carrot wine

As beetroot wine (old) but with 3 kg (6 lb) of roots, and without spice if preferred.

Currant wine (garden)

  2 kg (4 lb) bursting-ripe currants (black, red, white, or a mixture
     of all three)
  1·5 to 1·75 kg (3–3½ lb) sugar
  Yeast nutrient
  Pectin degrading enzyme
  All-purpose yeast, prepared as a starter

Prepare the yeast starter.

Strip all the stems from the berries, crush the berries, and put them in a plastic bucket. Cover the berries with boiling water, cover the bucket, and leave the mixture to cool.

Next day, stir in the yeast, yeast nutrient (3·7 g, or 1 tsp, or one nutrient tablet per 5 litres (1 gal)) pectin degrading enzyme and 250 g (½ lb) of sugar.

Keep the bucket well covered. Stir daily.

After a week, press the berries, either in a wine-press or in a piece of strong net, such as terylene. Pour the resulting juice into a 5 litre (1 gal) jar, add 1 kg (2 lb) of sugar made up as a syrup (as detailed on page 70); make sure the mixture is thoroughly mixed. Top the jar up to shoulder level with water. Fit a fermentation lock. Leave the jar in a warm place until the first vigorous fermentation is over. Add the remaining sugar as syrup, either in one stage or in two, at intervals of a week or two (the timing is not critical).

Rack when a noticeable sediment forms, and again as necessary, topping up the jar each time. Give this wine plenty of time to mature in bulk, and do not bottle until it is star-bright and fermentation has long ceased.

Black currants on their own, or as the predominant partners in a blend, do not make a pleasant dry wine. Red currants, white currants, or a blend of the two, do make a good dry wine, and the above recipe, using 1·25 kg or 2¼ to 2½ lb of sugar, can be used.

If you wish to make a dry black-currant wine, then use a quarter of the quantity of the fruit, and 2 kg (2 lb) of sugar. This is a very economical wine, with sufficient flavour and a pleasant colour.

Date wine – as dried fruit

Dried fruit wine (basic)

500 g (1 lb) dried fruit
2·25 kg (2½ lb) sugar
Yeast nutrient (3·7 g, or 1 tsp, or one tablet)
3·5 g (1 tsp) citric acid
0·5 g (¼ tsp) tannin
Wine yeast, as starter

Prepare the yeast starter.

Chop the fruit up into small pieces, put in a pan, cover with water, and bring through the boil. Simmer at boiling-point for two or three minutes. Pour the panful of fruit into a plastic bucket, and stir in the nutrient, citric acid and tannin. When the pulp is cool, add the yeast starter.

Ferment on the pulp for a week, stirring the 'mush' daily, and keeping it well covered. Press as much of the juice out as possible, either with a wine-press or through strong netting, such as terylene. Put the juice in a 5 litre (1 gal) jar; wash the pulp through with warm water; strain the resulting juice into the jar.

Add the sugar, prepared as syrup in the way described on page 70, either in one lot or, more prudently, in two batches, the second after vigorous fermentation has died down.

The first racking is needed in a week or two, when a thick soft sediment forms. After that, rack the wine on into another jar (topping up each time) only when a noticeable sediment forms.

Bottle when fermentation has ceased, and the wine is star-bright.

This wine can be made with dates, currants, raisins, etc. Apricots (and figs) should be treated as suggested in the recipe for fig wine.

Note that the pulp, which still contains some residue of sweetness and flavour, can be added to the pulp fermentation of another batch of wine – perhaps a fresh fruit or vegetable wine – if you are preparing one *right away*.

Elderberry wine (basic)

2 kg (4 lb) very ripe elderberries
1·5 kg (3 lb) sugar
Yeast nutrient (3.7 g or 1 tsp or 1 tablet)
3·5 g (1 tsp) citric acid
Pectin degrading enzyme
Wine yeast – e.g. Burgundy – prepared as a starter

Prepare the yeast starter.

Strip the elderberries from the stems, put the fruit in a plastic bucket, and cover them with boiling water. Stir thoroughly, cover, and leave overnight. Next day, stir in the acid, the nutrient, the pectin degrading enzyme and 500 g (1 lb) of sugar. Add the yeast, and keep the bucket for a week, well covered, in a warm place, stirring daily. Note that shortening this period to say, four days, results in a less highly flavoured and quicker-maturing wine, not so high in tannin.

Press as much juice as possible from the berries, either in a wine-press or through a strong piece of netting, such as terylene. Mix in the remainder of the sugar, prepared as syrup as described on page 70, and pour the sweetened juice into a 5 litre (1 gal) fermentation jar.

Fit a fermentation lock, and leave until any frothy fermentation has died down before topping up to just below the stopper with warm water.

Rack when a noticeable sediment forms, topping up the new jar each time.

Give this wine plenty of time to mature in bulk, and bottle it only when it is star-bright.

This is a very flexible wine. Elderberries can be used with other autumn fruits, and they can be used by themselves in much smaller quantities, as low as 500 g (1 lb) per 5 litres (1 gal). Low-fruit wines mature more quickly, but rarely become 'big' wines as the full-fruit wines sometimes do.

Elderberry wine (boiled)

2 kg (4 lb) thoroughly ripe elderberries
1·5 kg (3 lb) sugar
Yeast nutrient (3·7 g or 1 tsp or 1 tablet)
3·5 g (1 tsp) citric acid
Pectin degrading enzyme
All-purpose yeast, prepared as a starter

Prepare the yeast starter.

Strip the stems from the elderberries, and put the fruit into 1·5 litres (3 pt) of water boiling in a pan. When the contents of the pan come back to the boil, briskly crush the berries against the side of the pan with a wooden spoon, and then quickly press or strain out the juice. Dissolve 1 kg (2 lb) of sugar, and the acid and nutrient into it, and when it has cooled so that the glass will not break, pour it into a 5 litre (1 gal) jar and top it up with water to shoulder-level. Fit a fermentation lock.

When the liquid has cooled to blood heat, add the yeast and a generous amount of pectin degrading enzyme – in other words at least the full quantity recommended in the instructions supplied.

As the gravity drops, feed in the remainder of the sugar as syrup (made as described on page 70), either in one lot or in two or three spaced 'doses'.

Rack when a noticeable sediment forms, topping up the new jar each time. Bottle when the wine is star-bright, and when you are certain that fermentation has ceased.

This is an easy wine to make – easier than the instructions might indicate – and likely to be drinkable long before elderberry wines made after long fermentation on the pulp. The pectin degrading enzyme is very necessary, for you can sometimes see the juice beginning to jell as you press it from the berries.

Elderflower wine (light)

> 1 litre (1 quart) of elderflower blossoms, stripped of stems
> 500 g (1 lb) white sugar
> 250 ml (1 cup) orange juice
> Yeast (All-purpose or champagne)

Put the elderflower blossoms in a bowl, cover them with boiling water, and leave the bowl, covered, for three or four days, stirring daily. Strain the liquid into a 5 litre (1 gal) jar, add the orange juice and the sugar made up as a syrup, as detailed on page 70, and make up the quantity with warm water. Fit a fermentation lock and place the jar where it will keep warm.

When the hydrometer reading drops to 1000 or below, and the wine is clear, bottle in strong screwtops or in champagne bottles with corks that can be tied down, putting 5 ml spoonful (1 tsp) of sugar in each bottle before filling it.

This priming sugar, as with home-brewed beer, will ferment away to give a pleasing sparkle.

This is a very light wine – hardly more than a 'pop' – but it can be relished in hot summer weather only a few weeks after it is made.

For a bigger wine, 250 ml (1 pt) of white grape concentrate, preferably muscat which reinforces the elderflower aroma, can be added to the basic ingredients.

Fig wine (basic)

> 500 g (1 lb) dried figs
> 1·250 kg (2½ lb) sugar
> 1 g (½ tsp) tannin
> 3·5 g (1 tsp) citric acid
> Yeast nutrient (3·7 g, or 1 tsp, or 1 tablet)
> Pectin degrading enzyme
> Wine yeast, prepared as starter

Prepare the yeast starter.

Boil the figs for twenty minutes in enough water to cover them well. As soon as they are cool enough to handle, mince them and put them back in the water in which they were boiled. Put the pulp in a polythene bucket, then, when it has cooled to below blood-heat, stir in the nutrient, the yeast, the acid, the tannin and the pectin degrading enzyme. Put in a warm place, carefully covered, and stir daily for a week.

Press out as much juice as possible from the pulp, either with a wine-press or through a piece of strong net such as terylene. Give the pulp a wash with a little warm water, and add the washings to the juice.

Place in a 5 litre (1 gal) jar with the sugar, prepared as syrup in the way described on page 70. Fit a fermentation lock and proceed as usual, but note that the first racking may have to be after a week or two, because fig wine tends to drop a heavy sediment at the start.

Rack only when a noticeable sediment forms. Bottle only when the wine is star-bright, and after all fermentation has ceased.

This wine is quickly drinkable, but matures well. If you make it with the intention of maturing it, double the quantity of citric acid, or, better still, add equivalent quantities of lactic or succinic acid.

The pectin degrading enzyme may seem a strange addition for a dried-fruit wine, since no-one makes fig jelly. But figs and apricots contain enough pectin to cause a troublesome haze if not dealt with.

The pulp of fig or apricot, retaining some sweetness and flavour, can be added to the pulp fermentation of the next wine you make – for example rose-hip or rowan – if you are preparing one *right away*.

Flower wine

(Suitable, in particular, for rose-petals)

> 5 litres (1 gal) petals, lightly pressed down
> 1·25–1·5 kg (2½–3 lb) sugar
> 2 lemons
> Yeast nutrient (3·7 g or 1 tsp or 1 tablet)
> Benerva tablets (approx 9 mg)
> 150 ml (¼ pt) strong tea
> Yeast, prepared as a starter

Prepare the yeast starter.

Put the petals in a plastic bucket and pour about 3 litres (6 pt) of boiling water over them. Stir thoroughly and leave, covered, to cool. Next day, strain the liquid from the petals, gently pressing the last of the water out of them. Put the water in a 5 litre (1 gal) jar and add the yeast nutrient, the yeast, the tea, the dissolved Benerva tablets, and the juice of the lemons. Top up the jar into the base of the neck with sugar made up as syrup, as described on page 70.

When the fermentation dies down, add more sugar syrup.

To most tastes, petal wines are the better for being slightly sweet.

Lemon juice and the Benerva tablets are recommended in this

recipe to supplement the yeast nutrient, since the flowers and the sugar contain, in themselves, very little nutrient to maintain a sound fermentation.

Flower wines have their place as 'single' wines, but are more valued to blend with other wines and give them a more delicate and subtle nose.

The common marigold (*Calendula officinalis*) is easy to grow and prolific. It can be stripped of its petals, and the petals used to make a wine with an unusual tint and flavour – again a good blender.

Gooseberry wine (green)

2·5 kg (5 lb) gooseberries, topped and tailed if patience allows
1·25 kg (2½ lb) sugar
German wine yeast (e.g. Hock, Bernkastler) prepared as starter
Yeast nutrient (3·7 g or 1 tsp or one tablet)
Pectin degrading enzyme

Prepare the yeast starter.

Put the gooseberries in a plastic pail, pour warm water over them (sufficient to cover them) and leave them to steep overnight.

Pour away the steeping water, and crush the softened berries (they may be put in a strong plastic bag and thumped with a heavy piece of wood). Put the crushed berries in the plastic pail, cover them with boiling water, and stir in the yeast nutrient. When the pulp is cool, add the pectin degrading enzyme and the yeast starter. Keep the pail closely covered. Stir the pulp at least once a day.

After three days, strain the juice from the pulp and press the remaining juice from the pulp, either with a wine-press or through a strong piece of net, such as terylene. The juice from the straining and pressing is placed in a 5 litre (1 gal) jar and topped up with *cool* sugar syrup made from the 1·25 kg (2½ lb) of sugar.

Fit a fermentation lock and place in warm surroundings.

When vigorous fermentation has died down, top the jar up with water.

Rack when a noticeable sediment forms, topping up the jar each time. Bottle the wine only when it is star-bright and fermentation has ceased.

This can be one of the most enjoyable of country wines, impressive in its balance and character at its best. It provides a basis for experimentation – for example, some of the sugar can be replaced by an equal weight of white grape concentrate.

Gooseberry wine (sweet)

3 kg (6 lb) gooseberries (red or white) bursting-ripe
1·5 kg (3 lb) sugar
3·5 g (1 tsp) citric acid crystals
0·5 g (¼ tsp) tannin
Yeast nutrient (3·7 g or 1 tsp or 1 tablet)
Pectin degrading enzyme
Sauternes yeast, prepared as starter

Prepare the yeast starter.

Mash the gooseberries thoroughly in a plastic bucket and cover them with approximately 2·5 litres (4 pt) of boiling water. Stir in the citric acid, tannin and yeast nutrient. When the pulp is cool, add the pectin degrading enzyme and the yeast starter. Keep the bucket covered, except when stirring daily.

When the fermentation is going briskly, stir in 500 g (1 lb) of sugar.

Ferment on the pulp for a week, then press out the juice, using a wine-press or a piece of strong net such as terylene, add the remainder of the sugar and place the liquid in a 5 litre (1 gal) jar and fit a fermentation lock. When vigorous fermentation has died down, top up with water.

When a heavy sediment forms, rack the wine into another jar and top up again with water. Thereafter, rack only when a noticeable sediment forms.

Do not be in a hurry to bottle this wine, nor to drink it. It can taste heavily fruity and almost oily when young, but it matures to a beautiful silky roundness.

Another wine, but also a good one, can be made by substituting a Tokay yeast starter and carrying out the fermentation in much warmer surroundings. Up to a further 500 g (1 lb) of sugar may be required with this hard-driving yeast.

Grape concentrate

Most suppliers include recipes with the concentrate, and it is advisable to follow these instructions – at least until you have proved them for yourself. Some tend to be a little optimistic about the amount of wine that can be made from a small amount of concentrate.

The amount of grape juice concentrated in each type of concentrate tends to vary, but a rule-of-thumb method is to exchange 500 g (1 lb) of grape concentrate for a similar weight of sugar in a recipe, to give a fuller and more vinous wine. The addition of even a cupful of concentrate to 5 litres (1 gal) of wine improves the speed of fermentation and the resulting flavour and bouquet.

Mint wine

> 500 g (1 lb) freshly picked mint
> 1·5 kg (3 lb) sugar
> 2 lemons
> 500 g (1 lb) black ripe bananas
> 3·7 g or 1 tsp or 1 tablet yeast nutrient
> 250 ml (½ pint) strong fresh tea
> Wine yeast, prepared as starter

Prepare the yeast starter.

Slice up the bananas, including the skins, and boil them for half an hour with the mint in ample water.

Strain the juice into a plastic pail, cover well, and leave overnight. Next day pour or siphon the comparatively clear juice into a 5 litre (1 gal) jar, leaving the soft sediment behind. Add the tea, nutrient and the sugar (prepared as a syrup as described on page 70) and swirl the jar until the contents are well mixed. Squeeze in the juice of the lemons, add the yeast starter, and fill the jar to shoulder level with additional water if necessary.

Fit a fermentation lock, and put the jar in a warm place. If a vigorous frothy fermentation takes place, wait till it dies down before topping the jar up into the neck.

Rack when a thick sediment forms, topping up the jar again as necessary with water. Thereafter, rack only when a noticeable sediment forms. Bottle only when fermentation has ceased and the wine is star-bright.

In this wine, the mint gives a pungent herbal flavour and the bananas give body. The recipe can be adapted to other herbs, parsley being an outstanding example – and, by cutting back the sugar to 1 kg (2 lb), a dry wine, rather strongly flavoured, is obtained.

Other variations include the deletion of the bananas, and the substitution of an equal weight of grape concentrate for up to 500 g (1 lb) of the sugar.

Orange juice wine (simple)

500 ml (1 pt) unsweetened orange juice
1 to 1·5 kg (2 to 3 lb) sugar
Yeast nutrient (3·7 g or 1 tsp or 1 tablet)
Yeast, prepared as starter

Prepare the yeast starter.

Pour the orange juice into a 5 litre (1 gal) jar. Add 1 kg (2 lb) of sugar prepared as syrup (as detailed on page 70) and the nutrient. Mix well, and top up the jar into the shoulder with water. Add the yeast starter.

Fit a fermentation lock, and put the jar in a warm place.

When fermentation has slowed down, top up with water (if you are making a dry wine) or with the remainder of the sugar syrup (if you are making a sweet wine).

There can be no easier wine to make than this!

Using more orange juice, or less, alters the flavour and particularly the acidity. Different yeasts can also be tried, and if you use no more than a kg (2 lb) of sugar, and make certain that the wine ferments to dryness, this is the basis of a good sparkling wine.

Orange wine

12 sweet oranges
1 to 1·5 kg (2 to 3 lb) sugar
Yeast nutrient (3·7 g or 1 tsp or 1 tablet)
Yeast, prepared as a starter

Prepare the yeast starter.

Peel or grate the peel of six of the oranges, trying to avoid adding any of the white pith, which is often blamed for making orange wine bitter.

Pour 1 litre (1 quart) of boiling water on the peel, and allow it to stand overnight, then strain the water into a 5 litre (1 gal) jar. Cut all twelve oranges in half, and squeeze the juice into the jar through a plastic funnel. Add the nutrient, and 1 kg (2 lb) of sugar made up as syrup (as described on page 70). Fill the jar up into the shoulder with water, and swill the jar round to mix the contents, then add the yeast starter and fit a fermentation lock. When the most vigorous early fermentation has died down, top up the jar with water (if you are making a dry wine) or with the remainder of the sugar syrup (if you are making a sweet wine).

The first racking may need to be done in two or three weeks, because the solid matter in the orange juice will settle out. Thereafter, rack only when a noticeable sediment forms.

Bottle only when you are sure that fermentation has completely finished, and the wine is crystal clear.

This is a flexible basic recipe. You can vary it by substituting grape concentrate for an equal weight of sugar, or using a few bitter Seville oranges, or one or two lemons, in the wine.

Nor need you waste the residue of the fruit. Grate the peel from the unpeeled oranges, push the peel into a bottle, and fill it up with an undistinguished sweet white wine. The alcohol in the wine will draw the flavour from the peel to give new zest to that otherwise undistinguished wine.

Parsley wine – as mint

Parsnip wine – as beetroot (basic)

Peach wine – as plum (but add 3·5 g (1 tsp) of citric acid and a pinch of grape tannin)

Plum wine

  2 kg (4 lb) plums or greengages, or 1·5 kg (3 lb) damsons or
       bullaces, or a proportionate mixture of fruit
  1–1·5 kg (2–3 lb) sugar
  Yeast nutrient (3·7 g or 1 tsp or 1 tablet)
  Pectin degrading enzyme
  Yeast, prepared as a starter

Prepare the starter.

Stone the fruit, crush them between your hands, put them in a plastic bucket, and cover them with boiling water. Next day, stir in the nutrient, the pectin degrading enzyme, and the yeast starter. Keep the bucket, well covered, in a warm place, stirring the contents daily, for up to a week.

Press as much juice as possible from the pulp, using a wine-press or a strong piece of net such as terylene. Pour it into a 5 litre (1 gal) jar and add 1 kg (2 lb) of the sugar, made up as a syrup as described on page 70. Swirl the jar to mix the contents thoroughly. Fill up to the shoulders with water, if necessary, and fit a fermentation lock.

Keep the jar in a warm place.

If you wish to make a dry wine (though most winemakers would agree that plum wine is better when sweet) top the jar up with water when the first vigour of the fermentation has died down. If you wish to make a sweet wine, top up with sugar syrup.

If the wine 'eats up' the sugar in the recipe and is still dry, then add more sugar syrup in stages, until the wine ferments down to around 1015 on the hydrometer, and stays there.

Rack when noticeable sediment forms, topping up each time with water. Bottle only when fermentation has definitely stopped, and when the wine is star-bright.

The whole plum family provides an excellent feed-stock for wine, the black 'Czar' plum being especially popular.

If you intend to allow plum wine to mature for some years, add 3·5 g (1 tsp) citric acid, or a proportionate amount of other acids, as detailed on pages 72–3. Add also 0·5 g (¼ tsp) grape tannin. Those additions can be made to the juice when pressed. The recipe including the acid and tannin can be used for a full-fruit peach wine.

Raspberry wine (sweet)

2 kg (4 lb) ripe fruit
1·5 kg (3 lb) sugar
Pinch of grape tannin
Yeast nutrient (3·7 g or 1 tsp or 1 tablet)
Pectin degrading enzyme
Yeast prepared as a starter

Prepare the starter.

Clean the fruit of any 'livestock', such as grubs and greenfly. Put the fruit in a plastic bucket and cover with a solution made by dissolving one Campden tablet in 2·5 litres (4 pt) of warm water. The colour may fade slightly, but will return.

Next day, give the contents of the pail a vigorous stir, before stirring in 500 g (1 lb) of sugar, and the tannin, nutrient, pectin degrading enzyme and the yeast starter.

Cover the bucket and keep it in a warm place for a week, stirring at least once a day.

Press the juice from the pulp as thoroughly as possible, either with a wine-press or through strong netting such as terylene. Add the remainder of the sugar to the juice as syrup (prepared as described on page 70), stir thoroughly, and pour the liquid into a 5 litre (1 gal) jar and fit a fermentation lock.

A vigorous frothy fermentation is likely to occur. When it is over, top up the jar to just below the stopper of the fermentation lock with water.

Rack when a heavy sediment appears, topping up with water. Thereafter, rack only when a noticeable sediment appears, again topping up. Do not bottle until fermentation is well completed and the wine is star-bright.

This is an enjoyable fruity wine, of rich colour. The recipe is also suitable for loganberries, and can be used for brambles (blackberries) by omitting the tannin and reducing the pulp fermentation to three days.

Rhubarb wine (basic)

3 to 3·5 kg (6–7 lb) young rhubarb
1·5 kg (3 lb) sugar
125 ml (¼ pt) strong fresh tea
Yeast nutrient (3·7 g or 1 tsp or 1 tablet)
Yeast, prepared as a starter

Prepare the yeast starter.

Mash the rhubarb thoroughly – in quantity this can be done with a wringer or mangle! – put it in a plastic pail and cover with approximately 3 litres (5 pt) of cold water in which a crushed Campden tablet has been dissolved.

Leave the pail, closely covered, in a warm place for three or four days, giving the rhubarb a daily stir and squeeze. Then press as much juice as possible from the pulp, either with a wine-press or through a strong piece of netting, such as terylene.

Dissolve the sugar, nutrient, tea and yeast in the juice and pour it into a 5 litre (1 gal) jar. Fit a fermentation lock. When vigorous fermentation is over, top up the jar with water into the neck.

Rack when a heavy sediment appears. Thereafter, rack only when a noticeable sediment forms, again topping up. Do not bottle until fermentation is well completed and the wine is star-bright.

This basic recipe is capable of infinite variation – for example 500 g (1 lb) of malt extract can be substituted for the same weight of sugar, or fruit juice, for example orange juice, can be incorporated in it.

Though rhubarb rarely makes an outstanding wine, it almost

always makes a drinkable wine – one which by its nature is ideal for blending with fuller and flabbier wines.

Though, in this recipe, the sugar has been incorporated in one batch, prudent winemakers may wish to feed it in, perhaps 1 kg (2 lb) to start with, and then 500 g (1 lb) when this has fermented away.

Rhubarb wine (by osmosis)

1·5 to 2·5 kg (3–5 lb) fresh young rhubarb
1·5 kg (3 lb) sugar
Yeast nutrient (3·7 g or 1 tsp or 1 tablet)
Wine yeast, prepared as a starter

Prepare the yeast starter.

Chop up the rhubarb into thin slices, as for jam, and place in a plastic bucket. Cover the rhubarb with the dry sugar, cover the bucket, and leave it for at least a day.

When the sugar has drawn the juice from the rhubarb the contents of the pail will be almost liquid. Strain off the sugary pink liquid into a 5 litre (1 gal) jar, then replace the pulp in the bucket, cover it with warm water, stir thoroughly, and strain again.

Add the yeast nutrient and the yeast to the contents of the jar (the first and second strainings) and put it in a warm place, fitting the fermentation lock.

Rack when a thick sediment forms, and thereafter only when a noticeable sediment forms.

This recipe produces a light-flavoured wine, pleasant to drink almost as soon as it has cleared. If you wish to convert it into a long-keeping wine, use the higher amount of rhubarb and include either grape tannin or fresh strong tea.

This wine is an ideal blender, to be used for 'stretching' wines made from more expensive ingredients.

Rose-hip – as elderberry wine (basic)

Rowan wine (Mountain Ash) – as elderberry wine (basic)
with three days pulp fermentation

Vine prunings (Folly wine)

2·5 kg (5 lb) vine prunings, tendrils and unripe grapes
1–1·5 kg (2–3 lb) sugar
Yeast nutrient (3·7 g or 1 tsp or 1 tablet)
Wine yeast, prepared as a starter

Prepare the yeast starter.

Put the cuttings into a plastic bucket, pressing them down well, and pour enough boiling water over them to just cover them. Cover the bucket and put it in a warm place for two or three days, giving the mash a stir daily. Strain the liquid off and squeeze as much juice as possible from the prunings. Dissolve 1 kg (2 lb) of sugar in the liquid which has been strained and pressed from the prunings, add the yeast and the nutrient, and pour into a 1 litre (1 gal) jar. Top up to shoulder level and, in a few days, when any violent fermentation is over, top up again – with water, if you are making a dry wine, or with sugar syrup if you are making a sweet wine.

Folly wine can be successful either as a sweet or a dry wine.

For a dry wine, a German yeast such as Hock or Bernkastler can be used – for a sweet wine, either All-purpose or Sauternes is suitable.

The dry wine, with not more than 1 kg (2 lb) of sugar, can be used as a base for a sparkling wine, following the process outlined in the text of this book.

21

Brewing – the Sister Craft

Brewing and winemaking are not two separate crafts, hence much of the information in earlier chapters on equipment, hygiene and ingredients like sugar and water, apply to both. In 1834 W. H. Roberts, the author of the first modern treatise on both subjects, commented: 'Brewing and winemaking are so nearly allied that, literally speaking, making ale is nothing more nor less than making wine from malt by the process of fermentation, instead of making wine from the grape, by the same process.'

There is, however, one key difference. You can pick grapes from the vine, but malt has to be made out of grain, and so it is plain that before you can brew ale you must first know how to make malt.

How, then, did the earliest brewers discover how to sprout grain to make malt? They did so not to brew beer but for food. They found that if wheat or barley was moistened and left to sprout it produced a sweeter dish than the dry, starchy, unsprouted grains. The sprouted grains were, in effect, green malt. They were over the first hurdle and on the way to their first pint of ale.

Beer, so many thousands of years later, is still a food as well as a drink. It has been calculated that commercial beer is equivalent in calories to its volume in milk, or a quarter of its weight in chocolate!

Neolithic man surmounted the first hurdle in brewing beer through his discovery that bread made from sprouted, dried and ground grain was tastier than bread made from flour, and by the time the first cities had appeared brewing was well established. In ancient Sumeria, for instance, there were eight types of barley beer, eight types of wheat beer and three beers made from mixed grain. With the rationalisation of breweries Britain (but for home brewing) may end up with fewer types of beer than the Sumerians!

In fairness to the commercial brewer, it should be said that he has handicaps that the home-brewer does not have. He must pay heavy duty, make a profit and keep his beers uniform. We are happy if our successive beers made according to the same recipe are broadly similar and palatable, but the commercial brewery goes to great trouble to ensure that Bloggs Best Bitter tastes the same week in, week out – no worse, no better, but identical.

Some people tend to feel that the great advantage of home-brewed beer is that it can be made much stronger than commercial beer. The original specific gravity of most commercial beers falls between 1030 and 1040. Beers made from commercial kits may be around 10° stronger. What about home brews? No one has carried out a poll, and it would be very difficult to do so with any accuracy, but their specific gravities probably fall anywhere between 1035 and 1085, with the average somewhere between 1045 and 1055.

Nowadays, home-brewed beer does not depend only on its strength to commend it. An interesting hint of the rise in status of home brewing could be seen a few years ago, when Guinness showed large posters of their product with the words 'Our Home Brew'. Although most home-brewers have their reservations about commercial brewers, few have ill to say of that bitter stout, and Guinness advertising is well known to be astute as well as amusing. So when Guinness compare their product with our home brew, it is obvious that the old image of home-brewed beer as being strong, pungent, cheap, cloudy and not very good has gone, at least as far as Guinness and their advertising agents are concerned.

The home brew market, still very small compared with the huge commercial brewery trade, grows faster as the price of pub beer rises.

Many people come to home brewing through trying a beer kit, but they are extensively used by many home-brewers simply because of the convenience they offer.

Sooner or later, however, most people begin to devise their own brews. They may be high in hops but light in alcohol and thus fit for quenching a summer thirst. Or they may be like the ale that George Borrow described (recipes for both types are given later in this book):

'The ale which I am fond of is ale about nine or ten months old, somewhat hard, tasting well of malt and a little of the hop – ale such as farmers, and noblemen too, of the good old time, when farmers' daughters did not play on pianos and noblemen did not sell their game, were in the habit of offering to both high and low and drinking themselves.'

A happy result of brewing your own beer is that you have plenty to offer to both 'high and low', and to drink yourself.

22

Beer – Barley and the Bitter Vine

There are very wide variations in personal tastes in beer. English draught beers are not cold, are not bubbly, are bitter and quite strong (to quote Boston on Beer in the *Guardian*). Draught lagers, on the other hand, which are increasingly popular, are cold, are bubbly, are not bitter and are often far from strong. And on either side of these drinks lie even more extreme differences, from home-brewed 'winter ales', stronger than table wines, to American 'near beer', with a legal upper limit of half 1% volume of alcohol. In addition, there are what can only be described as freak beers, such as banana ale or the famous English Cock Ale (the recipe for which is given on page 207, more for amusement than for imitation). Drinks including meat have parallels in other civilisations, such as Asian deer wine, tigerbone wine, tortoise wine, snake wine, dog wine and mutton wine, and no doubt Cock Ale could easily be modified to allow the use of a surplus tortoise!

Happily the home-brewer can now make beer to please himself, with a strength and flavour anywhere along the range.

Let us look at some of these types of beer.

Types of beer

Light ale, with an original specific gravity of around 1030, merges into **pale ale** (1038 to 1042), which enthusiasts maintain is the crown of the home-brewer's art and can only be reproduced by using the best of pure malt at about 750 gm to 5 litres, or 1½ lb to the gallon, with no added sugar but with ample good hops.

Bitter beer is a description that covers a variety of brews, the original gravity being a little higher than that for pale ale.

Mild ale takes its name from the fact that it *is* low in hops, and is the closest successor to the old ales, which were unflavoured. Mild ale and **brown ale**, in flavour and strength, are very much a matter of taste. The commercial mild ale and brown ale of southern England can seem very insipid to folk from the north. Newcastle Brown Ale is very different from other brown ales, and its commercial missionaries are spreading its fame far outside north-east England. Its success does not depend merely on advertising, for it cannot be damned (like some commercial brown ales) as 'good tap-water spoiled'.

Sweet stouts (1035 to 1040) are dark, sweet and almost innocent of hop flavour.

In contrast, **dry stout**, of which Guinness is the great example, is stronger, less luscious, markedly flavoured of roasted barley and (though the fullness of flavour tends to mask it) well hopped. The water for Dublin-brewed Guinness comes not, as legend has it, from the Liffey but is piped from County Kildare. The yeast (which many home-brewers have 'pirated' by a method to be described later) has been used by the firm for 300 years. Guinness' original gravity is around 1046.

Strong ale, with an original gravity of 1055 upwards, merges into **barley wine**. With these, a very high hopping rate is needed to balance the sweetness and fullness of body. Once brewed, they need months to reach their full potential, and will sit happily on the cellar shelves gaining in maturity and apparent potency for many years.

And **lager**, which is becoming more and more popular in the pubs. It can be anything from a fizzy drink the colour of pale straw, and with less flavour than straw, to a golden-brown liquid which winks in the glass and seduces you into drinking more than you should, then leaves you feeling surprised at the after effects of an original gravity of 1080.

By definition, lager is a stored beer (a lager is a place where beer is laid away, and the word has interesting parallels with the lair of an animal and the lager into which the Afrikaner drew his wagons as a guard against attack).

Because of the danger of infection by flowers of wine and the vinegar bug, most home-brewers like to hustle their beer down to bottling gravity as quickly as possible, but lager enthusiasts prefer to give their brews a long, slow fermentation. It is literally true that a lager yeast, once started, would keep a brew fermenting on the sunny side of an iceberg, though there would be little use in trying to start a fermentation at that temperature. In commercial breweries the last stages of lager fermentation are carried on in premises just above freezing-point.

Of course, many of the home brews that are made for the pleasure of the brewer rather than the approval of a judge at a circle or a national show do not fall neatly into any of the commercial categories and are none the worse for that. It is only when you are brewing competitively that you need to worry about your brew ending up right in the centre of a classification.

Ingredients

Hops
Hops are the essential flavour of all types of modern beer. They belong to the same family as marihuana, and, like marihuana, the female flower head is valued for its complex oils.

Hops were originally grown to provide greenery for a tasty salad. They were first used to flavour drink many centuries ago, and the captive Jews in Babylon are said to have remained free from leprosy by drinking barley beer made bitter with hops. Home brewing is not advanced as a preventive for leprosy, however!

Other nations had adopted the idea of flavouring their ale with hops long before the British took it up. Various rhymes say that the new 'hops', 'Reformation', 'baize', 'beer', 'turkey', 'carp', 'pickerel' and 'heresies' all came to England in the same year. So, although nothing could sound more English than the blunt word 'hop', we took the word from Low German and the practice of hopping our ale from the Continent too.

There are alternatives if you care to experiment. The aromatic leaves of the bog myrtle or sweet gale, which grows in bogs and marshy places and looks like a low willow bush, were used to flavour beer long before hops were introduced. Perhaps, during a day on the hills, you would enjoy gathering the foliage with its sweet resinous aroma and trying it in a brew?

Nettles, too, are a traditional ingredient in country brews. A gallon of young nettle tops is needed to make a gallon of beer – and wear rubber gloves when you gather them, for those little springtime nettles have a fierce sting. The old jingle 'Gently gently touch the nettle and it stings you for your pains; grasp it like a man of mettle and it soft as silk remains' should be revised so that the last line reads 'grasp it like a man of mettle and it stings you just the same'!

A recipe for nettle ale is given on page 205, but most home-brewers who have experimented with the old substitutes for hops, from willow-bark to new hay and from nettles to sweet gale, know at the end of their experiments why hops finally won the day.

It is not many years since the home-brewer had to content himself with whatever anonymous hops he could get, but named varieties are readily available today through the specialist shops.

How important is it to use a named variety? Well, a skilled commercial brewer will quite often be able to tell which varieties have been used in a beer by assessing the taste and smell. Some home-brewers can recognise *some* varieties, and many could guess whether the hops were English or Continental. But every beer-drinker can tell you whether the amount of hops in his pint is too much, too little or just right.

If you like a brew that is pungent with hops, then a pint with too little hopping will taste slightly insipid but will be drinkable. If, however, you like no more than a hint of hops, then a pint of highly hopped beer will assault your palate with its emphatic coarse taste.

So, if you are beginning to brew or are changing over to a new variety of hop, err on the low side in your hopping. It is almost certain that, when you have been weaned away from the 'all things to all men' mildness of pub beer, your liking for well-hopped beers will increase and after your first few brews you will be stepping up the hopping rate.

The amount of hops used can vary from as little as 30 gm in 5 litres (1 oz in 5 gal) to as much as 180 gm in 5 litres (6 oz in 5 gal). The lower level might be adequate in a very light lager, while the top level would be none too much in a very full-bodied malt wine intended to mature in bottle for a year and a day!

Hops do not only flavour a brew but also help to preserve it – it was this quality that first brought hops into favour with the brewers (their brews did not go sour so quickly) and their customers then came to like the bitter tang.

The hop plants grow in favoured parts of England and on the Continent, and the flower-heads are harvested (mainly by machinery now) and dried at carefully controlled temperatures.

The dried hops come from the hop-garden to the supplier in pockets of approximately 75 kg (1½ cwt). On the outside of the pocket is the name of the variety. Still the most common British hops supplied to home-brewers are Fuggles and Goldings.

Fuggles have abundant resins, and give a heavier and coarser flavour. They end up in stout, brown ale, porter and similar brews.

And if you find the name amusing, it's simply an old English surname meaning 'birds'.

Goldings, smaller and more compact, are good for high-quality light ale or bitter – the Continental Goldings (from Styria, for example), being seedless, can be used at a lower rate, perhaps 15 gm in 5 litres (½ oz in 1 gal).

Northern Brewer is a hop that finds its ideal niche in full-bodied strong stouts, and even here less than this amount is sufficient.

Bullion is a good hop but one to be wary of. It has a very emphatic flavour and bitterness – one of its parents was a wild hop from Manitoba. But that 'rank American flavour' can mellow very acceptably in a really strong beer.

Lager, yet again, falls into a category by itself. Many lager brewers would put Saaz hops first, with Hallertauer a close second. Taste, once again, comes into it – there is no necessity to make home-brewed lager so mild that the hop tang is almost undetectable, but the tang should be that of Continental seedless hops.

Since hops grow wild in many parts of Britain, the flowers can be gathered and used fresh. If you do this, remember that fresh hops have a stronger herbal flavour, and be cautious. It is, however, hardly worth picking the green 'cones' from the hop bines that climb clockwise through many an English hedge and drying them for winter use – it needs too exact a control of temperature.

If you find that all you can buy in your neighbourhood is a nameless type of hops, do not despair. Many a good pint of home brew was made before named varieties were available. Do try to avoid hops that look like badly dried hay. If they are packed in a polythene bag, there should be some yellow powder along the bottom seam, and when you take them home and open them they should have a strong hop 'nose' and leave your hands slightly sticky when you rub them between them.

Since evaluating hops is a craft for the professional, the best that the amateur can do is to keep going back to the shop or the supplier who has consistently sold him acceptable hops in the past.

Mention has been made of Continental hops. The chief difference between them and English-grown hops is that the latter are allowed to set seeds. It is said that in the British climate this is necessary to prevent disease but the immediate result is that a third of the weight of English hops is made up of seeds, which serve no useful purpose in brewing.

The Continental hop-gardens, from which male plants are stringently excluded, supply us with seedless hops. They do not bulk up as heavily, but the hopping rate can be cut back by at least a third.

Hops, named or nameless, are worth storing carefully. Breweries go to great trouble and some expense to make sure that their hops are kept in a cold dark place, and it is prudent for amateurs to follow their example. Hops should be stored in polythene bags, with the necks knotted, or sealed with a rubber band or a twist of wire, or they can be pressed into an airtight jar or tin.

If you buy your hops in bulk, then store them carefully. This gives you the opportunity to make a test brew and to find the exact hopping rate that suits your palate, knowing that you have more of exactly the same type of hop to use in subsequent brews.

Hops *have* to be boiled in order to extract the flavour. If you use hop extracts, this is not strictly necessary (though desirable).

Hop extracts, when they first came on the market, were unpleasant greenish liquids that looked like cascara sagrada and produced beers with uncouth flavours. Now, these extracts are replacing more and more hops in commercial brews – a fact that, though not a recommendation, shows that they can produce a drink recognisably like beer!

You can now buy hop extracts obtained from named hops, and you may use them to supply all the bitterness and flavour of a brew or, if you prefer, part of the bitterness and flavour, with the same named variety of hop supplying the rest.

An old custom in brewing is to 'dry hop' the beer. This consists of adding a handful of hops at a very late stage in boiling the hops, or even in the barrel when the beer is maturing. The dry hops give a fresh aroma to the beer, but it is a wasteful process since such a small proportion of the hop oils and resins is extracted.

The alternative to doing this is to add a very small amount of hop oil to the brew a day or two before the beer is bottled. Hop oil is a very highly concentrated extract, and a drop to the gallon gives the beer a noticeably improved 'nose'. To add this, fill a jug with the beer and drop the oil into the middle of the jugful, stirring well to ensure that it is well dispelled through the sample, then add the jugful to the bulk of the beer and give it a thorough stir.

Do not, when using extract or hop oil, put the extract or oil into the jug first and top up. A plastic container that has come in contact with either will retain the flavour for a surprisingly long time, and the tang will even cling to glass or metal.

Note again that, although hop extract *can* be added direct to the unhopped wort, it is preferable if the extract is added at the very beginning and boiled up with the malt extract.

Malt extract

Hops in some form or another provide the authentic flavour of beer, but the basis of beer is barley. One reason for the wide availability of beer is that barley grows in very varying climates and soils.

When any seed is damped and put in a warm place, it will start to grow. This is what happens at the beginning of the malting process – the barley is damped and encouraged to sprout. The little shoot creeps along the surface of the grain, under the husk, and when that shoot is a certain length the maltster checks the growth by heating the barley. It is barley no longer, but malt.

On this simple foundation a huge superstructure of technology has been built to ensure that the commercial brewer can buy malt of the exact nature he wishes.

Increasing amounts of malting barley go to the malt-extract makers. Malt extract, either as a powder or as a sticky liquid, is familiar to all home-brewers, but it also goes by the hundred gallons and the ton into commercial breweries.

The process of making malt extract begins with mashing. The grain malt is ground to the right consistency, then covered in water and held at a carefully regulated temperature until the enzymes turn the starches into fermentable sugars. The sugary liquid is then washed out of the grain and the surplus water is evaporated until a syrup is left. Powdered malt is carried a stage further.

It is worth noticing that different brands of malt extract please different home-brewers. One famous brand, which delights hundreds of brewers, reminds many others of malt loaf every time they taste beer made from it. This difference of taste applies to hopped malts, hopped worts and beer kits. Experiment until you find a brand that suits your own tastes and stay with it.

Many people start by using the liquid malt extract and then go on to experiment with dried extract, which tends to ferment out more completely to give a drier and stronger brew. Because of the absence of water, four parts by weight of dried malt is approximately equal to five parts by weight of liquid malt.

Roughly 500 gm (1 lb) to 5 litres (1 gal) of either type of malt extract is a reasonable maximum for a home brew – some brewers would argue that half that weight is plenty.

Crystal malt

Another very familiar form of malt in home brewing is crystal malt. It has an attractive biscuity taste and flavour, and the use of even 30–60 gm in 5 litres (1–2 oz in 1 gal) gives a brew an extra richness of colour and roundness. It is made by heating sprouted barley (green malt) to 66°C (150°F) or more, at which point the starch turns into sugars, and then lightly roasting the grain.

If you buy it crushed, or crush it before use, you naturally get a better extraction of flavour and sweetness. Straining, however, is more difficult. Use the grain whole and step up the amount, and though you may waste some of the extraction you save yourself trouble in straining.

Crushed crystal malt rapidly loses its freshness on the suppliers' shelves.

Grits

The word 'grits' covers several useful ingredients in home brewing – ingredients like flaked barley or brewing flour. The most useful are the flakes, barley and maize. Flaked barley can be used in beers but is particularly at home in stout formulations. Flaked maize gives a characteristic tang to a brew, and can best be used in light ales and beers of this type. In round figures, 4 oz to the gallon is a rule-of-thumb maximum for both. Be sure to buy pre-cooked flakes, otherwise you may find you have starch hazes. Flakes from specialist shops cost markedly more than flakes from a grain store, but you know what you have got.

Shredded wheat, cornflakes, brown bread and the like have been used experimentally but are unlikely to replace the commonplace adjuncts.

Since torrified barley and torrified maize are simply grains that have been 'popped' by heat, there is nothing (other than expense) to prevent the brewer bringing home a big bag of popcorn from the local cinema and using this instead! Torrified grains give a brew a distinctive flavour and, like all the grits, should be used with discretion until you discover what suits your own taste.

Bran, which is the ground husk of grain, is readily bought from specialists, from health-food shops and from pet stores. It gives a beer extra body and helps with head retention, and it contains so little starch that when a small amount is boiled up with malt extract it rarely gives any trouble from starch hazes.

Brewing flours (of which Brumore is the best-known brand) are specially selected flours of graded particle size, and, because they contain starch, they have to be used along with grain malt or diastatic malt extract so that the starch can be converted to sugar. Even when used in small amounts, they give a brew smoothness and help with head retention. Used too liberally, they can cause a 'set mash' which is difficult to strain.

Brewing syrup

A very useful type of adjunct is brewing syrup. The principal syrups available, at the time of writing, are barley syrup, the one naturally linked with beer but which can be used experimentally in wines; maize syrup, which has something of the grainy dry flavour we associate with American beers; and wheat syrup, which should be used discreetly – its flavour is not to everyone's taste.

(Wheat, though it can be malted, is not much used in British commercial brewing, but the Germans make an all-wheat beer, Weissbier, which was traditionally fermented with wild yeasts – perhaps because of its sour flavour, it was sometimes 'improved' with a shot of raspberry juice!)

These grain syrups can be added directly to a brew, for the starches have been converted into sugar and they do not need to be mashed. They can replace in a beer recipe about 80% of their weight in sugar, but not all this sweetness is available to the yeast, so the hydrometer does not fall as low as it otherwise would and the resulting beer has a trace of sweetness.

Like malt extract, the syrups are much cheaper if bought in bulk, but since they are inclined to set solid or to oxidise if exposed to the air, it is more economical in the long run to buy the syrup in small quantities and use it as you need it.

Dextrin

Soluble dextrin (glucose polymer) is a comparative latecomer on the scene. It is almost unfermentable by brewing yeasts and gives body to a brew without adding any strong flavour of its own. Some beer-drinkers are disappointed to find that their home brew drinks very thin, and soluble dextrin at around 30 gm to 5 litres (1 oz to the gallon) helps to avoid this disappointment.

Flavourings and colourings

Roasted barley is just what it sounds – barley roasted to charring-point. It adds flavour and an intense black colour to stout, and also helps stout to keep that creamy head. Its predecessor was patent black malt, which is malt roasted equally drastically – which accounts for the characteristic charred taste in stout. A very small amount will give a beer a darker colour. Patent black malt is more easily obtained than roasted barley, but for most purposes you will find roasted barley is preferable.

Roasted barley and patent black malt cannot give a brew colour without adding flavour as well – this is not undesirable with some brews, such as brown ales. However, a beer can also be tinted without altering the colour.

One way is to add artificial colouring, but although such colourings are used in ice lollies and brightly coloured cakes, they are not likely to attract the home-brewer. Caramel, which is produced from burnt sugar, gives exactly the right kind of colour without any discernible change in flavour, at the concentration needed. Gravy browning (unseasoned!) has been used for many years in the craft, but caramel intended for the purpose can be bought from supply shops and through the mail-order trade.

Lactose

Although caramel is made from sugar, it does not sweeten the beer. Adding sugar will not achieve this purpose either, for the yeast will continue to break down the sugar into alcohol and carbon dioxide until a very alcoholic and completely still hopped-malt wine results. There is one sugar that is not fermented by the yeasts we use – lactose or milk sugar – and this can be used to sweeten a brew. Milk stout (which can no longer be called by that name commercially because it contains no milk) and sweet stout are examples of the kind of beer in which it might be used. It takes only 30–60 gm in 5 litres, or an ounce or two in a gallon to round off the dry taste.

Heading liquid

Some people prefer sweet stout, others do not, but the difference in attitude to a head on a pint seems to be geographical. In some parts of Britain, they say approvingly 'Fine creamy head! Follows you right down the glass', while in other parts they scowl at the head on the glass and ask the barman pointedly if his father was a vicar.

To judge by conversation, questions at meetings and correspondence in the trade press, most home-brewers belong to the former group. They want a head on their beer, they have difficulty keeping one, and they will have nothing to do with arguments that no other sparkling drink is expected to have a head of froth and that a pint with a good running bead of bubbles is not really improved by a collar of foam.

The problem of head retention is a vexed one, involving many factors. Several points are clear: the head on the last bottle of a batch is always better than the head on the first bottle, because maturity helps head stability; high malt content, and the use of Brumore and other adjuncts, also helps; detergent in the glass often causes what would otherwise be a good head to be disappointing and fleeting; malt beers probably have a better reputation than beers made from malt extract, but slack and damp malt give poor results, and brewers who use grain malt should ensure for this and other reasons that it is fresh and dry.

Chemical aids to head retention have a long history. Publicans used to put a froth on their beer by doctoring it with sulphate of iron, the poisonous green vitriol. Home-brewers have a gentler substance – heading liquid, derived from quillaia bark, the bark of a Chilean tree whose other name is soap-bark. The use of heading liquid does not make the beer any more brisk, but it does hold a frothy air-bubble on the surface after the beer is poured vigorously.

Brewing salts

Another type of additive, used meticulously by some keen brewers but neglected by others, is brewing salts.

The purpose of these salts is to adjust the water from the tap so that it is more suitable for the type of beer you aim to make. Unfortunately, this is a much more complicated business than it might seem. The water authority (instead of simply saying that the water is very soft, moderately hard, very hard, etc.) may give you a detailed analysis, and unless you worked as an analytical chemist in a brewery you will find yourself faced with a mass of facts and puzzled by their apparent lack of connection with what you wish to do. You will be back to rule-of-thumb adjustments on the recommendation of the maker of proprietary softeners or hardeners – and this is probably the easiest way.

On this pragmatical basis, many brewers use a little table salt – perhaps 3 gm in 25 litres (½ tsp in 1 gal) – in the belief that this brings up the flavour of the beer, in the way that a pinch of salt is reputed to improve coffee. Health-food enthusiasts carry this a little further and say that the salt should be sea-salt, which contains traces of thirty elements including magnesium, calcium, iron and iodine. It is unlikely that the difference would be noticeable but it might be worth trying experimentally (there is no need to go further and use herb salt, which also includes celery, onion, parsley, carrot, paprika and other plants).

Irish moss
What have edible sausage skins, ice-cream and blancmange got to do with the clarity of beer? The common factor is seaweed. When carragheen is picked from the rocks on the Irish shores it is purple-red or green and tastes of salt and iodine. By the time it has been processed, it is brownish-white and is sold either as a powder or in little hard shreds which dissolve in the hot wort. Carragheen or Irish moss is added while you are boiling up your malt and hops, and some of the substances that might otherwise make your beer cloudy settle out when the wort is left to stand. It helps to achieve what the commercial brewer calls 'a good hot break'.

It is not strictly necessary to use Irish moss, but if you are boiling up the ingredients in any case, it is cheap and easy to do so, and thus give the beer extra clarity and polish.

Yeasts
Much of what has already been said about yeasts in general applies also to beer yeasts.

The division between wine and beer yeasts is not quite as deep and wide as is sometimes made out – for instance, a champagne yeast is excellent for a heavy lager that is going to be given plenty of bottle maturity, and an all-purpose wine yeast is suitable for the heavy malty beers that verge on malt wine in character.

The main division in home brewing is between top-fermentation yeasts and bottom-fermentation yeasts. They can be distinguished from each other by the way they work – as their names indicate – and also by complicated biological tests.

Most home-brewers use bottom-fermentation yeasts. They, like wine yeasts, lie at the bottom of the fermentation vessel and work away. They will work in lower temperatures than top-fermentation strains (once the first fermentation is established); they produce a beer that tastes more highly hopped than a beer made with the same amount of hops and a top-fermentation yeast; and they tend to stick down better in the bottle.

Top-fermentation yeasts, on the other hand, work throughout the brew. They multiply in the beer and ride to the top on the streams of bubbles. As a result, a layer of yeast builds up, and a brew with a good rocky head can look solid enough to trot a mouse on. In a brewery the surface of the fermenting vessel may be covered a foot or more deep in 'cauliflower-head', but amateurs will find that the layer is only 50–75 mm (2–3 in) deep.

Top-fermentation yeasts are happier in higher temperatures than bottom-fermentation strains – 21°C (70°F) perhaps rather than 15°C (60°F). They have to be skimmed when a good solid crust forms. And the brew also needs to be regularly roused up – even once or twice a day – otherwise attenuation will be slow.

The top-fermenting strains have tended to be more mixed than the others and thus more variable in action. Some top-fermentation yeasts need to to be skimmed several times and roused up at least once a day, whereas others need one skimming and no rousing.

In ideal conditions, the top-fermentation yeast process is the quicker. Usually, however, home-brewers find bottom-fermentation yeasts quicker and very much easier to use, and perfectly suitable for most types of beer and stout.

Theoretically, once you have made one brew of beer you have far more yeast than you will ever need, because the layer that settles at the bottom of every bottle contains millions of yeast cells raring to spring to active life in a new batch of wort.

On the face of it, too, it seems obvious that, by using the yeast that has stuck to the bottom of the bottle, you are selecting a good sedimenting strain. But this is not necessarily so, for when you think about it you realise that the yeast in the bottom of the bottles is, in fact, the very last to settle out of the entire bulk of the beer and that the best sedimenting yeast strains may already have been discarded.

However, there is no doubt that 'bottle bottoms' have been satisfactorily used by generations of home-brewers without trouble.

One of the snags is that trouble may come undetected – the yeast may change very gradually and you may not notice. Wild yeasts may establish themselves among the selected strain and with them, worse still, bacteria and other organisms. Your beer may develop a sharp or sour taste so slowly that you may not notice – or you may come to like it. The chances are that your best friends won't tell you, though they may no longer welcome an invitation for a pint with the same enthusiasm as before.

You should therefore assess each successive brew with a very critical palate, prepared to say 'Yes, it's a good pint, but I think I detect just a trace of vinegar, so I'll stop using the bottoms of bottles and start up a new yeast culture.'

Where does the home-brewer get his yeast?

Sometimes he is advised to get a lump of fresh yeast from his local brewery if possible, but – perhaps because of specialised conditions in the brewery, or because of the fact that commercial beers now start at lower gravities than most home brews – these samples are sometimes disappointing.

Should he get it from other home-brewers? If their brews are sound, then probably yeast from the bottom of a bottle would be satisfactory. But it is a chancy method, with pounds' worth of raw materials at stake.

The simplest way is to buy yeast from the specialist supplier or big chemists. Edme top-fermentation yeast is a good worker – you buy it in a colourful foil envelope. Vierka yeast and Leigh-Williams lager yeast are satisfactory bottom-fermentation strains. Make up a starter bottle with a tablespoonful of malt extract and a squirt of lemon juice boiled up in ¾ pt of water.

You can amuse yourself by 'capturing' yeast from a bottle of naturally conditioned commercial beer – Bass Red Label, Worthington's White Label or Guinness. You buy a bottle and leave in a quiet cool place for two or three days, then carefully pour off all but 12 mm (½ in) of the beer or stout. Pour it into a glass for future enjoyment, of course.

In the small amount left there will be a high proportion of the yeast cells that have settled out of the beer. Make up a starter liquid similar to that described above, pour it (cool) into the beer bottle and plug the bottle with a twist of cotton wool or tissue. In a day or two the bottle, left in a warm place, will contain a lively culture of your selected yeast.

Does the type of yeast you use – top or bottom – and the particular strain, affect the character of the beer you make? Yes – but not recognisably as much as the type of malt, hops and adjuncts, and your choice of technique (long vigorous boiling, slow stewing or plain hop essence).

The hydrometer

The basic theory of the hydrometer has already been dealt with, but this is certainly the point to emphasise again that a hydrometer is desirable for winemaking but *essential* for home brewing. This is not so much to assess the original gravity (one can do this easily enough by reckoning the total poundage of 'sugars', such as malt and white sugar) as to make sure that the brew has reached bottling-point.

The use of soluble dextrins and other unfermentable substances clouds the issue a little – and beers made from grain malts do not generally ferment down so far – but the rule-of-thumb figure of 1005 on the hydrometer is a safe bottling-point to aim for with extract brews.

Methods of making beer

Having surveyed the basic ingredients for home brewing, let us take a look at the different methods of achieving a satisfactory pint, starting with the simplest – hopped malt or hopped wort.

Hopped malt or wort

Sometimes this basic material comes in tins, sometimes in plastic packs. The instructions vary slightly from one to the other, but basically all you need do is dissolve the sticky malt with its bitter hop flavour in hot water, add the amount of sugar suggested in the instructions, wait until the liquid is cool, add the yeast, wait until bottling-point is reached, and bottle!

If you make sure that your plastic bucket and your bottles are sterile, and if you take care to keep the bucket covered while it stands in a warm place, you are sure to end up with drinkable beer.

There are, of course, refinements in the technique. Before you have made many brews you will have discovered that malt extract runs from a tin or jar much more easily if it is first gently warmed.

This is brewing-made-easy, and many home-brewers never move past this point. They try one or two hopped malts or worts until they find the one that suits them best, and they make a regular weekly brew. It is not unknown for people who have made the full range of home brews to come back to the hopped wort for their regular bread-and-butter beer and to make a more elaborate batch only occasionally. From which it is easy to gather that beer of this kind is sound and pleasant but that it rarely wins prizes.

Hop tea

The next step forward is to make a brew by the hop-tea method.

Let us assume that the aim is to make 20 litres (4 gal) of a full-bodied strong beer.

The first step is to obtain a suitable brewing vessel – a 20 litre (4 gal) white plastic bucket with a close-fitting lid is ideal.

The necessary ingredients are 2 kg (4 lb) of liquid malt extract, 120 gm (4 oz) of hops, 1 kg (2 lb) of white sugar, 3 gm (½ tsp) of citric acid crystals and a bottom-fermentation yeast.

Dissolve two Campden tablets and a pinch of citric acid crystals in ½ litre (1 pt) of warm water, and rinse the fermentation vessel.

Stand the jars of malt extract in a basin of hot water.

Put the hops in a light-meshed bag (a piece of muslin or terylene netting, or even a well-boiled nylon stocking) and put the bag in the biggest pan you have. Nearly fill the pan with water, bring the water to the boil and keep it boiling for an hour. During this time the house will smell like a small brewery (which it is), but the odour is not unpleasant to those who are going to drink the resulting brew.

While the hops are boiling, pour the malt extract into your sterilised fermenting vessel. Wash the jars out with hot water and pour the washings into the vessel. Add more hot water, and stir the malt and water until the malt dissolves.

Now add the kilo (2 lb) of sugar and the citric acid, and stir these into the liquid.

Pour the water in which the hops have been boiling onto the dissolved malt extract and sugar. Fill the pan with hot water and squeeze the bag of hops with the back of a wooden spoon to extract the last of the 'goodness', then add this hot water to the brew.

Fill the fermentation vessel to within an inch or so of the top. In theory you should use boiled water, but in practice most municipal water supplies are sterile enough to be used safely direct from the tap.

Add the yeast when the temperature of the wort has dropped to below 26°C (80°F).

Put the vessel in a warm place, with the lid on. Warm room temperature is ideal. The time the beer will take to ferment out varies from two or three days to, more probably with a strong brew like this, about ten days.

As bottling-time approaches, make sure that you have enough strong screwtop bottles – cider, beer or lemonade bottles, but *not* whisky bottles. They must be strong, otherwise you will literally be making a bomb.

Wash them thoroughly and rinse them with Campden tablet solution – and soak the stoppers in sterilising solution too. Sterilise your siphon tube – 2 m (6 ft) or so of rubber tubing.

There are rule-of-thumb ways of checking when bottling-point is reached. The bubbles gather into a ring on the centre of the vessel. The surface of the beer begins to clear . . . Ignore such methods and instead float a hydrometer in the brew. When the line of the surface cuts the hydrometer at 1005, the brew is ready to bottle.

Into each bottle put a little sugar – a teaspoonful into a quart cider flagon, half a teaspoonful into a pint beer bottle.

Put the bottles in the kitchen sink. Lift the fermentation vessel, without shaking it, onto the draining board. Put one end of the siphon in the beer and suck on the other end until the beer rises to your lips, then pinch the end of the siphon close to your lips, between thumb and forefinger, and lower the end to the mouth of the first bottle. When you release your pinch-grip the beer will run steadily into the bottle.

Fill each bottle to a level 25 mm (1 in) or more below the stopper. This is important since a small 'expansion chamber' must be left to allow for a build-up of pressure.

Screw the stoppers down very firmly – they are going to retain a pressure equal to the air pressure in a car tyre.

Shake each bottle thoroughly to dissolve the priming sugar, which is then broken down into alcohol and carbon dioxide. The gas cannot escape and gives the home brew its sparkle.

Stand the bottles in a warm place so that the yeast is encouraged to get to work. Then, after a couple of days, move them to a cool place. A cellar is, of course, ideal, but anywhere will do, provided that the beer will be kept cool and quiet in the dark.

With a heavy brew of this kind, three weeks in the cellar is none too long to give it before opening the first bottle. Because of the sediment at the bottom, it is simpler to decant the beer steadily into a big glass jug and to fill the glasses from the jug. They need not be pint glasses, for this is a heavy brew, almost half as strong again as pub beer. It has some great advantages as a pilot experiment.

In the first place, the method is very simple, and the ingredients are just as uncomplicated. In the second place, it produces the layman's idea of a home brew – something that is strong and highly hopped. And in the third place, the method and recipe are ideal springboards to more advanced craftsmanship.

The first advance is to discard the bag in which the hops were enclosed. Boiling the hops loose and then straining the liquid means that you get a much more effective extraction from the hops.

The second advance is to boil the malt and hops together. The more of the wort you can boil up with the hops, the better. If you boil the whole 'length', the total amount of the brew, you make sure that every drop is thoroughly sterilised so that the invading wild yeasts and bacteria are less likely to invade the tempting liquid (as happy a home for them as for beer yeast, given any encouragement). By boiling the malt and hops together vigorously in this way, you do not only extract the bitterness and the tannins from the hops (you did that by stewing the hops alone in a pan) but you also make the proteins in the malt coagulate and fall out of the wort, leaving a star-bright brew.

(One side-effect of boiling the malt with the hops and, if you wish, adding the sugar to the contents of the boiler is that you raise the temperature of the sugary liquid to well above the boiling-point of water, thus helping the extraction rate. The amount of sugar left behind when you wash out the hops is negligible.)

You can even elaborate on the hop-tea method itself. Some home-brewers put the hops in a pan with a tight-fitting lid. They cover the hops with boiling water, fit the lid and leave the hops to infuse like tea for ten minutes or so. Next they strain off the liquid into a jug and put it to one side. The hops are then boiled up in the usual way, either with the malt extract or by themselves.

When the rest of the wort is prepared, the jugful of hop extract is poured into it. This extra process, its advocates claim, preserves the volatile oils that would otherwise go to waste – instead of boiling off and scenting the whole house, the oils are in the 'tea' which is poured into the wort.

Before leaving the subject of the 'hop-tea' method, it is worth reminding the reader that, although the process of boiling all the ingredients in a large boiler is likely to give a better and brighter beer, and although many home-brewers would dismiss the 'hop-tea' method as slovenly, uncraftsmanlike, unhygienic and so forth, the fact remains that since home brewing became legal (and, indeed, long before) beer has been made and enjoyed by this method.

Experienced home-brewers will agree that another advance can be made on the basic method outlined – an advance in formulation. The same amount of malt, hops and sugar would make 30 litres (6 gal) of beer instead of 20 litres (4 gal), and the beer would still be high enough in hops and in body to be very palatable. Some enthusiasts would go even further and say that the malt and hops, with no sugar, would form a good basis for 40 litres (8 gal) of beer!

Crystal malt

If you are going to reduce the malty part of the wort to this extent, it is time to introduce crystal malt. This malt, cracked or uncracked, can be boiled up with the hops. Thus 2 kg (4 lb) of liquid malt extract, 500 gm (1 lb) of crystal malt (boiled along with the hops if the hop-tea method is used), 120 gm (4 oz) of hops and 2 kg (4 lb) of sugar would make 40 litres (8 gal) of a very acceptable pub-type ale.

(The fact that the recipe has now crept up to 40 litres (8 gal) when the brewing vessel only holds half that is no handicap. Simply split the quantities in half and, if you wish, make two brews a fortnight apart.)

The basic formulation can be further developed by using bran in a brew instead of the crystal malt – or, indeed, along with it.

And a further development in technique. Once the gravity has dropped to around a fifth of the original gravity (say, from 1040 to 1008) and the beer shows signs of clearing from the top, many home-brewers now introduce an extra process into the sequence – they rack the beer into smaller containers and leave it to settle in them.

Whatever you use, make sure that the vessel is full right up into the neck, because at this stage the brew is very subject to infection, particularly from flowers of wine.

The beer can be left for a couple of weeks or more and will be much clearer when you come to bottle it. There *should* be sufficient yeast still in suspension to break down the priming sugar in the bottles, but the way to ensure that the beer develops condition is to make up a starter of bottom-fermentation yeast, put it in the fermentation vessel with the priming sugar (15 gm to 5 litres (½ g to 1 gal)) and carefully rack the beer from the vessels in which it has been clearing into the fermentation vessel, giving it a good stir to make sure the live yeast and the sugar are well dispersed through the bulk. You can then bottle the beer, either through a siphon, or if you find it quicker and easier, with a jug and funnel.

(It is worth noting that, even though a top-fermentation yeast has been used in the original fermentation, the yeast added at bottle-point should be bottom-fermentation because it sticks down in the bottle better. For a really strong beer, the ideal yeast for this 'krausening', as the process is called, is a champagne culture.)

Diastatic malt extract

The next development of the basic method is the use of diastatic malt extract and brewing from grain malt itself, but so many competent brewers are frightened away by the idea that this is an extremely difficult process that a separate section is devoted to this development. The theory of the mashing process is extremely complicated, and whole books have been written about its chemistry and biology, but the practice is a good deal easier than the theory, as you will see from the next chapter.

In the meantime, let us take a closer look at the bottling process, and the bottles to use.

Bottling your beer

If you find that you cannot bottle your beer on the day when you discover its gravity has dropped to bottling-point, do not despair –

but do not just walk away and leave the beer either. Boil up a little sugar (30 gm for 5 litres, or 1 oz for 1 gal, is ample) in a little water and add this syrup to your brew. This will keep the fermentation moving for another day or two until you have time to bottle the brew.

The alternative is to rack the beer into gallon jars or other containers which can be filled right into the neck, as described above.

If you leave a brew in the fermentation vessel after active fermentation has ceased, it is very likely that flowers of wine will establish itself.

A thick felt of flowers of wine on the surface of a brew is a sign that that batch is beyond saving, but a few little islands of the white film is a warning that you must carry out a rescue operation.

Bottle the beer right away, with a little priming sugar even though the gravity may be rather high, and put the bottles in a cool place. All being well, the combination of the drop of temperature and the formation of carbon dioxide under pressure in the atmosphere above the beer in the bottle will keep the disease in check. But it is important to test bottles at random at least once a day to make sure that excessive pressure has not developed. A hurried rescue operation can mean that every bottle is drinkable. At the very worst, the beer will still develop a thick film and you will have to throw away the whole batch and sterilise every empty bottle with great care – but at least you will have *tried*.

Normally, the bottling process is a much more leisurely matter, especially if you have 'dropped' the brew so that it can clear for a week or two and then krausened it.

The technique of checking a bottle a day, at random, applies whenever you have bottled a brew much above 1005. Sometimes a high proportion of unfermentable solids means that the gravity will never fall below, say, 1010 (perhaps because soluble dextrin has been added to give the beer roundness, perhaps because a mashed beer has a high amount of dextrinous material or perhaps simply because too much crystal malt has been included in the formula). In that case, be wary after bottling – take a random bottle and try the stopper. If the gas comes out, as you unscrew the stopper, with something between a sigh and a hiss, all is well; if the gas whistles out or comes shrieking out, then go round the entire batch releasing the tops and quickly tightening them. This reduces the pressure – but it may build up again.

Beer bottles with screwtops are the obvious choice for home brews – if you can get them. They are made of green or amber glass, and this can cause a little difficulty when you are bottling – it is not always easy to see when the level of the beer is high enough in the bottle and you may overfill it. The semi-opaque glass also makes it more difficult to see the first signs of yeast when you come to pour your beer. The screwtop soft-drink bottle, being clear, is better but these bottles are becoming increasingly scarce.

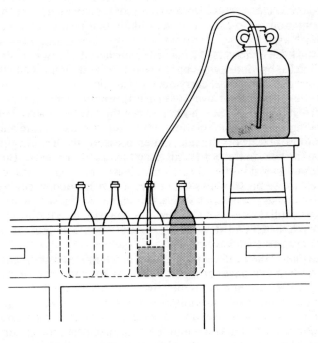

Bottling: jar of wine raised 60–90 cm (2 or 3 ft), with bottles in sink. The wine is then siphoned into them

The often-recommended cider flagon is ideal for home brew, if you always split a bottle with a friend, a pint apiece, or if you have a quart tankard of your own and the thirst to empty it.

Be wary of the screwtops on the bottles. As soon as you suspect that the plastic or metal screwtops are getting past their best, throw them out and replace them. The cost of doing so is much less than the cost of spoiling two or three bottles in every batch because the gas escapes and they turn into 'sleepers' – and the cost of these 'sleepers' is all the greater if you take a chance, split the quiet bottle round four or five glasses and *then* find that the contents taste pungently of vinegar.

You wouldn't take the silly chance of dividing an extra-quiet bottle in that way? Congratulations; but experienced home-brewers have done so and have had to lead a melancholy procession apologetically to the sink, where all the wasted beer is poured out and washed away amid the shudders of the guests who were rash enough to take a swig.

Similarly, with screw stoppers fitted with a rubber ring, do not be slow to replace a ring if you think the old one is perished. The way to ensure that you can make the change is to keep a good stand-by stock of washers. This is easy if you have standardised on one type of bottle but less easy if your stock varies from beer bottles to pop bottles and from internal screw stoppers to female caps with a threaded flange fitting over the bottle-neck. Perhaps standardisation is a counsel of perfection, for most home-brewers build up their stock from various sources, including the gifts of friends who know they need bottles.

A bottling session can become a geography lesson (as well as an exercise in ingenuity to fit the right cap to the right bottle), for 'Skottikoke' from Achentottie can rub shoulders with 'Cornish Pop', a souvenir of a holiday in the south-west.

Bottles, when obtained, should be washed and sterilised as a matter of routine. But what about the bottles the home-brewer empties?

Some home-brewers wash out each bottle as it is emptied, put a squirt of sulphite solution into the bottle from a 'squeezy-type' container and replace the cap. Some leave the inevitable beer and yeast deposit in the bottle (arguing that the presence of carbon dioxide in the air in the bottle will inhibit any moulds or bacteria) and then wash a big batch of bottles at one time. Others rinse out the bottle, squirt in a 'shot' of bleach and fill the bottle with water. Before bottling a brew, they pour out the solution and rinse each bottle very thoroughly. And still others submerge their empties in a bin of strong bleach solution until they need them.

All these systems seem to work – and all have their occasional failures. The first is one of the easier and more craftsmanlike methods; the second is more casual and means that part-emptied bottles are left around – but it works.

Whichever method is used, it is imperative that the bottles are sterile and free from any taint of bleach before they are filled.

Crown-corked bottles are likely to take over from screwtops as time goes on. A crown cork can only be used once, but it is not too expensive to replace. If you do decide to standardise on crown-corked bottles, be prepared to go to the expense of a proper crown-corking machine. It is true that you can hammer a crown cork into place with a shaped die and a mallet, but the tool for the job makes it simpler and easier. The metal crown cork is held in place by a magnet while you position it above the neck of the bottle; then, by pressing down on two handles, you simultaneously push the crown cork firmly down on the neck, while three shaped arms grip the rim of the neck. The edge of the cork is crimped into place with no fuss and no blackened nails.

Screwtops need to be sterilised, preferably by being soaked in sulphite solution. Crown corks can be used straight out of the polythene pack with the minimum of risk, but if you wish to be safe you can sulphite them or bring them through the boil in a pan of hot water.

Kegs

Bottles are, in effect, small pressurised containers, and it is safe to say (though no statistics have been gathered) that far more beer goes into these containers than into the bigger ones with taps.

It is also safe to say that the proportion is likely to alter, with the swing more and more to draught beer. Washing bottles is nobody's favourite task. Pulling a pint has a special thrill that pouring a pint does not have. And, most important of all, the bulk containers coming on the market are becoming more reliable.

It is disappointing enough to find that one bottle out of thirty is a sleeper. It is much more disappointing to find, at the end of the waiting-time, that the beer in a 25 litre (5 gal) container is dead flat when you turn on the tap.

The most stylish method of dispensing beer from bulk is the Beersphere – as spherical as its name implies. It is made of translucent plastic, stands on three neat legs, and is fitted with a strong sealed hatch on top, and a well designed tap.

The 25 litre (5 gal) keg is probably the commonest type for producing draught on tap. These plastic barrels are attractive and *are* improving in quality, though they are still not 100% dependable. Gas under pressure is not easy to hold in.

The general practice when using these kegs is to fine the beer first – the proprietary finings are stirred into the beer a couple of days before racking it into the keg.

The beer is primed with 15 gm (½ oz) of sugar, and this priming provides the original pressure in the keg.

The screwtop cap of the keg is pierced to take a fitment which holds a CO_2 bulb or cylinder. When the first pints have been drawn from the keg, the valve is opened and the gas is admitted into the space over the brew. Not only does this keep up the pressure, so that the beer draws briskly and with plenty of condition, but it also excludes air and airborne infections.

What are the pros and cons of serving beer in this way?

One keg is a great deal easier to wash than thirty-odd screwtop bottles. The beer does develop a 'draught' flavour and is noticeably different from the same brew matured in bottles. It is easier to pull a pint at a tap than to pour a pint from a bottle. It looks impressive!

On the other side of the coin there is the undoubted fact that many brewers who have gone over to draught beer have been disappointed by the difficulties they have had with the equipment, chiefly in maintaining pressure. Once you have your stock of bottles, it is cheaper to use them, since you do not need to buy CO_2 bulbs to keep up the pressure (and the bottles are, in fact, cheaper than the keg and equipment). And a pressure failure spoils only one bottle, whereas a failure in the keg can spoil an entire brew.

The enthusiasts for beer made from mashed grain malt maintain that only beer made in this way tastes as it should when served from bulk, and that draught beers made from malt extract drink too thin and dry and lose their condition too quickly, whereas beer made from mashed grain is full-bodied, slightly sweet and holds its condition better. This is a matter of taste – and certainly malt-extract beer out of a pressure keg would need to drink very thin and gassy to compare with some commercial keg beers.

The height of luxury for home-brewers is provided by the expensive Cornelius pressure system, which consists of a stainless steel cylinder to hold the beer, a CO_2 regulator to control the pressure from a gas cylinder and reinforced nylon beer lines leading to a variable-flow tap which enables you (as in a pub) to control the flow of beer into the glass and give a final burst, which puts a 'parson's collar' of creamy head on top of the beer. Basically, this is similar to systems used commercially throughout the world.

Again, as with bottles and plastic kegs, home-brewers can rack the finished and fined beer into the cylinder (leaving a 75 mm (3 in) space at the top), and create gas pressure by adding priming sugar. A secondary fermentation takes place (just as it would in a bottle or a keg) and when sufficient pressure is created the beer will flow briskly when you link up and operate the tap. The CO_2 cylinder can then be used to supplement the pressure created by the fermentation in the cylinder.

Do *not* be tempted to devise your own system, using a pub gas cylinder direct. There have been fatal accidents caused by the sudden release of the pressure without the use of proper breaking valves.

Wooden casks

Most home-brewers and winemakers have a nostalgic feeling for the 'good old days', and it is tempting to consider serving beer from the wood – drawing it from a tap in an oak cask.

There are two societies devoted to the propagation of the idea that this is the ideal way to serve beer in pubs – but even they would admit that beer in casks presents problems.

The Campaign for Real Ale agree that ale will not keep long once a cask has been tapped and spiled; that landlords have to be skilled in storing real ale in casks because of the sediment; and that they have to be very careful with their ordering so that they are not left with beer that has gone off. At pub level, this is more than balanced in CAMRA's eyes by the fact that beer stored in casks is 'living' beer, meaning that it is still fermenting gently right up to the moment when it is drunk, and thus has a distinctive character and flavour. They claim that keg beer is fizzy and tainted by being stored under pressure.

The first consideration – that beer spoils quickly once air is admitted – is the one that defeats the home-brewer with the notion to serve beer regularly from the wood. Even if large amounts of carbon dioxide are used to blanket the surface of the beer in the cask, the porous nature of the wood admits more air than the beer requires. A case can be made for brewing beer in a cask if you can do so regularly enough to keep the cask sweet; but unless you are going to empty your cask in one well-lubricated party, it is as well to forget the notion of 'home brew from the wood'.

Labels

One label is enough to identify a keg of home brew. What about bottles?

Shelf after shelf of bottles, each neatly labelled, looks well – very craftsmanlike. Then, as time goes on, you are faced with the chore of scraping off the old tatty labels, and what seemed in the first flush of enthusiasm to be a great idea becomes a waste of time, cash and trouble. Keep a stock of attractive labels for the beers you intend to make – stout, strong ale, lager and so forth – and use one when you give a bottle to a friend. It does enhance the gift.

If you wish to keep the shelves looking tidy and uniform, then soak the labels off the bottles when you bring them into use so that they do not proclaim the brand of beer or lemonade they previously held.

If you use crown corks, you can 'label' types of beer by using crown corks of different colours and bearing the name of the type of brew.

Storing your beer

Unlike wine bottles, beer bottles are stored upright, and most of the sediment falls to the bottom to gather in a thin firm layer. Some yeast may lodge on the minute roughnesses on the inside of the glass – you can see the film when you hold the bottle up to the light.

This very thin skin of yeast particles can be dislodged when you pour the beer and can give the pint a slight cloudiness before the main yeast has crept along the bottle to the neck.

This is not at all important when you are pouring a pint for your own enjoyment, but at a show this film can lead to your beer being down-pointed. A new bottle collects less yeast on its walls than one that has been used for successive brews. A soak with Chempro or Silana helps to freshen an old bottle, and a bump (not a hard thump) administered a couple of times during the bottle's first week in the cellar will move the yeast down to where it should be, on the base of the bottle.

Cellarage for beer is much like that for wine – cool, dark and free from disturbance.

And do remember that beer, especially a high-malt strong brew, is well worth longer maturation than it sometimes receives. Look on three weeks in the cool as a minimum. The really heavy brews are still gathering quality and apparent strength a couple of *years* after they are bottled – though this, in a household with small storage space and large thirsts, is a counsel of perfection.

Pouring your beer

A good pint of home brew can still be spoiled at the last stage – the pouring. Once you learn the art it can be very exasperating to see others pull the crown cork off a bottle, or untwist the stopper, and then stand around discussing irrelevant subjects while the bubbles stream up through the beer, bringing the yeast from the bottom to cloud the pint.

Do not follow their example. Take the bottle gently in hand, open it without violence and immediately tilt it and pour the beer into the pint glasses or a large jug. Do not stop pouring until the first trail of yeast has crept up to the lip of the bottle.

Pouring beer gently like this, with the bottle-neck against the rim of the glass, does not give the maximum head. To achieve this you need to pour from a height, so that a combination of gas bubbles and air bubbles gives an impressive collar. (Whether you think this is a good thing or not is a matter of opinion – many home-brewers think it is a pity to thrash the condition out of a pint, and thrash the air into it, by pouring from a height like a mini-Niagara.)

In any case, to achieve the maximum head the beer must be poured into a glass that is not only dry but also polished (a rare occurrence in pubs, and none too common in most homes, where the beer glasses are washed with the rest of the crocks in water containing a lavish amount of detergent).

Troubles to avoid

A fleeting head is not the worst trouble that the home-brewer can encounter. Most of the diseases that affect wines also affect beer – the winemaker has the preservative effect of the high alcohol content on his side, but the home-brewer has the balancing advantage of the preservative effect of the hop oils. Of course, the fact that home brew tends to be stronger than pub beers makes the home-made product more robust and able to fight off infection. Again, beer while it is fermenting, and while it is under pressure in bottle or keg, is partly protected by the thick layer of carbon dioxide that, being heavier than air, lies on the surface.

If you wash your brewing equipment thoroughly and rinse it with sulphite solution; if you keep fermenting brews covered; if you make up a yeast starter so that the yeast can establish itself quickly; if you use a sound recipe; and if you do not introduce 'bugs' from outside, you should rarely see any signs of trouble.

As with wine, hygiene is the first line of defence.

Some troubles are not bacterial.

Yeast-bite, a sour offensive bitterness, is a term in the home-brewer's vocabulary which covers several troubles. It is encountered sometimes when top-fermentation yeasts are allowed to

Pour beer gently – and continuously. (1) Get your glasses all ready *before* you start pouring. (2) Pour the beer *gently* down the side of the glass, bringing the bottle only slowly to the near-horizontal. (3) Fill the first glass: *do NOT return the bottle to the upright* or the beer will cloud: go straight on to the second glass. (4) Continue thus, being careful not to let any sediment pass out of the bottle

ferment too closely covered or are not skimmed, or when the temperature of a brew is allowed to creep up to around 26°C (80°F).

Its sickly bitterness can be encountered in individual bottles when they have a heavy sediment and have been left too long in a warm place (this heavy sediment often occurs in the last dozen bottles from a batch that has been bottled straight from the primary fermentation vessel).

'Cold haze' is another trouble that has nothing to do with bugs. If you make a strong heavy beer and move it to a cold place, you may be dismayed to find that it becomes almost opaque. This is due to the cold and does not affect the flavour, though it may affect your pleasure in your pint because the pint will lack eye-appeal. Bring the beer back into a slightly warmer place and the haze will dispel, leave it in its cold cellar and the haze will also eventually dispel, but much more slowly. This haze (it is some comfort to know) is primarily a trouble in really good full beers, not in the hopped-water brews.

If you find that every bottle in a brew is flat, the options are that you were too late in bottling, that you did not add enough priming sugar or that you moved the bottles straight out into the cold instead of giving them enough time in a warm place to enable the yeast to multiply.

If you find that an occasional bottle in a brew is flat, then perhaps you forgot the priming sugar in that one, or perhaps the closure is leaking because it is defective; or possibly you left some grains of priming sugar on the rim of the bottle and the closure has not sealed properly.

If the bottles burst or are foaming gushers, the chances are that you bottled too soon and did not check a bottle or two at random during the conditioning period, as recommended above. With 'gushers' you can take each bottle individually and let the excess pressure and some of the beer blow to waste in froth and foam, then screw the top down again and leave the bottles to settle. Any attempt to recover the waste beer, for instance by standing the bottles in a plastic basin, is likely to be nullified by the danger of infection. Burst bottles, being potentially lethal, are more serious than gushers – you may have bottled too early, you may have used weak-walled bottles such as whisky screwtops or you may have failed to leave that 1-in expansion chamber between the surface of the liquid and the base of the cork.

If you detect a smell of vinegar in every bottle, the vinegar bug has been at work. With wine you can, if you wish, make vinegar from what should have been a pleasant wine, but with beer the remedy is to pour the offending brew away and sterilise everything with which it has been in contact.

Loss of head has been mentioned above. It is a trouble that can cause neurotic symptoms in home-brewers who cannot accept that a pint of home brew which has a steady rising head of CO_2 does not need the publican's profitable inch of carbon dioxide foam on top of it.

To recapitulate, loss of head can be caused by low malt content, insufficient maturing time, the slightest trace of the wrong kind of detergent or of grease, a damp glass, overfining (which may cause lack of flavour and character as well as of head retention) and, to make life more complicated, other minor factors which would be difficult to isolate.

One of those factors, reducing condition and head, is excessive cold. Beer can be enjoyed by most Britons at a little below room temperature (around 10°C or 50°F), but lager should be stone-cold.

Beer that is too cold goes 'dumb', and its quality only shows up in the last quarter of the glass, when the liquid gets some chance to warm up.

Lager, on the other hand, is intended to be drunk cellar-cold, though the late veteran globe-trotting journalist James Cameron did once say that *hot* lager beer goes with fried locusts, which are rather like scampi because the legs fall off!

The sulphite fumes which affect wines that have been too liberally dosed with Campden tablets can be detected in beers too. Wines and beers can both go ropy through the attentions of slime-forming bugs, but, like wine, beer almost always survives the obstacle-course of possible diseases and troubles from bad technique to end up, very acceptably, sparkling in the glass.

23

Mashing for Quality

Since acceptable beer can be made from hopped worts and malt extracts, and very good beer from malt extract, hops and such additives as crystal malt, why should anyone go further and resort to the more complicated process of mashing the makings of his brews at carefully controlled temperatures?

Cost is not a big factor. Although use of the process does reduce the price of some brews, this is more than matched by the extra trouble involved. The chief consideration is that the mashing process, which is by no means as difficult as it seems, does produce beer that is distinctly better.

Once again, it is a matter of personal preference whether you feel, once you have experimented with it, that the extra quality is worth the extra trouble.

Most home-brewers are gently introduced to the practice by using diastatic malt extract. Diastatic extracts are carefully prepared so that the enzymes that turn starch into sugar are still present and ready to burst into activity when given the right conditions.

If you take diastatic malt extract (Munton and Fison's Century or Edme's Diastatic Malt Syrup, for example) you can use starchy grits, like flaked barley and flaked maize, along with it. Dissolve the malt extract in warm water, stir the flakes into it, raise the temperature of the mixture to approximately 66°C (150°F) and leave it at that temperature for an hour or two. The enzymes in the malt get to work on the starches in the flakes and break them down into fermentable sugars.

As a rule of thumb, do not use more than 1 part of starchy grits to 4 parts of diastatic malt extract, even though the extract might be able to convert slightly more.

It seems, to begin with, difficult to hold the temperature of a mash at such an exact level, but it proves easier than expected. You can put the pan on a low gas and juggle the control until you reach the exact level; you can pour the mash (at 150°F) into a plastic bucket and put the bucket in a haybox; you can work out a timing for short bursts of heat on the electric stove; you can stir in small quantities of boiling water to raise the temperature as it falls.

The simplest method, however, is to put the pan and its contents in an oven at a pre-set level.

Some electric ovens are fitted with 'simmerstat' fitments, which can be set at 66°C (150°F). The setting *should* be accurate, but before trusting a mash to the oven, put a bowl of water at the required temperature in the oven and stand your brewing thermometer in it. Then go away for an hour. When you come back, the thermometer should still read 66°C (150°F). If the temperature has moved up or down a degree or two, adjust the setting accordingly and take a clear note of the setting required to hold this temperature – and put the note where you will be able to find it the next time you wish to mash a brew.

In the same way, gas ovens can be adjusted to hold the desired temperature – you may find, for example, that the 'R' on the WARM setting is exactly right.

Once this setting is achieved, successive mashes can be placed in the oven and left to work. You can even put the mash in the oven in the morning before you go to work and know that it will be there, with its starches converted into sugars, when you come home.

In times of crisis, people rediscover the haybox principle – they find that it is possible to keep food hot, and even to cook it slowly, by setting the pot in a thick, warm nest of hay. The idea can be brought up to date by the home-brewer who lines a box of suitable size with polystyrene sheeting (like ceiling tiles) or fibre-glass and then stands the bucket he is using as a mash-tun in the snug box.

If the bucket has a watertight lid, the same idea can be used by letting the mash-tun float in hot water – the bulk of hot water will be slower to cool than the smaller mass of malt and grits.

More simply still, you can invest in one of the insulated containers designed for keeping picnics warm (or cold) and put the mash direct into that. Remember when washing them that they will generally not stand boiling water. Bruheat-Brewers Bucket, in polypropylene, can be used to boil 25 litres (5 gal) of wort, but the thermostat can also be set at mashing temperature.

It is advisable to phase your beermaking so that you do not have to hurry the mashing process when using grain malt or malt extract. If you move on to the next stage before all the starch is converted – before starch end-point is reached – you will find that the beer has a particularly stubborn haze. This starch haze will not affect the flavour of the beer too drastically, so the remedy is to drink that brew, perhaps out of pewter or pottery mugs, and make sure by the iodine test that the next mash is fully converted before the wort is boiled.

Whichever method of temperature control you use, you will ultimately have to check that the last of the starch has been converted into sugars, and it is here that the iodine test comes into its own.

Put a few drops of the wort from the mash-tun on a white saucer and add a drop of iodine – the old-fashioned tincture used for cuts! If starch is present, the liquid will turn a dirty blackish blue. 'Indigo' is the colour usually mentioned, and this is flattering but fairly close. If the liquid is free from starch, one may still see little flakes of blue where the iodine has reacted to tiny specks of grain in which the starch is not completely converted. This does not matter, provided that there are not too many such grains.

The next stage, when using malt extracts and starchy grits, is to strain the malt extract from the residue of the flakes. This can be done by pouring the contents of the mash-tun through a coarse strainer – the flakes left on the surface of the strainer can be rinsed with warm water.

The malt extract is now boiled with the hops, as described before.

The next step forward in technique is to make a brew from grain malt. At first glance, barley and malt look alike, but a grain of malt is noticeably lighter in weight and when cracked with the teeth is softer, with a pleasant malty taste instead of the barley's flinty rawness.

Most home-brew suppliers sell malt intact, like this, but before it can be used it has to be crushed. Commercial breweries go to great trouble to ensure that the particle size is exactly right. If the particles are too big, extraction is lost and trouble from starch hazes is likely; if the particles are too small and floury, there is every chance that a 'set mash' will result, when the mashed malt sets like paste and will not allow liquid to drain through it.

It is easy to talk lightly of cracking the grains with a rolling-pin, a bottle, a coffee-grinder, a liquidiser or whatever, but much more difficult to do so, without discouraging effort, and achieve the right 'semolina' particle sizes.

If you can find a supplier at all convenient to you who sells his malt ready-ground and whose stock is fresh, then buy the malt ready-ground. It will save you trouble, at little extra cost. Alternatively, go to the other extreme and buy yourself a little mill with the proper clearance. You may be able to find one through the health-food stores.

Grain malt mashed at the 'standard' figure of 66°C (150°F) is likely to yield three-quarters maltose and one-quarter dextrins. This is reflected in the speed of fermentation – the readily fermentable maltose is quickly converted into carbon dioxide and alcohol, so that the beer attenuates rapidly to about a quarter of its original gravity, at which point fermentation slows drastically as the yeast gets to work on the less readily fermentable substances. If you lower the mashing temperature, more maltose is produced, fermentation is quicker and more complete, but the final beer is likely to drink thinner. Dextrins, which give body and sweetness to a brew, are produced by enzymes which like a markedly higher temperature, up to 77°C (170°F). Theoretically, too, mashing for maltose and for dextrins requires differing acidities, but most home-brewers feel that they are going a long way into the realms of abstract science if they check the acidity of the wort with pH comparison papers and adjust to just over pH 5.

The consistency of the mash is a more easily adjustable way of altering the balance of the brew. A mash the consistency of thick porridge produces more dextrins, and a fuller sweeter flavour. If you add more water to make the mash up to the consistency of thin porridge, and keep the original mashing temperature down to 65°C (148°F) for the first half hour, you will produce more maltose – and, therefore, a more completely fermentable brew which will drink thinner when mature.

Just as 66°C (150°F) is a good guide to mashing temperature, until you feel confident to vary it, so 3 kg (7 lb) of crushed malt stirred into 5 litres (9 pt) of water at 77°C (170°F) produces a reasonable porridge-like consistency.

The same methods of keeping the malt mash at 66°C (150°F) can be employed as were listed for malt-extract mashes – the most useful probably being the use of an oven at pre-set and pre-checked temperatures.

Starch end-point is checked in the same way, with a drop of old-fashioned brown iodine in a few drops of the wort on a white surface. The scientist uses a special tile for this purpose, but a white saucer serves just as well.

Having mashed the grain, with up to 1 part in 5 of starchy grits such as flaked maize or barley, you have the task of separating the malty liquid from the mash. Nowadays in commercial breweries this is done by watering the surface of the mash with a very fine mist of hot water. This gently leaches the sugary material out of the mash, leaving the spent grains (tasting of cardboard) behind. The sparging liquor is around 77°C (170°F) which, by a happy chance, is just about the heat at which some domestic storage heaters or geysers discharge their contents.

It is difficult to equal the thoroughness of the commercial brewer's thin fine rain – but old brewers can recall when sparging was done in some breweries with a hose! Something between the two extremes is easily obtained.

The first task, however, is to provide a perforated bed for the mash to lie on. A nylon strainer with high wooden sides, a plastic basin liberally perforated with holes made by a 9/42-in bit, or a wooden frame laced across with nylon tapes, on which a piece of netting can be laid, are all possibilities. Try to arrange the strainer so that it fits exactly on the top of a suitable vessel, such as a 25 litre (5 gal) plastic container.

When the mash is evenly distributed on the straining-bed, but not pressed down, start to spray it with the sparging water. A garden sprayer, bought specially for the purpose, can be used – but be warned that it takes a fair amount of elbow-grease to sparge a brew. The best tool for the job is a plastic water-can fitted with a plastic T spray-bar of the kind used for applying weedkiller. Again, buy one specially for the job.

Fill the water-can with water at around 77°C (170°F) and sprinkle it gently onto the surface of the mash. As soon as any liquid gathers on top of the malt, stop spraying for a few seconds to let the moisture seep through.

Ideally, the first cloudy wort that drains through the malt should be refiltered by pouring it very gently back on top of the bed of grain – taking this precaution certainly cuts down the amount of sludge that may end up in the fermentation vessel.

The greater part of the malt sugars are sparged out by the first gallon of sparging water, and the yield grows less and less as sparging continues. The commercial brewer goes for the last trace of sugars in the mash, but this is unnecessary in home brewing, since it costs far more to boil the wort down to the proper 'length' than to add a small amount of sugar to make up any shortfall in extraction.

The sweet wort that you have sparged from the malt grains is now

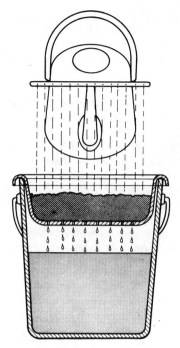

Simple apparatus for 'sparging' when brewing by the mashing method – a
watering-can fitted with a weeding bar, a perforated plastic handbasin
fitted into right-sized plastic bucket

boiled – as was done with the malt extract whenever possible – with
the hops. When the hops are strained out they, too, can be sparged
with about 1 litre (a couple of pints) of very hot water to wash out
any malty liquid and the last of the flavour.

As a rough guide, 500 gm (1 lb) of malt extract in a recipe can be
replaced by 600 gm (1¼ lb) of malt grain – so a beer made with
600 gm (1¼ lb) of malt grain to the 5 litres (1 gal) would give you a
very pleasant pub-strength beer without any added sugar, crystal
malt or other adjuncts.

Most home-brewers would prefer something a shade stronger,
and this gives you scope for infinite permutations, 100 gm (¼ lb) of
flaked maize, flaked barley, flaked rice, crystal malt, torrified grain,
bran, popcorn – they would all be appreciably different.

If you start with a basic recipe – say, for argument's sake, 750 gm of malt, 100 gm of crystal malt, and 30 gm of Goldings to 5 litres (1½ lb malt, ¼ lb crystal malt, 1 oz Goldings to one gallon) – and you decide to experiment, do not alter all the factors at the same time, otherwise you will never know just exactly what makes the improvement.

Next time, substitute 100 gm (¼ lb) of flaked maize for the crystal malt – the colour will be lighter, and the palate cleaner but thinner.

If you are in a soft-water area, try hardening the mashing liquor by adding 5 gm (1 tsp) of gypsum and 2·5 gm (½ tsp) of Epsom salts to 25 litres (5 gal) of water, and use it for mashing and sparging. If you find that this improves the extract and flavour, stay with it!

Somehow, when one makes beer from malt extract, it is comparatively simple to find a recipe and a method that is satisfactory, and to stick to it. With grain malt beers (as with winemaking) the temptation to go on and on trying to improve on what is already very satisfactory can become something of an obsession.

An enjoyable obsession – but it does not always add to the quality of the beer.

24

Beer Recipes

Notes on the Beer Recipes

The beer recipes are merely some representative examples of what can be done. Experimentation is half the pleasure in home brewing, once a grasp of the basic technique has been obtained.

It is suggested that, because of its easy management, bottom-fermentation yeast or lager yeast should be used at least to begin with.

The liquid which is to become beer is known as *wort*.

Brewers should note that the metric and imperial quantities are not, strictly speaking, interchangeable, though little harm is likely to result from the slight variation between them.

The teaspoon of the recipes is the 5 ml teaspoon which is now common. Some domestic teaspoons are slightly bigger.

Lager (simple)   (*to make 25 litres or 5 gal*)

2·5 kg (5 lb) light dried malt extract
45 g (1½ oz) Continental hops
Lager yeast

Boil the hops and the malt together for an hour in as much water as possible, strain into a fermentation vessel, and wash out the hops to obtain any remaining sweetness and flavour. Add the lager yeast, preferably prepared as a starter (see pages 87–8). Bottle at 1000 on the hydrometer, adding 2·5 ml (½ tsp) sugar to each screwtop bottle as priming sugar.

Leave the bottles in a warm place for two or three days, then move them into the cool to settle and mature.

(This quick and easy recipe makes a lager comparable to some commercial lagers – which may be no wild compliment.) It can be made stronger, without altering the flavour, by adding white sugar. One kg (2 lb) is quite enough; 2·5 kg (5 lb) will more than double the original strength of the lager.

Lager *(to make 25 litres or 5 gal)*

3·5 kg (7 lb) lager malt (crushed grain)
60 g (2 oz) good Continental hops
Lager yeast

Despite the simplicity of the ingredients, this recipe is more complicated than others because it involves mashing by decoction in the Continental way. This difference is not due to some foreign perversity but to a difference in the nature of the true lager malt – the malting process has not been carried so far forward, and the malt accordingly has a larger proportion of unconverted starches.

Mix the ground malt with enough cold water to make a stiff mash, then heat it to 49°C (120°F) and hold it at this temperature for a quarter of an hour. During this 'rest', enzymes start to work on the nitrogenous part of the mash.

Take approximately a third of the mash and heat it slowly in another vessel – the process has to be slow, as anyone who has made thick Scottish porridge will appreciate.

Boil this portion for a quarter of an hour, then return it to the mashing vessel and stir it in. The temperature of the bulk rises to around that familiar figure of 66°C or 150°F. Hold the bulk at that temperature for an hour.

Take some of the bulk (approximately a quarter this time) and bring it gradually to the boil, and boil for quarter of an hour. Return it to the bulk and stir it in.

The temperature of the bulk will rise to around 77°C (170°F).

A little of the liquid can be tested for starch, using a drop or two of iodine on a bright background such as a white saucer. If the sample turns blue-black, the mash must be sustained at this temperature until all the starch is converted into sugars.

When this point is reached, the sweet wort can be sparged out of the malt as described on pages 198–9, but the sparging water may be as hot as 88°C (190°F).

Boil the wort with the hops for an hour, strain, and make the quantity up to 25 litres (5 gal). Pitch with a lager yeast starter. When fermentation in the primary fermentation vessel is well established, rack the brew into a 25 litre (5 gal) container which can be fitted with a fermentation lock and put it in a cool place to continue working closely under the protection of the lock.

This lager is light in colour, in flavour and in alcohol – but heavy in time!

Mashing by decoction is a good deal more complicated than by the usual method of mashing, which in itself is more complicated than using malt extract without mashing. Worth doing? The experimentally minded brewer will enjoy it at least once, and it is a useful method to have in hand if you obtain grain malt which you suspect is high in nitrogen and more lightly cured than usual.

Workaday beer (*to make 30 litres or 6 gal*)

3·5 kg (7 lb) Edme DMS malt extract or similar extract
60 g (2 oz) Bullion hops, if obtainable
Vierka bottom-fermenting yeast, or lager yeast

Boil the malt extract and the hops together in as much water as possible – say, 20–25 litres (4–5 gal) for at least an hour. Strain the wort into the fermentation vessel, wash the hops through and add the washings to the brew. Make it up to the total and add the washings to the brew. Make it up to the total quantity with water as necessary.

When cool, add the yeast. When fermentation is complete, and the hydrometer reading is down to around 1000, bottle the beer or put it in kegs.

Despite the low finishing gravity the beer does not drink thin. Although it is only of pub strength by the hydrometer, it has to be treated with a little caution (the hydrometer won't be drinking and driving).

The special beauty of this brew is that the ingredients can be bought in advance and stored indefinitely, hence its name – it is a good workaday beer to make regularly and ensure that you never run short of a pint, even when you have no time to make more experimental and varied brews.

Scuppet beer   (*to make 25 litres or 5 gal*)

2·5 kg (5 lb) Munton and Fison Century or similar malt
1 kg (2 lb) flaked maize
Bottom-fermentation or top-fermentation yeast, as preferred
90 g (3 oz) Styrian Goldings hops

Mash the malt and the maize as recommended in the text on pages
194–9. For instance, they can be blended together with water at
around 82°C (180°F) in a preserving-pan, and the pan can then be
placed in an oven at 66°C (150°F) maintaining that temperature for
at least two hours.

Sparge the extract from the mash, as described on pages 198–9.
Boil the wort and the hops in as much of the 25 litres (5 gal) of water
as your boiler will allow, for an hour or more.

Transfer to fermentation vessel. When the wort is cool, add the
yeast and ferment in a warm place. When fermentation is complete,
bottle the beer or transfer it to a keg.

This is a 'beer-drinker's beer', being golden, grainy and highly
hopped. It needs care in mashing, because you are asking the
diastase in the malt to break down a fair amount of starch in the
maize.

The high hopping gives the beer its name. A scuppet is a large
shovel with a wooden frame and a canvas cover, with which dried
hops are shovelled through a hole in the oasthouse floor into a
pocket below.

And using 90 g (3 oz) of Continental hops gives the impression
that they have been shovelled into the brew.

This is a beer in which the use of Irish moss, for maximum clarity,
two drops of hop oil, for an extra-good nose, and six weeks in bottle,
for maturity, will put the finishing touches to the kind of beer that
you cannot buy in a pub nowadays.

Shale ale   (*to make 25 litres or 5 gal*)

This recipe was sent to the author by the late 'boosewright' Ken
Shales, with the enthusiastic comment 'Beat that if you can'.

1·5 kg (3 lb) diastatic malt syrup (Edme DMS)
620 g (1¼ lb) crystal malt
45 g (1½ oz) Hallertauer or Styrian hops
Pale ale water treatment
1 kg (2 lb) glucose chips
Lager yeast

'Boil malt, crystal malt and hops for one hour, strain on to 2 lb chips, make up to 5 gal. Adjust pH to 4·5 with citric acid. Pitch with a lager yeast. Start in open fermenter, rack at half original gravity into ex-wine five, and let it gang its ain gait.' Those were Ken Shales' instructions. He advised bottling at 1002 and giving the beer six to nine weeks to mature in the cellar.

For those who do not wish to test the pH of the wort, the addition of a routine level teaspoonful of citric acid crystals (3·5 g) should serve.

The water treatment, following the instructions on the packet, should be applied to all the water used for boiling, and for making the brew up to its 'length' of 25 litres (5 gal).

Nettle ale

5 litres (1 gal) young nettle tops
500 g (1 lb) malt extract
250 g (½ lb) sugar
15 g (½ oz) hops
Lager yeast

Boil the nettles in enough water to cover them, for a quarter of an hour, then strain off the liquid and discard the nettles unless you wish to experiment with them as a vegetable.

Boil the hops in the nettle tea for half an hour, then strain the hop-and-nettle tea onto the malt extract and sugar in a plastic bucket. Stir thoroughly, then when the liquid is cool, pour it into a 5 litre (1 gal) container. Add the yeast, top the jar up with water if necessary, fit a fermentation lock, and, when gravity falls to 1005, bottle in strong screwtop bottles, into which you have put 2·5 ml (½ tsp) sugar. Keep in a warm place for two or three days, then move to a cool place.

This small brew is a simple way to discover if you like the flavour of nettle ale, which is reputed to 'clear the blood' in the spring. If you discard the hops, the nettle flavour is even more obvious. And, if you discard the nettles, the result is a very pleasant light beer, slightly underhopped (to some tastes) for its strength.

Sweet stout   *(to make 25 litres or 5 gal)*

3·5 kg (7 lb) malt extract
500 g (1 lb) patent black malt or roasted barley
500 g (1 lb) crystal malt
60 g (2 oz) Fuggles hops
Top or bottom fermentation yeast, as preferred

Boil up the malt extract, the patent black malt or roasted barley and
the crystal malt with the hops for an hour or more, with plenty of
water – certainly 5 litres (1 gal) or more.

Strain the wort into the fermentation vessel and wash the residue
through with repeated small amounts of hot water. Make up to
25 litres (5 gal), add the yeast, and proceed as usual. If a really sweet
stout is wanted, lactose at up to 60 g to 5 litres or 2 oz to the gallon
can be added. Remember, however, that the lactose affects the
hydrometer reading, so it is advisable to ferment the brew down to
bottling-point (about 1006) before adding the lactose.

When bottling, you still need 2·5 ml (½ tsp) of sugar per bottle.

Like most recipes, this is a good basis for experiment. The same
ingredients, with the amount of hops doubled, and the addition of
2·5 kg (5 lb) of brown sugar, makes 50 litres (10 gal) of a less
full-bodied sweet stout, which is slightly more economical in price
per glass.

Irish stout   *(to make 25 litres or 5 gal)*

3 kg (6 lb) diastatic malt extract
500 g (1 lb) roasted barley
500 g (1 lb) flaked barley
5 ml (1 tsp) salt
60 g (2 oz) Northern Brewer hops or 120 g (4 oz) Fuggles hops
Top fermentation yeast – e.g. Guinness yeast, cultured from a
    bottle of Guinness as described on page 177

Mash the malt extract, the roasted barley and the flaked barley
together at 66°C (150°F), as described in detail on pages 194–6, for an
hour or longer until starch endpoint is reached. Add the hops and
the salt, and boil the mash plus added water as necessary for an
hour. Strain the liquid out of the mash, and make the 'length' up to
25 litres (5 gal) by washing the mash through with successive small
amounts of hot water.

When the wort has cooled, add a top-fermentation yeast culture, rouse up once or twice a day and, when the gravity has dropped to around 1010, rack into suitable closed containers (such as jars fitted with fermentation locks) and leave to clear.

You may find that the final gravity is still high, because of the amount of solids in this brew. Bottle as usual, adding 2·5 ml (½ tsp) of priming sugar to each screwtop bottle, but after they have been two or three days in a warm place, check the bottles for excessive pressure. If you find they are too highly primed, release some pressure by screwing open the top briefly. Repeat this if necessary.

Three weeks later, you can gently pour your stout, but it improves with further maturing.

Cock ale   (an updated version of an ancient recipe)

Ingredients as on page 160, plus:

> 500 g (1 lb) of chicken giblets, scraps, etc. (cooked)
> 500 ml (1 pt) grape concentrate

Make up the 20 litres (4 gal) brew described on page 178. When the gravity has fallen to approximately 1010, dissolve the grape concentrate in a little of the beer, add it to the fermenting wort, and hang the chicken scraps in a piece of netting in the brew. Ferment on as usual, and bottle at approximately 1006, priming each bottle with 2·5 ml (½ tsp) of sugar.

Though the presence of the chicken scraps does give flavour and 'body', the idea is not to everyone's taste. An excellent, but very potent, beer can be made simply by adding the grape concentrate to the basic brew – and eating the chicken as soup or sandwiches.

25

Showing Your Wine and Beer

Not every winemaker or home-brewer has any inclination to enter his best produce in a show, local or national. When the keen showman says 'But don't you want to know if your wine or beer is good?' he answers 'I already know it's good, and I'm not interested in proving whether it is better than yours or not!'

Sometimes it seems that the craft is divided between those who make small quantities of excellent wine and beer with the aim of collecting cups and those who make lavish quantities of good wine and beer with the aim of filling glasses.

The best way to learn how to show successfully – and this applies whether you are showing beer or budgies, wine or Wyandottes, sherry or Shire stallions – is to enter again and again, and learn intelligently from your failures and successes.

The first step towards success is to adhere closely to the rules as laid down in the show schedule. The rules may vary from show to show, and even from year to year at the same show, so study them carefully before you enter your exhibit.

You are likely to be required to give the assurance that you made the wine or beer yourself.

In wine classes, you may be required to use clear white wine bottles of standard size (approximately 700 ml or 26 fl oz) with rounded shoulders; to cork them only with natural cork stoppers; to fill them so as to leave between ¼ in and ¾ in (6–18 mm) air-space under the stopper; and to label them with their class numbers, and perhaps a descriptive label.

White wines are likely to take in all shades from clear white to gold, but tawny wines may be excluded – they may either have a class of their own or simply have no place in the show.

Red wines are self-explanatory. Rosé wines are expected to be a true pink colour with no hint of brown.

Sparkling wines will be exhibited in champagne-type bottles, with an air-space of between 25 mm (1 in) and 38 mm (1½ in), and corked with a champagne stopper, a plastic or natural cork.

In most shows, exhibitors are restricted to one entry per class.

Beer classes, too, are usually closely regulated. Beer must be entered in 1-pt beer bottles, either clear, green or amber – the only exception is barley wine, which is entered in bottles containing 10 fl oz.

For safety's sake, the bottles must be sound, and must be filled no fuller than 12 mm (½ in) to 19 mm (¾ in) from the bottom of the screwtop or closure.

And, of course, beers and wines must conform to type.

Bottles are more likely to please the judge's eye if they are polished – although it is infuriating to buff up a bottle till it shines and then watch the stewards put enough fingerprints on it to keep Scotland Yard busy for a week.

Most shows have arrangements so that any aggrieved exhibitor can protest timeously. This should only be done when the grounds of the complaints are worth while. An 'I was robbed' attitude does nothing to endear an exhibitor to judges, show authorities or fellow exhibitors. If a real point of principle is involved, then protest and make your point.

Otherwise 'better luck next time' is a happier attitude.

26

Penalties – Legal and Otherwise

Although we are free to brew beer and to make wine in Britain, the craft does have its penalties, some obvious and some less obvious.

It would be interesting, but difficult, to find out whether there was any correlation between the winemaker's busy vintage season and the birthrate. Hugh Johnson, the voluminous writer on wine, has no doubt about such a relationship: 'The wine-harvest is the jolliest romp of all – witness the yearly spate of babies nine months after the vintage, my own included.'

That 'penalty' – if that is the just word – is hypothetical. But there is nothing hypothetical about the severity with which the law would treat the sale of home-made wine and beer, though the village constable *might* overlook the odd bottle in a raffle for a good cause.

Until 1963 home brewing in Britain was so hedged about with regulations as to be, for all practical purposes, illegal. Only a beer of very low alcohol content could be brewed without restriction, and it is interesting to note that some well-known commercial brews are only marginally above the level that successive Chancellors took as representing the minimum for 'real' beer. If, then, we start to sell the wine and beer we make, we stand in danger of the commercial producers and the temperance advocates making common cause to have our craft restricted. A heavy fine might be a temporary and personal inconvenience, but trammels on the craft would affect millions of people.

The winemaker's next commandment is 'Thou shalt not still'. Britain's first distiller was St Patrick, who, by blessing a cup of wine, turned it into ice. He then poured off the 'poison' – presumably the alcohol – thawed the wine and drank it. This process of congelation (concentrating the alcoholic content of a beverage by freezing) is sometimes discussed by winemakers, who presumably have quietly tried it in the odd domestic deep-freeze. Congelation, as distinct from distillation by the usual method, retains all the constituents of the original liquid (wine, cider or grain wash) except the water.

Why not do it? Because if you were caught, while your deep-freeze might not be confiscated as an unlicensed still, you could be heavily fined for possessing spirits on which duty had not been paid.

Distillation by heat works because alcohol vaporises at 78°C (173°F), well below the boiling-point of water. If you heat your wine to about that temperature and condense the vapour, you *may* make an excellent brandy. But you will also lay the foundation for a court case that will put you in prison and, much more important, discredit the winemakers' craft, giving its opponents ammunition. Of course, by concentrating the congenerics (such as the alcohols which are jointly described as fusel oils), you may make a drink that will put you and your friends in hospital, instead of in prison. Many a man has qualified for a white stick by drinking a glass or two of home-made hooch.

So remember: *separation of alcohol by freezing and distillation is both strictly illegal and highly dangerous.*

Since wine fermented with a good driving yeast and fed with sugar as the gravity drops can become a drink more than half the strength of pub whisky (surely strong enough for anyone), there seems to be no point in risking the heavy legal and physical penalties of distilling at home.

You could get about a litre of brandy of a kind from 8 litres or 9 litres of good wine, but the brandy would then need to mature for years – unless you wished to drink it raw as American bathtub gin, which during Prohibition was allowed to 'stand and age for as long as ten minutes'.

Pushed to over 20% alcohol, wine reaches the strength at which it is absorbed very quickly by the body – whisky-and-soda in half-and-half quantities is faster in its effect because of the effervescence. This means that you can soon reach the breathalyser limit if you drink country wines and strong home-brewed beer. The familiar 'rule of three' (no more than three single whiskies or three half-pints of beer) gives very little indication of how much home-made drink one may safely consume, except to show that the answer is 'very little'. And if you are unwise enough to take on a really heavy cargo of home-made wine or beer, you could still be over the breathalyser limit thirty-six hours after your last drink. By then, you would also know the dismal feeling that Frenchmen sum up as 'My eyes aren't opposite the holes' or that Cyril Ray described as 'a small, personal, black thundercloud, made to measure'.

Wearing an amethyst is supposed to prevent a hangover. So, too, is drinking a couple of pints of water before going to bed or eating fructose (fruit sugar), which is reputed to double the rate at which alcohol is broken down in the body. But surely anyone who is sober enough to remember to take some spoonfuls of fructose or to drink a couple of pints of water 'the night before' is not in any danger from the worst kind of hangover.

Morning-after remedies vary from the nauseating (1 kg [2 lb] of honey, a really hot curry or raw herrings) to the more relaxing (a Turkish bath) and 'the hair of the dog' (brandy and ginger ale, or champagne, or a mixture of Crème de Menthe and Fernet Branca, which looks like a scooping from a disused duckpond). Anti-acid and aspirin, dissolved in plenty of water, has been medically recommended. One doctor has pointed out that such a mixture is to be found in Alkaseltzer, though he adds that other, and cheaper, blends might be made by those who propose to undergo *frequent* intoxication – and hangovers. Happily, few home-brewers and very few winemakers fall into that category.

Just as ways of totally beating the medical penalties of over-indulgence are suspect, so are *all* the ways of keeping below that breathalyser level – eating yoghourt, mashed potatoes or a large meal, or drinking pints of milk. They *may* help, but is it worth risking the heavy penalty of disqualification, disgrace and a very high insurance premium?

The law applies with equal severity to the home-brewer and the drinker of commercial products.

Why does that warning need to be so strongly stressed here? Because some people seem to feel, quite wrongly, that home made wines and home-brewed beer do not really count as 'drink' – in much the same way as it is said that, by the merciful dispensation of Allah, alcohol turned to pure water as soon as it passed the Aga Khan's lips!

To paraphrase St Paul, when driving you are better to take only 'a little wine for your licence sake'. Or perhaps you should drink water, which, as Mark Twain says, taken in moderation cannot hurt anybody.

United States weights and measures

When converting British imperial measures or metric measures to American, a close approximation is all that is necessary – there is no need to work to four decimal points. The vigour of the yeast, the acidity of the basic ingredients, and all the small variables are likely to have much more effect than minute differences in conversion.

As has been made clear, the imperial and metric measures in this book are independent, and are not conversions. It is advisable, then, for US readers to convert from one of them, preferably the imperial figures.

As in many aspects of the two nations' lives, the measures of volume are similar enough to be confusing. An American gallon is four-fifths of a British gallon, so the weight of sugar, etc., should be adjusted proportionately. The American gallon, like the British gallon, is eight pints – and thus, once again, the American pint is four-fifths of a British pint. Fluid ounces are the same, but there are twenty in a British pint, sixteen in an American pint.

Since the 5 ml teaspoon has become standard in Britain, this is the teaspoon used in the recipes. It is suggested that no attempt need be made to adjust those for the American gallon, since the difference is likely to be minimal.

The Fahrenheit and Celsius (Centigrade) temperatures are given throughout, so winemakers and brewers in America can use which they choose.

Britain and the United States, instead of using the straightforward figure of percentage of alcohol by volume, both have arbitrary systems of degrees proof. Percentage alcohol by volume is converted into UK degrees proof by multiplying by 1·75, or into US degrees proof by multiplying by 2.

Index